Sex Tourism in Bahia

NATIONAL WOMEN'S STUDIES ASSOCIATION /
UNIVERSITY OF ILLINOIS FIRST BOOK PRIZE

Sex Tourism in Bahia

Ambiguous Entanglements

ERICA LORRAINE WILLIAMS

University of Illinois Press

URBANA, CHICAGO, AND SPRINGFIELD

Library of Congress Control Number: 2013949200

Maferefun gbogbo eggun que timbelese Olodumare.
James McCrae, ibae. Lorenzo Patterson, ibae.
I dedicate this work to my grandfather and uncle,
who became ancestors
before they had a chance to see how their inspiration
and encouragement
would shape me into a scholar.

Contents

Acknowledgments   ix

Introduction   1

Chapter 1.   Geographies of Blackness:
             Tourism and the Erotics of Black Culture in Salvador   18

Chapter 2.   Racial Hierarchies of Desire
             and the Specter of Sex Tourism   44

Chapter 3.   Working-Class Kings in Paradise:
             Coming to Terms with Sex Tourism   64

Chapter 4.   Tourist Tales and Erotic Adventures   83

Chapter 5.   Aprosba: The Politics of Race, Sexual Labor,
             and Identification   97

Chapter 6.   *Se Valorizando* (Valuing Oneself):
             Ambiguity, Exploitation, and Cosmopolitanism   126

Chapter 7.   Moral Panics: Sex Tourism, Trafficking,
             and the Limits of Transnational Mobility   141

             Conclusion. The Specter of Sex Tourism
             in a Globalized World   159

             Notes   169

             Bibliography   179

             Index   201

Sardenberg of the Women's Studies Institute at the Federal University of Bahia for granting me the status of visiting researcher during my year of fieldwork. Ultimately, I thank everyone in Brazil who took time to sit and talk with me while on vacation or on the job. I am especially grateful to Arlete Ferreira dos Santos and her family in Estrada Velha do Aeroporto, who became my Bahian family.

My deepest gratitude goes out to my dissertation committee members at Stanford for all of the guidance and support over the years: Paulla Ebron, Liisa Malkki, Shiho Satsuka, and Sylvia Yanagisako. They always pushed my thinking and helped me to consider things from new and different angles. I also thank Amalia Cabezas and Kia Lilly Caldwell for taking the time to offer support, encouragement, and advice and to read my work. I would be remiss if I did not mention Robin D. G. Kelley, Lok Siu, and Angela Zito, with whom I had the opportunity to study as an undergraduate at New York University. These professors provided me with excellent examples of intellectual rigor and innovative teaching and inspired me to pursue the path of a scholar-teacher. I was also fortunate to be a part of NYU's Academic Achievement Program (AAP), a program designed to provide resources to retain first-generation students of color from working-class backgrounds. Through the AAP, I received the Robert Holmes Travel and Research Grant, which enabled my first foray into international research in Venezuela. This experience sparked my interest in research and exposed me to the field of cultural anthropology.

Thanks to all of my close friends from New York, the Bay Area, and all points in between who have been cheering me on for years: Kelvin Black, Sheriden Booker, Martina Fongyen, Monique Hazeur, Zakiyyah Jackson, Imara Jones, Alicia Kester, Joshua Leach, Howard Rambsy, Gabriela Richard, Alex Salazar, Latham Thomas, and countless others. To the Stanford friends and colleagues who have been with me through thick and thin: Micaela Díaz-Sanchez, Mike Dunson, Babajide Kolade, and Valerie Jones Taylor. Christen Smith has been a relentless sista/friend/colleague who has offered me tough love, constructive criticism, praise, and nuggets of wisdom to help me navigate the terrain in Brazil, in graduate school, in my writing, and on the job market. As a graduate student at Stanford, I benefited greatly from the camaraderie and support of some of the best colleagues anyone could ask for—the "monster cohort" who began this journey with me in September 2003: Tania Ahmad, Stacey Camp, Mun Young Cho, Rachel Derkits, Oded Korcyzn, Serena Love, Ramah McKay, Zhanara Nauruzbayeva, Kevin O'Neill, and Thet Shein Win. I could count on them for humor, good food

xii

and company, clarification of anthropological theories, café writing sessions, and feedback on dissertation chapter drafts.

Last but certainly not least, I give many thanks to my spiritual, given, and newly expanding family. To my *ocha* family: *mi padrino* Peter de Jesus, Alyssa, Scotty, Dolores, Bashezo, Naomi, Mkonu, and *iyawo* Michelle. To Aisha Beliso de Jesus, my colleague/*madrina*, who has been an inspiration and has helped me both intellectually and spiritually. To my given family, especially my parents, Brenda Lee Williams and Eric Peter Williams, for a lifetime of encouragement and support. And also to my newly expanding family—my fiancé and best friend, Terence L. Courtney, and stepdaughter, Kaeming Courtney, for supporting and encouraging me as I revised this manuscript. I am forever grateful for so much love. So many people holding me up. *Obrigada/Modupe.*

Sex Tourism in Bahia

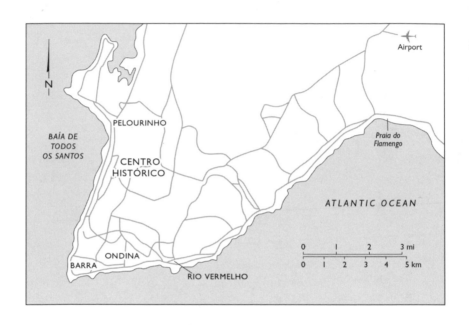

Introduction

Pérola's Story

One day while attending a weekly meeting of the Association of Prostitutes of Bahia (Aprosba), I met Pérola,[1] a black Brazilian woman in her mid-thirties. Wearing a white miniskirt and red tank top, she sat next to a woman she referred to as her wife, a muscular, masculine woman with cornrows. After the meeting, I accompanied Pérola to distribute condoms to sex workers in the bars and brothels of Cidade Baixa (Lower City), near where she lived. During the day, Pérola sold drinks and food in her one-room house, and at night, she went to Barra beach to solicit *gringo* (foreign) clients. She showed me several pictures of a slim, elderly man whom she referred to as "o holandes" (the Dutchman). She told me that they were "together" for two months, during which time he treated her and her son to dinners at fancy restaurants, took her for yacht excursions, paid for her to learn English, and even bought her a house on Mar Grande island. He left Salvador with promises to return but died of a stroke shortly thereafter.

Fabiana's Story

One day, Fabiana, a cofounder and lead organizer of Aprosba, was on the beach sunbathing with a group of female friends. She was the only white woman, the only sex worker, and the oldest. She noticed a European man looking in their general direction, but she was sure that he was looking at the younger, brown-skinned women, not at her. However, when she went to take a dip in the ocean, the tourist quickly joined her. "He said he liked me. He said, 'Those girls look like prostitutes, and I don't like prostitutes.' I was revolted." Fabiana assumed that a European tourist could not possibly have preferred her to the young women of African descent. Conversely, the foreign tourist assumed that the other women were prostitutes because of their blackness. Fabiana was "revolted" by what she called this tourist's "puta-phobic" comments. Drawing inspiration from the term *homophobic*, Fabiana coined *putaphobic* to signify a fear or hatred of *putas* (whores/prostitutes). She decided to play a game with him: she lied and told him that she was from a neighboring town, Feira de Santana, so that he would pay two hundred reais for her taxi ride home.[2] Over the next few days, the man took her to expensive restaurants, gave her money, and bought her clothes and shoes. The night before he left, he invited her to his luxury hotel room. When it was clear that he wanted to have sex with her, she feigned shock and retorted, "What do you think I am—a prostitute?"

My Story

In 2001, I studied abroad in Salvador, the capital of the state of Bahia, in the northeastern region of Brazil. One day, my friend and I were relaxing on Barra beach, one of the primary beaches in the tourist district. As African American women who could easily blend into Bahian society, we preferred to communicate in Portuguese to avoid standing out as *gringas*. A group of middle-aged Italian male tourists soon approached us and initiated a conversation. Within a few minutes, they were aggressively inviting us back to their hotel. Incredulous, my friend and I slipped back into English, causing the men to apologize profusely: "Oh, you're American? We're so sorry, we thought you were Brazilian!" But that did not make their assumption that we were sexually available and eager any more acceptable. Did these Italian tourists think that any and every black Brazilian woman was available for sex at any moment? The questions resulting from this visceral experience ignited my intellectual curiosity about the sexual economies of tourism in Salvador. I wondered how assumptions of black hypersexuality have come to characterize foreign tourists' imaginaries of Brazil as a racial-sexual paradise. These questions persisted after I returned to the United States. I noticed that after learning about my stay in Brazil, heterosexual men—regardless of race or age—often responded with enthusiastic exclamations like, "Oh! I've heard about the women over there!"

*   *   *

The stories of these two Brazilian sex workers as well as my story of being mistaken for a sexually available Brazilian woman reflect some of the racial dynamics and ambiguities of sex tourism in Salvador. Pérola's encounter with the Dutchman reveals how the touristic neighborhood of Barra functions as a site where black Brazilian women can procure *gringo* clients. Her story also highlights the ambiguity of "sex tourism," in which intimate encounters with *gringos* range from one-time *programas* (commercial sex transactions) to more open-ended relationships (*namoros*).[3] Furthermore, her queer sexuality and female partner problematize many scholars' assumptions of the heterosexuality of sex workers who are engaged in heterosexual commercial sex. In a context where practices of gendered racism (and racialized sexism) characterize all black and brown women as sex workers, Fabiana's story reveals how white women sex workers presented white foreign tourists with a conundrum. Her whiteness allowed her to escape the *prostitute* label even though she was the only member of her multiracial group of friends who identified as such.

In my case, the Italian tourists assumed that my friend and I were Brazilian and therefore available for quick and easy sex. To be sure, this is a common story that many women of African descent routinely experience all over the world. As cultural anthropologist Kia Lilly Caldwell points out in *Negras in Brazil: Re-Envisioning Black Women, Citizenship, and the Politics of Identity*, "Diasporic anthropologists" are often "subjected to many of the same racialized and gendered discourses and practices that we set out to examine in our research" (2007, xxii). Furthermore, Caldwell notes that her positionality as a woman of African descent is integral to her understanding of Brazilian racial and gender dynamics. My experience is also indicative of what I call the specter of sex tourism, the broad and wide-ranging implications of sex tourism that go far beyond self-avowed "sex workers" or "sex tourists." In foregrounding the specter of sex tourism, this book explores the meanings and implications of the phenomenon of sex tourism for daily life, romantic relationships, and the transnational mobility of multiple actors in Salvador.

As the first full-length ethnography of sex tourism in Brazil, *Sex Tourism in Bahia: Ambiguous Entanglements* explores the sexual economies of tourism in Bahia, touted as the "Black Mecca" of Brazil (see Piscitelli, Assis, and Olivar 2011). This book is about sex tourism, yet it is also about much more. I utilize the phrase *ambiguous entanglements* to include the broad range of liaisons and relationships forged in this "ethnosexual frontier" (Nagel 2003, 14). Ambiguity comes into play in the context of the globalized tourism industry when sexual relations move beyond mere commercial exchanges to encompass intimate and emotional exchanges as well. The notion of ambiguous entanglements highlights the difficulty of identifying people's motivations, desires, and intentions in these encounters and relationships that often bridge boundaries of age, race, class, and nationality. Sometimes there are even mixed messages and a lack of clarity between the two people involved in these encounters. A foreign woman who starts "dating" a black Bahian capoeirista may wonder if his feelings for her are genuine when she discovers that he keeps company with several *caça-gringas* ("hunters" of foreign women tourists). A black Bahian woman who meets an American man online may question his assumptions about Brazilian women. A European man who meets a Bahian woman on the beach may not know whether she is a sex worker since she has never explicitly asked him for money (even though he has paid for her dinners, taxis, and shopping trips and given her gifts).

This book draws on eighteen months of ethnographic field research between June 2005 and August 2008 to explore sex tourism from various perspectives: foreign tourists and tourism industry workers, sex workers who engage in ambiguous entanglements with foreigners, everyday Afro-Brazilian men and women who must contend with foreigners' stereotypical assumptions about their licentiousness, and government and civil society efforts to eradicate sex tourism and trafficking. By analyzing my interviews with a broad range of people (tourists, tour guides, sex workers, representatives of nongovernmental organizations), I map out diverse and at times conflicting understandings of sex tourism. As a cultural anthropologist, I seek not to make normative judgments about people's behaviors, desires, and sexual practices but rather to understand the cultural worlds in which people construct their experiences, pleasures, and anxieties.

The cultural and sexual economies of tourism are inextricably linked in Salvador's tourism industry. While studies of black Brazil have been dominated by a focus on African cultural practices, identity, and mobilization, this book explores the nexus among racism, eroticization, and commodification. Studies of sex tourism in other parts of the world have often focused exclusively on the sexual and gendered aspects of the industry, without considering the significant role that race and culture invariably play. Furthermore, governmental and civil society campaigns against sex tourism in Brazil tend to define it as something that happens when the state turns away its watchful eye. These campaigns often limit the scope of sex tourism to the sexual exploitation of children and adolescents. Moreover, they often construct cultural or heritage tourism as a more wholesome alternative to sex tourism. However, other scholars have noted that rather than being an anomaly, sex tourism is in fact merely "one strand of the gendered tourism industry" (Enloe 1990, 36) in which sexual services are "part of a range of informal services" available to tourists (Kempadoo 2004, 118).

The city of Salvador exemplifies not only the gendered nature of the tourism industry but also its racial nature. The eroticization and commodification of black culture combines the tourist's desires for "exotic culture" and for erotic, hypersexualized black bodies. What I call the touristscape of Salvador is characterized by both the lure of Afro-Brazilian cultural heritage and the possibilities for sex. The dynamic between cultural and sexual tourism is not either/or but rather both/and, as the two are often mutually imbricated. The search for the "primitive erotic Other" as well as notions of "touristic intimacy" (Harrison 2003: 51; Frohlick 2007, 152) and authenticity unite the realms of culture and sex in Salvador. Similarly, in *Pretty Modern: Beauty, Sex, and Plastic Surgery in Brazil*, Alexander Edmonds observes that "the boundaries between the entertainment, culture, and sex industries are becoming more permeable" in Brazil (2010, 31). My ethnographic research with tourists, tour guides, and tourism industry workers reveals how the desires for "exotic" bodies, "mystical" cultural practices, and natural landscapes are often connected in the tourist's desire for intimacy and alterity.

Salvador can be considered what Lenore Manderson and Margaret Jolly (1997) call a "site of desire" in the global tourist imaginary. Manderson and Jolly define the "site of desire" as a place that is eroticized and imagined as a site for romance, sexual adventure, and license. They highlight the example of the "libidinization of Thailand," which has led to the firm association of this country with sex tourism (17). Though Manderson and Jolly originally formulated this concept with Asia and the Pacific region in mind, the fact that sites of desire are "formed by confluences of cultures" makes it a concept that can easily be applied to other places (1). In 2004, Brazil surpassed Thailand as the world's premier sex tourism destination in the aftermath of the devastating Indian Ocean tsunami (Rogers 2010), perhaps lending more credence to this connection. I conceptualize Bahia as a site of desire as a consequence of the widespread circulation of myths of black hypersexuality as well as the ways in which the Bahian state government utilizes an eroticized blackness and Afro-Brazilian culture to sell Bahia to foreign tourists. These processes of racialized eroticization render black Bahian men and women both objects and agents of desire in the sexual economies of tourism.

This book interrogates crucial questions of globalization, political economy, and transnationalism by investigating the racialized and sexualized dynamics of Salvador. It follows in the footsteps of scholars such as Mark Padilla (2007a) and Dennis Altman (2001) in advancing a political economy of sexuality that recognizes the linkages among political, economic, and cultural structures. The concepts of sexual economies and of a touristscape are crucial here. The "sexual economies of tourism" highlights the "intersections between economic systems and social life" (Ara Wilson 2004, 9). My understanding of this concept also draws from the work of M. Jacqui Alexander (2005) and of Adrienne Davis, who describes slavery in the antebellum U.S.

South as a sexual economy because of the "interplay of sex and markets" that converted "private relations of sex and reproduction into political and economic relations" with regard to enslaved black women (2009, 217). My use of *touristscape* draws from the scholarship on the anthropology of globalization and global ethnography. Arjun Appadurai defines an *ethnoscape* as "the landscape of persons who constitute the shifting world in which we live: tourists, immigrants, refugees, exiles, guest workers, and other moving groups and individuals constitute an essential feature of the world and appear to affect the politics of (and between) nations to a hitherto unprecedented degree" (1996, 33). *Touristscape* encompasses the many sites within the city of Salvador where the tourism industry is a central focal point—beaches, bars, cybercafés, plazas, and cultural institutions—as well as the many people who occupy and move through these spaces on a daily basis. Like ethnoscapes, touristscapes are never stable and are always in flux, as exemplified by the constant comings and goings of foreign and domestic tourists, sex workers, and workers in hotels, restaurants, and bars and in the opening and closing of internet cafés, restaurants, hostels, and cultural spaces. Furthermore, as Zsuzsa Gille and Seán Ó Riain contend, global ethnography conceives of places as "globalized with multiple external connections, porous and contested boundaries, and social relations that are constructed across spatial scales" (2002, 291). I conceive of a touristscape in the same way.

In *What's Love Got to Do With It?: Transnational Desires and Sex Tourism in the Dominican Republic*, Denise Brennan refers to the town of Sosúa as a "sexscape," or a "new kind of global sexual landscape and the sites within it" (2004, 15). Sexscapes highlight the connections between sex work and the forces of the globalized economy, and they are places where the "exotic is manufactured into the erotic" and "the sex trade becomes a focal point of a place" (16). Sexscapes are characterized by international travel from developed to developing countries, the consumption of paid sex, and inequality (16). While my work is deeply influenced by Brennan's compelling ethnography, her concept of sexscapes does not clearly apply to Salvador. Consequently, I prefer *touristscape* because it does not privilege sex as the primary feature of Salvador as a tourist destination. Rather, it highlights the intersections between the cultural and sexual realms of the transnational tourism industry. Salvador has much more than just the exchange of sex; there is also the eroticization of culture and racial heritage.

This book also considers the far-reaching implications of the specter of sex tourism in Salvador, which creates widespread anxiety about the validity and authenticity of romantic relationships between foreign tourists and Bahians. Consequently, sex tourism also profoundly affects how people relate to each other across transnational borders. One day, I was sitting at an outdoor café in Pelourinho; two black Bahian women and two European men were sitting at a neighboring table. An elderly white Brazilian woman walked by, selling necklaces, and stopped and stared rudely at the four people. One of the men asked her in flawless Portuguese, "Do you have a problem? You're looking at us as if you don't like what you see. This is my *wife*." His emphasis on *wife* implied that he knew what assumptions the elderly woman was making.

As this incident illustrates, the specter of sex tourism produces anxiety for those who must contend with strangers' assumptions about the validity or authenticity of their relationships. The prevalence of sex tourism, the sensationalist media that surround it, and even the campaigns to stop it have created a moral panic about black sexuality that unwittingly reinforces stereotypes as well as notions of who is worthy of the privileges of transnational mobility. Discourses on globalization often tout people's increased ability to traverse international borders as one of the benefits of interconnectedness. However, a great deal of inequality remains in terms of who has access to the privilege of international travel. In this book, I document the creative and sometimes overlooked ways in which Bahian women and men express their cosmopolitan aspirations within the socioeconomic conditions and structures that may limit them. Thus, I go beyond an understanding of cosmopolitan subjects as globe-trotting, multilingual passport holders with the financial resources to afford the privileges of globalization (Ong 1999; Saraswati 2010). Many of the people who participated in my research sought access to cosmopolitanism by expanding their network of international friends, acquaintances, and lovers through ambiguous encounters with foreign tourists who would take the Bahians to expensive shopping malls and restaurants and on vacations to the islands of Itaparica and Morro de São Paulo that were beyond the reach of most low-income Brazilians.

This book offers important ethnographic material to help us make sense of how race, affect, and cultural production play out in the context of transnational tourism. Although sex tourism occurs in various parts of the world—Thailand and the Philippines, the Dominican Republic, Cuba, and Colombia—Brazil is a significant site of sex tourism. With few exceptions (Piscitelli 1996, 2001, 2006, 2007, 2008; Blanchette and da Silva 2011), the anthropological literature on sex tourism in Latin America focuses almost exclusively on Cuba and the Dominican Republic (see, for example, Allen 2011; Cabezas 2009; Padilla 2007a, b). There is a surprising dearth of scholarship on sex tourism in Brazil, particularly in English. This introductory chapter offers an overview of the tourism industry and tourism studies scholarship, summarizes a few of my major arguments and theoretical frameworks, and concludes with a note about the methodological challenges of doing this type of ethnographic research.

The Tourism Industry and Tourism Studies Research

The tourism industry is currently the largest employer in the global economy, yet it remains a relatively undertheorized field of study (Ness 2003). With the largest economy in Latin America, Brazil is an increasingly important global player, experiencing unprecedented levels of economic growth and becoming the world's sixth-largest economy by 2012 ("Measuring" 2011). Nevertheless, the country maintains persistent racial and socioeconomic inequalities (Edmonds 2010). In 2010, Brazil ranked 73rd among 169 countries on the Human Development Index (which measures health, education, and income) and eighth in the UNESCO ranking of illiteracy (United Nations Development Programme 2010). In the state of Bahia, where people of African descent comprise nearly 80 percent of the population, this inequality has racial overtones. According to anthropologist Cecilia McCallum, nearly "80% of Salvador's 2.5 million residents are black or brown and low-income" (2007, 61). Salvador has experienced one of the nation's highest unemployment rates: in 2010, the unemployment rate for all of Brazil was 7 percent, while the rate for the Salvador metropolitan region was 12 percent ("Salvador" 2010).

However, while many countries have been hit hard by the global economic crisis that began in 2007, Brazil was one of the last of the emerging market economies to be affected by the financial and economic crisis and one of the first to emerge relatively unscathed (Roett 2010).The Brazilian federal government is ostensibly working toward using the tourism industry to reduce inequalities in Brazilian society. Brazil's *2007–2010 National Tourism Plan: A Journey towards Inclusion* refers to tourism as "an important tool for achieving the Millennium Development Goals, particularly in regards to the eradication of extreme poverty and hunger, the guarantee of environmental sustainability and the establishment of a global partnership for development" (Brazil 2007, 15). The *National Tourism Plan* also emphasizes that "Brazilians should be the main beneficiaries of tourism development in their country" (15). My conversations with sex and tourism industry workers reveals that tourism has in fact improved the living conditions of Brazilian citizens.

Tourism studies theorists have conceptualized tourism as a "sacred journey" (Graburn 1977), as consumerism-inspired pleasure seeking (Urry 2002), and as a ritual experience that transforms its participants (Bruner 2005). Others have highlighted the class dynamics of tourism by calling it "conspicuous consumption in front of the deprived" (Crick 1989, 317). Many of the characteristics that tourism studies scholars have articulated about the nature of tourism can certainly be applied to Salvador. A common scene in Salvador's touristscape is a group of tourists sitting down to a meal at an outdoor restaurant to enjoy the ocean view or the scenic cobblestone streets and vibrant nightlife in Pelourinho. Before long, poor, marginalized, typically Afro-Bahian street children approach the diners, begging for money or food. Salvador's tourism industry is a particularly interesting site for investigating sex tourism because of the ways in which race, gender, nationality, and class inequalities intersect with the racialized eroticism of black cultural production.

Scholarship on sex tourism has explored how the mere idea of travel and tourism often invokes notions of sexuality, play, risky behavior, and a temporary respite from the ethical constraints of work and moral expectations of society (Brennan 2004; Frank 2007). The tourist experience has been constructed as a liminal phase in which travelers may experiment with their identities, lose their inhibitions, and become more sensual (Bauer and Mc-Kercher 2003; Lofgren 1999; Turner 1966). As Hastings Donnan and Fiona Magowan point out in *The Anthropology of Sex*, the tourism industry often "encourages, nurtures, and endorses sexual experimentation" (2010, 71). In other words, the oft-cited idea that "what happens in Vegas stays in Vegas" can also be applied to virtually any place to which a person travels.

While scholars of tourism have often felt compelled to choose between a focus on tourists or on locals (or guests versus hosts), this book calls attention to the interactions and relationships between tourists and locals. It explores the subjectivities, motivations, and perspectives of both the foreign tourists who come to Salvador in search of erotic adventures and the sex workers (and non–sex workers) who have ambiguous entanglements with the visitors. Furthermore, the book focuses on how both tourists and locals mutually embody, interact with, and contest the touristscape through the production and consumption of Afro-Brazilian cultural practices and sexual/romantic encounters. Rather than seeing foreign and domestic tourists as a monolithic, homogeneous group, I see them as differentially situated individuals with subjectivities and identities that may be (partially) constituted through travel experience, visual representations, and romantic encounters. As Orvar Lofgren (1999) notes, rather than homogenizing tourists, scholarly analyses of tourism should recognize that there are different modes of being and becoming a tourist.

Arguments and Theoretical Frameworks

This book advances an intersectional, transnational, black feminist approach to sex tourism that is deeply influenced by feminist anthropology, queer studies, and activist anthropology. As Myra Marx Ferree and Aili Mari Tripp point out, transnational contexts are increasingly important sites for feminist work (2006, vii). My ethnography has significant implications for the anthropology of globalization, a field that Jonathan Inda and Renato Rosaldo describe as "exciting and rapidly growing" (2002, 36). The anthropology of globalization considers "the situated and conjunctural nature of globalization" and is concerned with the experiences of people whose "everyday lives are contingent on globally extensive social processes" (5). While social science scholarship on globalization often tends to focus on the macro level of nation-states, multilateral agencies, and transnational corporations, the anthropology of globalization is attentive to human agency, imagination, and the practice of everyday life. Anthropologists study globalization "at the level of real people who imagine new lives, make plans, travel, form networks, assume identities, and socialize their children" (Lewellen 2002, 26).

Despite the significant contributions of Inda and Rosaldo's collection, they openly admit that their volume does not adequately discuss gender, race, and sexuality. Jafari Sinclaire Allen (2009) makes the same critique of much transnational sexuality studies scholarship—that it silences and ignores blackness. Drawing inspiration from anthropologists whose work explores the connections between globalization and affect in people's everyday lives, this book fills this gap by offering rich, vivid descriptions of the voices, desires, lives, and experiences of the Afro-Brazilian women and men and the white and black foreigners navigating Salvador's touristscape (see, for example, Babb 2007; Brennan 2004; Cabezas 2009; Gregory 2007; Padilla 2007a). Furthermore, it fulfills what Florence Babb calls the "need for more detailed ethnographic studies that examine the nuances of socially and historically situated sex and romance tourism" (2010, 126).

While much research on sex tourism has focused exclusively on heterosexual encounters (for exceptions, see Allen 2007, 2011; Alexander 2005; Mitchell 2011a, b; Padilla 2007a, b), my work expands the analytical domain of participants in sex tourism by destabilizing heteronormative assumptions of sex tourism as involving exclusively heterosexual, transracial couplings. In conceptualizing my research, I did not limit myself to heterosexual encounters; rather, I was open to the various kinds of encounters that I might find while in the field. A significant number of my interviewees happened to fall into the local woman/foreign male dyad; however, I attempted to interview foreign women, local men, and tour guides specializing in black gay tourism. Jasbir K. Puar refers to tourism as "one of the most important aspects of the globalization of sexuality and sexual identities" and points out that tourism studies often ignore gays and lesbians (2002b, 935).

My project does not explicitly foreground gay and lesbian tourism, but it also does not explicitly foreground heterosexual tourism. Queer studies perspectives—particularly scholarship regarding queers of color—must be integrated into the study of transnational sexual economies even when not dealing explicitly with queer encounters. Queer of color critique offers crucial insights for the analysis of the relationship between race and sexuality (see Ferguson 2004; E. Patrick Johnson and Henderson 2005). Following Puar (2002b), I think about the *queer* in queer tourism as a methodological approach to the subject of tourism.

In this sense, queering sex tourism means not privileging or assuming heterosexuality and focusing on fluidity—behaviors and practices rather than fixed categories and concrete identities. Political scientist Cathy Cohen boldly argues that some heterosexuals find themselves on the margins of heterosexual privilege when their sexual choices are seen as abnormal or immoral (2005, 39). Likewise, in the context of the touristscape of Salvador, black women and sex workers of any race can be analyzed according to Cohen's logic of outlaw heterosexuals. Black Brazilian women—whether or not they are sex workers—are marked as outside of the bounds of sexual respectability simply because of assumptions about their hypersexuality. Similarly, sex workers (regardless of their race) are situated on the margins of respectability as a consequence of their stigmatized sexual practices.

Contrary to studies of sex tourism in other Latin American countries, I assert that sex tourism in Salvador is not limited to commercial sex work but also includes a broad range of ambiguous liaisons and relationships. The sexual economies of transnational tourism in Bahia are characterized by an ambiguity that is at times ethereal, intangible, and difficult to grasp. I often saw couples comprised of an older foreign male tourist and a younger, Afro-Bahian woman—on the street, in bars, cybercafés, and restaurants. How would I know which couples might be engaged in sex tourism, particularly given the racialized stigma that assumes that black and brown women in Bahia are either sex workers or at least sexually available?

Sex tourism does not constitute a new phenomenon but is actually a transnational reiteration of processes that have occurred historically in Brazil. The eroticization of women of African descent had a long history within Brazil before these images circulated transnationally. Scholars must understand the historical context in which black women's sexuality has been constructed. Gloria Wekker, Mireille Miller-Young, and other scholars of black women's sexuality have grappled with the question of how to study and write about the subject without "re-pathologizing an already stigmatized and marginalized population" (Miller-Young 2008, 119). We must take seriously black women's expressions of sexual agency and autonomy, even in the context of the phenomenon of sex tourism, which is often considered the epitome of exploitation and subjugation. In this way, my emphasis on agency brings together critical feminist scholarship with scholarship on race in Brazil. As Bernd Reiter and Gladys Mitchell (2010) point out in *Brazil's New Racial Politics*, one of the main characteristics of the new generation of Brazilianist scholarship is a focus on black agency. In other words, the scholarly work on Brazil has moved beyond merely describing or defining racism to considering how black Brazilians are challenging racism through mobilization, activism, racial identification, and agency.

Sex Tourism in Bahia contributes to the anthropological analysis of tourism and feminist scholarship by interrogating notions of gender, race, and sexuality that are constructed within sexualized tourist practices. As Inderpal Grewal notes, it is impossible to understand imperialism and travel without engaging issues of race and colonization (1996, 2). Grewal and Caren Kaplan also point out that "tourism is linked both to the colonial history of travel and to new forms of globalization in late capitalism" and that as such, it provides a "window onto specific connections among nationalism, political economy, and cultural formations" (2001, 673). While sex tourism is a transnational phenomenon, it is important to distinguish the local, historical, cultural, and political differences, particularly in Salvador. As Mark Padilla points out, sex tourism in the Dominican Republic could never be equivalent to sex tourism in Thailand because each place has a unique and particular history of sexuality (2007a, 6). Likewise, sex tourism in Brazil could never be equivalent to sex tourism in Cuba or the Dominican Republic or Thailand because of historical particularities of each place. I would also extend this analysis to a state/regional level within the vast nation of Brazil. Sex tourism in Bahia or the northeastern region could never be equivalent to sex tourism in Rio de Janeiro, for example, for similar reasons.

Methodologies: Challenges and Researcher Positionality

I utilized the ethnographic research methods of participant observation and in-depth interviews within Salvador's touristscape. My participant observation involved attending a wide range of activities promoted for tourists in Salvador and frequenting various touristscape locales. I visited the archive of tourist propaganda at the Bahiatursa library in Salvador and analyzed visual images and representations of the city as a tourist destination, highlighting the sexualized images of Brazil that are perpetuated in the international imaginary. In Salvador, I worked with two women's organizations, Aprosba and the Humanitarian Center for the Support of Women (CHAME), a nongovernmental organization that works to raise awareness about sex tourism and trafficking. In addition to interviewing CHAME's leaders, I consulted the organization's extensive archive of media coverage on sex tourism and trafficking to get a sense of the governmental and civil society debates and campaigns regarding these issues.

Aprosba was founded in 1997 by a group of sex workers to combat the violence that they confronted and raise awareness about safer sex practices. Despite the fact that adult prostitution is legal in Brazil, it is still stigmatized.[4] Since 2002, the Brazilian Ministry of Work and Employment has officially recognized prostitution as an economic activity, and the Classificação Brasileira de Ocupações (Brazilian Classification of Occupations) considers prostitution a professional activity. However, child prostitution and exploiting the sexual labor of third parties are criminal acts.[5] When I first approached Aprosba with the idea of becoming involved with them to pursue my research, I met with resistance, which I interpreted as resulting from what activist Joo-Hyun Kang (2009) calls "research fatigue": when academics continuously seek out grassroots organizations as subjects of research projects, but the organizations rarely see any benefits. Aprosba's president, Fabiana, told me directly that researchers frequently "used" her group's members as objects of study without providing anything in return. Fabiana requested that I submit a letter of intent on official letterhead from my institution outlining what kind of information I was seeking from Aprosba and for what purposes. In this letter, I expressed my interest in learning about Aprosba's history and activities and interviewing the organization's leaders and members. I explained my interest in understanding the relationship between sex workers and the tourism industry. Were foreign tourists a significant part of their clientele? How significant was the tourism industry in their daily lives? I added that if it were possible, I would like to attend organizational meetings and events.

In exchange for this access, I offered to teach a free English-language class for Aprosba members. Fabiana was enthusiastic about this proposal, since she and other leaders believed that knowing English was an important skill in a tourist destination. They actively encouraged Aprosba's members to take my class. One of the group's cofounders, Marisa, a brown-skinned woman of African descent considered *morena* by local color classifications, worked for a university-sponsored social project with substance abusers and believed that learning English would enable Aprosba's women to demand their rights and earn more money.[6] Bárbara, a bleached-blond young woman who had migrated to Salvador from the rural Bahian town of Joazeiro and who had a nine-month-old son, also enthusiastically encouraged Aprosba's members to take advantage of the opportunity to learn English: "It's summer. It's the season for us to go after *gringos*; we have to know how to ask for our money, to say how much we charge. Soon we'll need to be bilingual or trilingual."

These statements emphasize the significant and everyday presence of the tourism industry in the lives of sex workers in the Centro Histórico (Salvador's historic center).

Aprosba offered me access to a range of women's experiences and stories about their encounters with foreign tourists. I chose to interview professional sex workers to gain an empirical sense of the extent to which foreign tourists engaged in commercial sex rather than "dating" non–sex workers. I perceived a disconnect between my reading of sex tourism literature and what I witnessed in Salvador. In the literature, the idea of sex tourism was confined to those who have sex with prostitutes, while my observations seemed to indicate that any and all women of African descent were seen as sexually *disponível* (available). My interviews with sex workers opened my eyes to an understudied aspect of sex tourism of which I was previously unaware: *marinheiros*, or men from various countries who come to Bahia as ship workers. Once these men arrive in the port, people (some of them tour guides) welcome the men and take them to bars, restaurants, and brothels in the Centro in search of sex workers.

Aprosba members' stories of empowerment, police violence, romantic dreams, and complex desires challenged much of what is written about sex tourism in sensationalist media coverage. These women told me stories of falling in love with foreign ship workers, of traveling to visit their clients' home countries, of escaping police violence and abuse by domestic clients in the arms of a *gringo carinhoso* (caring, affectionate foreign man) who gave them access to their own city in a way that they had never before experienced. How was I to make sense of these complicated stories of affect, desire, strategy, and risk that did not fit into conventional narratives of a phenomenon that has been considered the dark side of tourism? These women's stories raise new questions about what exactly this transnational phenomenon entails and what impact it has on the lives of Brazilian women and men. Is sex tourism simply a manifestation of geopolitical racial and gender inequality, sexual exploitation, and the excesses of consumption and mass tourism? Or is something else going on here? This book works through some of these questions.

I ultimately interviewed four primary groups of people: (1) foreign tourists, (2) Brazilian sex workers, (3) Bahian men and women who had or sought out intimate liaisons and relationships with foreign tourists, and (4) tourism industry workers (hotel staff, taxi drivers, tour guides, street vendors). I conducted interviews or had informal conversations with seventy-two people: twenty sex workers affiliated with Aprosba, twenty tourism industry workers, ten foreign tourists, three people who worked for CHAME, one police officer from the Delegacia de Proteção ao Turista (Delegation for the Protection of Tourists) (Deltur), two *caça-gringas* (Bahian men who seek out foreigners for material benefits), and sixteen Bahians who either worked in the Afro-Brazilian cultural arena or had significant interactions and experiences with foreign tourists. Unless otherwise cited, all quotations are taken from interviews or conversations conducted as part of my fieldwork, and all translations are mine. Also, all anecdotes are taken from my field notes.

Doing ethnographic research on sex tourism is replete with many methodological challenges. First, there were issues of access. The benefit of working with Aprosba was that it gathered together a group of women who were politicized and who self-identified as sex workers. Conversely, it was much harder to gain access to women and men who did not self-identify as sex workers or who were not mobilized as a group. Furthermore, tourists are, by definition, a transient, mobile population—they leave. Studying tourism challenges the viability of long-term participant observation (Ness 2003). Moreover, sex workers are also transient, commonly shuttling among *pontos* (points where they solicit clients) within Salvador and sometimes even to different cities. They missed appointments, became drug addicts, or disappeared suddenly.[7]

Because of the taboo nature of sex tourism, it was often necessary to talk around the topic. The use of the term *sex tourism* could be problematic in the field. People often assumed that I was referring to European tourists who come to Bahia to have sex with children and adolescents. At other times, they understood the term to refer to European men who come to Brazil and "lure" Brazilian women to their home countries, making the women "victims of trafficking." Neither of these definitions of sex tourism is compatible with my working definition of the term. For this reason, I sometimes chose to say that I was interested in relationships and encounters between tourists and locals.

Because I interacted with sex workers in a nonjudgmental, open-minded way, my sexuality and identity were called into question. My positionality as a young, single, woman of color played a significant role in my fieldwork. In the course of my fieldwork, I learned that how people perceived me shifted according to my location, what I was wearing (particularly swimwear), and even my hairstyle.[8] Because of my appearance as a light-skinned black woman with natural hair styled in an afro or twists, I ran the risk of being mistaken for a Bahian woman—and thus perceived as sexually available—by European and North American men. At the same time, Bahian male hustlers who recognized that I was a *gringa* saw me as a potential conquest. My own sexual subjectivity was implicated at other moments in my research. At one weekly Aprosba meeting, two young black women looked in my direction and asked one of the leaders, "Does she do *programas*, too?" Marisa responded, "No, she's the English teacher." On another occasion, when I accompanied Aprosba organizers to a bar where foreign ship workers come to meet sex workers, a group of South Asian men kept glancing in my direction as I was interviewing a sex worker. Bárbara was flirting with the men, and she kept asking them to buy her a beer. When Fabiana saw them looking at me, she joked, "You might be able to make some money here." What struck me about these experiences was the contrast from the experience on the beach: there, the Italian tourists saw me as sexually available; in the bar, among sex workers, I was the unavailable foreign English teacher.

Overview of the Book

Chapter 1, "Geographies of Blackness: Tourism and the Erotics of Black Culture in Salvador," lays the groundwork for the rest of the book. It maps out Salvador's geography and political economy and provides historical background and ethnographic accounts that enable an understanding of how Bahia has been marketed in the international tourism industry as the Black Mecca. I discuss the shifts in how blackness and Afro-Brazilian culture have been treated by the state over time and how the tourism industry has explicitly used this culture to sell Bahia to the rest of the country—and the world—as a popular tourism destination. It also discusses the case of *caça-gringas* or *pega-turistas* (tourist grabbers), black Bahian male hustlers who use their Afro-Brazilian cultural expertise to attract foreign tourists with whom they seek to establish ambiguous relationships. Chapter 2, "Racial Hierarchies of Desire and the Specter of Sex Tourism," introduces the foundational concepts of racial democracy, whitening, and *mestiçagem* (racial mixing), which are important to understanding the Brazilian ideologies of race that shape the sexual economies of tourism. The chapter explores the racialized erotics of tourism propaganda and the construction of the *mulata* (a woman of mixed black and white ancestry) as Brazil's national erotic icon. Finally, the chapter reveals how Bahian women of African descent who are not engaged in sex work are implicated in the sexual economies of tourism because of assumptions about their licentiousness and availability. All of these phenomena set the stage for my ethnography.

Chapter 3, "Working-Class Kings in Paradise: Coming to Terms with Sex Tourism," draws on ethnographic interviews with tour guides and tourism industry workers to explore the parameters and structure of Salvador's sex tourism industry. It offers case studies of how Italian men are constructed as the quintessential sex tourists as well as how discourses of class status distinguish who may be considered a sex tourist. Chapter 4, "Tourist Tales and Erotic Adventures," offers a detailed exploration of a young white heterosexual male sex tourist from New York and an African American man who is not a sex tourist but who provides insights into the imagination of Brazilian women as exotic and hypersexual.

Chapter 5, "Aprosba: The Politics of Race, Sexual Labor, and Identification," explores Aprosba's role and activities as well as its impact on the lives of some of its members. The only organization in Bahia run by and for sex workers, Aprosba plays a powerful role in their politicization and health education. This chapter also explores the politics of naming in Aprosba's preference for the term *prostituta* (prostitute) over *profissional do sexo* or *trabalhadora do sexo* (sex worker), thereby highlighting the debates regarding the conceptualization of sex work—and by extension, sexuality—as identity or practice. Chapter 6, "*Se Valorizando* (Valuing Oneself): Ambiguity, Exploitation, and Cosmopolitanism," delves into the lives and experiences of some of the women of Aprosba to highlight the ambiguities implicit in their sexual and romantic encounters with foreign men. I ask how the ambiguous entanglements between sex workers and foreign men—both leisure tourists and *marinheiros*— complicate notions of power, agency, affect, desire, and cosmopolitanism. This chapter also discusses the racial politics of Aprosba, which has an overwhelmingly white Brazilian leadership and an overwhelmingly Afro-Brazilian membership.

Chapter 7, "Moral Panics: Sex Tourism, Trafficking, and the Limits of Transnational Mobility," explores how state and nongovernmental organizations' campaigns in Brazil construct sex tourism as a problem to be eradicated in part by conflating it with trafficking (Williams 2011a). How can we conceptualize sex workers' articulations of their right to migrate or travel abroad—often at the invitation of clients who visited Salvador as tourists—in the context of campaigns against "sex tourism" and "trafficking" that reaffirm patriarchal values and limit (particular) women's mobility? This chapter engages in textual and visual analyses of brochures from a nongovernmental organization's campaign to raise awareness about the dangers of sex tourism and trafficking. In depicting Afro-Brazilian women as naive, ignorant, vulnerable "victims" and European men as "evil" and "sinister" perpetrators, the sensationalist and totalizing narratives embedded within these materials create a "moral panic" (Cohen 1972 cited in Carby 1992, 740) about interracial sex and transnational border crossings that effectively reinforces notions of who is worthy of the privileges of transnational mobility. Finally, the conclusion, "The Specter of Sex Tourism in a Globalized World," ties together the chapters by emphasizing the connections between culture and sex in Salvador's touristscape. It also raises questions and implications for future research on issues of race, sexuality, and globalization within cultural anthropology. Ultimately, this book presents multiple perspectives on a phenomenon that has garnered tremendous worldwide media attention.

CHAPTER ONE

Geographies of Blackness

Tourism and the Erotics of Black Culture in Salvador

Setting the Stage:
Space and the Sexual Economies of Tourism

Site 1: Centro Histórico *(Historic Center)*

Walking toward Pelourinho from the bus stop, one passes by an area with fountains and several benches. At any hour of the day or night, dozens of women—black, white, mixed, young, old, thin, and overweight—always sit idly on the benches. Before delving into this research, I did not know who they were or why they were there. In the summer of 2005, I was taking an Afro-Brazilian dance class in Pelourinho twice a week at 6:30 P.M. On days when I was meeting Luana, a Bahian acquaintance, before the class to tutor her in English, I would wait for her on one of these benches, sitting quietly, observing, writing in my journal, or reading a book. One day, a man approached one of the women and engaged her in conversation. After a few moments, the woman laughed and walked past me, exclaiming, "He's crazy! He wants me to take him back to my house when there are all these motels right here!" At that moment, I realized that one of the major plazas, Praça da Sé, was a significant point of street prostitution in Salvador. Later, when I began my work with the Association of Prostitutes of Bahia (Aprosba), I discovered that this area was the *ponto* (point) for many of the sex workers affiliated with the organization.

Site 2: *The* Orla *(Coastline)*

The beachfront neighborhoods along the coast are prime locations for various types of exchanges and interactions between tourists and locals. In particular, the Castelo Velho, an internet café, *pousada* (inexpensive hotel), and restaurant located across the street from the beach, had a steady flow of foreign tourists and locals who seemed to be seeking out the company of tourists. I saw Rodrigo, a young, dark-skinned black Bahian man, sitting at a table by himself or with foreign tourists nearly every time I went into or passed by the establishment. Once, when I passed by him on the street, he said to me in his heavily accented English, "It's beautiful." When he was sitting alone, he never ordered anything, but he always approached foreign tourists—male, female, single, or in groups. On one occasion, he spotted an older white foreign woman sitting alone and sat at the table next to her and asked if she was American. Her response gave him all the permission he needed to join her at her table. They began to converse haltingly in English. When she left, Rodrigo promptly went back to what seemed to be his post at the front corner table.

Shortly thereafter, two Scandinavian-looking women with platinum-blond hair and blue eyes entered, and he fixated his eyes on these women. Without hesitation, he said, "It's beautiful. I wish to kiss you." The women did not respond. Rodrigo left the café for a while, and when he returned, he approached two foreign men sitting at a table and asked, "Italianos?" "No," they responded. He ventured a few more guesses before they revealed that they were from Argentina. Rodrigo smiled warmly, held out his hand to shake theirs, and joined them at their table. A few weeks later, I went into the internet café with a Canadian Latina acquaintance. Predictably, he attempted to speak to us in English. Having seen him do the same thing in multiple languages to other foreign tourists, I jokingly asked him in Portuguese, "Você aprendeu inglês só para paquerar?" (Did you learn English just to flirt?). His friend burst out laughing as he replied, "No," with a sheepish grin.

It is unclear whether Rodrigo's consistent and recurrent attempts to make connections with foreigners were motivated by a desire for sexual encounters or merely constituted an effort to expand his cosmopolitan network of friends and transnational connections. Nonetheless, his story alludes to an understanding of the sexual and cultural economies of tourism in Salvador as a diverse and complex social scene that encompasses a range of interactions, liaisons, and relationships. The fact that he could have approached these male and female foreign tourists with sex, flirtation, romantic relationships, hustling, or friendship in mind reflects the ambiguity that is central to the sexual economies of tourism in Salvador.[1]

Caça-Gringas (Hunters of Foreign Women)

One night while walking from the movie theater to my rented apartment in Barra, I passed by two black men and one black woman walking down the street, speaking English. I could tell that the men were Bahian, though one of them said loudly in English to the others that he liked my hair, which was styled in a large Afro. When I turned around to say thank you, they seemed surprised that I spoke English. I walked and talked with them for a bit, and they invited me to accompany them to an outdoor bar. As it turned out, the black woman was an African American exchange student who was dating one of the Bahian men. I was surprised at how well the two Bahian men spoke English. Wilson, the one who liked my hair, was in his early twenties and dressed in American hip-hop style. He was very flirtatious and repeatedly asked me for my telephone number. Although I was not interested in him, I gave him my number because I thought he might be a research participant. To my surprise, he called me the next morning to make plans with me. When I told him that I was conducting research on sex tourism, he said in a very detached, impersonal way, "Oh, I know some guys who do that."

I had a very strong inkling that Wilson was a *caça-gringa* (hunter of foreign women), also known as *caçador* (hunter) or *pega-turista* (tourist grabber). My intuition was confirmed after I found myself running into Wilson several times a week all over the tourist districts. One day I saw him in Pelourinho with a blond, foreign woman. The next day, I saw him in a beachfront neighborhood with an African American woman. He would avoid eye contact with me or look embarrassed, as if I had caught him with his hand in the cookie jar. Roughly a month later, I ran into Wilson at a *lanchonette* (snack restaurant) before my evening dance class. He joined me over coffee and finally revealed the truth. He said he knew I was a *gringa* the first night we met: "I can smell *gringas* from far away." He continued by explaining that he had complimented my hair so loudly in English so that he could prove to his companions that he was right in his supposition that I was American. On the one hand, I was astounded that something as simple as a compliment in English had been a part of his strategy to attract *gringas*. On the other hand, having seen so many of these types of encounters in Salvador, I was not surprised at all.

Keith, an African American tourist from Atlanta, seemed to be all too familiar with the work of *caçadores*: "I know a lot of Brazilian guys who all they do is look for tourists. . . . They look for American and European women. A lot of times they get with tourists to get clothes and money. In Pelourinho, I would see the same *caça-gringas* with a different girlfriend. They either teach dance, capoeira, or drumming. Their ploy is simple—they take the women to the beach because it's free and they'll see the women with little clothes. They'll pick you up at the hostel and take you around. Next thing you know, you find yourself paying for them—their coffee, food, water, and bus. After a while you get tired of it, but you're sucked in."[2] Keith's comment reveals the important role that Afro-Brazilian cultural production plays in the *caça-gringas'* ability to entice and seduce foreigners by teaching them capoeira, dance, and drumming. Foreigners wonder whether the feelings that the *caça-gringas* express are real or authentic or whether they are merely a part of the hustle. In other words, these ambiguous encounters with black Bahian men produce confusion and anxiety among foreign tourists, who may be swept up in a whirlwind of emotion, cultural exploration, and erotic adventure.

Two important sites in Salvador's touristscape are the Centro and the coastline. Sex workers who worked in Praça da Sé, in the Centro, saw it as a *ponto* that had certain benefits over other places they could procure clients, such as bars and brothels. Despite the risks associated with being in an open, public place, women who worked in Praça da Sé were generally able to keep all of the money they earned rather than giving a proportion to a third party such as an agent or pimp.[3] Gilmara, a young black sex worker with long braids, said that by working in the Praça, "you don't have to drink or listen to loud music," and violence was generally no longer a problem as a consequence of Aprosba's work.

My discussion of *caça-gringas* offers a lens through which to understand the intimate connections between the cultural and sexual politics of the transnational tourism industry in Salvador. Afro-Brazilian men commonly referred to as *caça-gringas* or *pega-turistas* capitalize on their cultural expertise to attract female and male foreign tourists by teaching capoeira and Afro-Brazilian dance and percussion. The *caça-gringas* illustrate how the figure of the black body/cultural expert is vital to the marketing of Bahia as the Black Mecca (Patricia de Santana Pinho 2004). Malik, an African American male expatriate in Salvador, said, "*Caça-gringas* are typically someone who does capoeira. It's easy to seduce and meet *gringas* because *capoeira* is exotic and physical." Fabiana, lead organizer and cofounder of Aprosba, knew a black man in Salvador who was the leader of a Carnaval group. He met a French woman who paid to take him to France with her. Fabiana also knew other capoeiristas who did *programas* (commercial sexual transactions) with this French woman, who, according to Fabiana, "established a capoeira school for male prostitutes in Europe!"

Jeremy, an African American man from Washington, D.C., who had come to Bahia in August 2005 for capoeira, told me that there is a lot of "situational bisexuality" in capoeira because many of those who have the resources to bring capoeiristas to Europe and North America are gay men. *Caça-gringas* can be seen as working-class Bahian men of African descent who attempt to reap some of the benefits of the transnational tourism industry in Salvador by capitalizing on the central role of Afro-Brazilian culture in shaping Bahia as a tourist destination. As Angela Gilliam (2001) argues, the commodification of Afro-Brazilian culture as a symbol of Bahia is intimately connected to the construction of stereotypes regarding the sexuality of black women and men that perpetuate and encourage sexual tourism.

This chapter explores the racial meanings attached to spaces of tourism and sex work in Salvador. It also provides historical background and ethnographic accounts that lay the foundation for understanding how Bahia has been marketed in the international tourism industry as the Black Mecca. I discuss the shifts in how blackness and Afro-Brazilian culture have been treated by the state over time and how the tourism industry has explicitly used that culture to market Bahia to the rest of the country—and the world—as a popular tourism destination. Heeding Clyde Woods and Katherine McKittrick's call for black studies scholars to pay attention to "how human geographies are integral to black ways of life" (2007, 7), this chapter engages black geographies scholarship to analyze how class, space, and race influence practices of sex work and sex tourism in Salvador. Black geographies scholarship enables an understanding of the multiple ways in which space is socially produced and perceived (Clyde Woods and McKittrick 2007; Lipsitz 2007). As feminist geographer Doreen Massey argues, "Spaces and places are not only themselves gendered, but . . . they both reflect and affect the ways in which gender is constructed and understood" (1994, 179). She encourages scholars to see the significance of class and gender relations in the structuring of space and place. Thus, drawing on these scholarly influences compels me to ask how Afro-Brazilians and sex workers (and Afro-Brazilian sex workers) negotiate and produce space. Furthermore, what practices do black women sex workers "employ across or beyond domination" to assert their sense of place in Salvador (McKittrick 2006, xvii)?

To articulate what distinguishes Bahia as a site of both sexual and cultural tourism, this chapter provides background on the history, political economy, and development of the region's tourism industry. It explores how class and race are used as signifiers to delineate spaces of sex work and describes the exclusion of marginalized black Bahians and sex workers in Pelourinho. This neighborhood offers a compelling example of the explosive consequences of the convergence of the tourism industry, sex work, and black cultural production. This chapter also interrogates how Afro-Brazilian culture is used to market Bahia to the rest of the world and how that approach plays out in the everyday lives of Afro-Brazilian tour guides, dancers, and Candomblé adherents.

Mapping Salvador: Space, Sex Work, and Exclusion

Salvador's touristscape is divided into carefully demarcated zones where class and race are crucial factors in determining who belongs and who is out of place. Praça da Sé, in the Centro Histórico, and Barra, on the *orla*, are two contrasting racialized spaces in the sexual economies of tourism. Despite the state's attempts to rid Pelourinho and Praça da Sé of sex workers, including persistent harassment by police, sex workers are still there, working with local and foreign clients alike. Salvador is divided into two parts—Cidade Alta (Upper City) and Cidade Baixa (Lower City). Cidade Alta, where the Centro Histórico is located, is considered more privileged, while Cidade Baixa is seen as more impoverished (*Cidade Baixa* 2005). Even as an early colonial settlement, the Cidade Alta was the administrative and religious center, while the Cidade Baixa contained financial, port, and market facilities (Hita and Gledhill 2009). The Centro Histórico, which encompasses Pelourinho, Praça da Sé, and Dois de Julho, is the site of hundreds of stores, restaurants, and office buildings, yet it is also run-down, with old colonial architecture in constant need of renovation. Conversely, the *orla* neighborhoods running from the southwestern part of the city to the northeast feature prime beachfront real estate that many locals and foreigners aspire to own or rent.

Tourists are expected to stay in the carefully circumscribed corridor between Pelourinho and Barra or in other neighborhoods along the *orla*, where hotels are plentiful; signs in English, Spanish, and Portuguese abound; and bus routes are easy for newcomers to navigate. When I first visited Salvador as an undergraduate exchange student, I lived in the middle-class *bairro nobre* (upscale neighborhood) of Graça, had classes every day in Pelourinho and Ondina, frequented the beach in Barra, and attended dance and music performances in Pelourinho and Campo Grande. I could take direct buses to get to my destinations with ease, and if I was willing to pay a few reais more, I could travel on compact, luxury air-conditioned buses with plush reclining seats. Only on subsequent visits to Salvador did I discover that there was much more to the city than the tourist district.

Tourist maps of Salvador show the populous neighborhoods where the vast majority of Salvador's Afro-Brazilian residents live as expansive stretches of green, as if they were parks, jungles, or otherwise empty spaces. In June 2011, I was codirecting a Spelman College summer study abroad program in Salvador. One day, we visited the Steve Biko Cultural Institute, where an Afro-Brazilian economist gave a presentation on racial inequalities in Salvador and in Brazil as a whole.[4] A young Afro-Brazilian woman who had recently graduated from college was translating the presentation from Portuguese to English for the students. When the economist showed the tourist map of Salvador, the woman interjected that her Cidade Baixa neighborhood, Paripe, was nowhere to be found. Her spontaneous outburst proved the economist's point about the racial and class demographics of Salvador's neighborhoods. This technique of making marginalized populations invisible on maps is not unique to Salvador. The popular Brazilian television series *Cidade dos Homens* (City of Men), a spin-off of the film *City of God*, included a scene in which the young black male protagonists Laranjinha and Acerola look at a map of Rio de Janeiro that does not depict their neighborhood and other favelas.

Black Brazilian feminist Lélia Gonzalez's work reveals the ways in which racism influences the constitution of places as well as the social and spatial dimensions of racial and gender inequality (Ratts 2011). She asserts that black Brazilians "are in the garbage can of Brazilian society" (Gonzalez 1980, 224). While "the natural place of the dominant white group are the healthy residences, situated on the most beautiful corners of the city or in the countryside and duly protected by different forms of policing," the "natural place of the black person is the opposite . . . from the slave quarters to the favelas, slums, invasions, wetlands and housing assemblies" (quoted in Ratts 2011, 2).[5] Pelourinho exemplifies this racialized distinction of neighborhoods.

Pelourinho (Whipping Post) was the center of the colonial elite. By the late nineteenth century, however, the collapse of the sugar market led to Pelourinho's decline as a site of wealth and power. The neighborhood suffered from decades of degradation, poverty, and social abandonment. In the period before military rule (1964–85), elite families began to move away from the old Cidade Alta and toward the Orla Marítima (Atlantic Coast), thereby "abandoning the historic centre to a growing number of lower class residents" (Hita and Gledhill 2009, 10). In the 1980s, the neighborhood became best known for gangs, petty crime, and prostitution before becoming a UNESCO World Heritage Site in 1985. Pelourinho then became a "priority in the preservation of historical patrimony and the implementation of tourism in the city of Salvador" (Teles dos Santos 2005, 85).

The transformation of Pelourinho from a decaying neighborhood to a pivotal site in the touristscape of Salvador was accompanied by the expulsion of poor, marginalized, black Brazilians as well as the attempted exclusion of sex workers (Kim Butler 1998; Collins 2008; Perry 2004). In 1992, the Bahian Institute of Artistic and Cultural Patrimony began block-by-block evictions that forcibly removed thousands of largely poor, black, working people from the city center to the distant slums in peripheral neighborhoods

(Collins 2008). Some scholars have referred to Pelourinho's "revitalization" as "a euphemism for a state takeover" (Kim Butler 1998, 170) or a "racist project of whitening the urban landscape in Brazil" (Perry 2004, 819). The process involved the exclusion of marginalized black residents so that tourists "would have unimpeded and untroubled access to places where they might wish to spend their money," illustrating what George Lipsitz calls the "spatial dimension" of the "lived experience of race" (2007, 11–12). It also demonstrates, as McKittrick argues, that traditional geographies essentially required "black displacement, black placelessness, black labor, and a black population that submissively stays 'in place'" (2006, 9).

The social exclusion of marginalized subjects from Pelourinho reveals how racism and sexism produce geographies that are "bound up in human disempowerment and dispossession" (McKittrick 2006, 3). According to Jorginho, an Afro-Brazilian dance teacher, after Pelourinho became a tourist site, "it was no longer a place for *baianos* [Bahians] to live—it was a place for tourists to do whatever they wanted." However, the state did not seek to completely erase the black presence in Pelourinho, as certain Afro-Brazilians were crucial to the marketing of Bahia as a Black Mecca (Kim Butler 1998). Those black Bahians who could be configured as "exceptional producers of Afro-Brazilianness," such as capoeiristas, stylized *baianas*, and musicians, were prioritized while others "came to be portrayed as dangerous backdrops to the exhibitions of Bahian folklore" (Collins 2008, 295). In this scenario, Jorginho was safe. Although he was from a majority black, peripheral neighborhood off the tourist beaten path, he could frequent Pelourinho to make a living from his cultural expertise.

In terms of sexual geographies, Praça da Sé was and still is a significant site of local commercial sex work, with a multiracial contingent of sex workers with both foreign and local clients. Barra, on the *orla*, conversely, was configured as a site that featured almost exclusively black Brazilian women and that held possibilities for much more ambiguous encounters that extended beyond commercial sex work, such as dating and intimate relationships. João, a middle-aged white Bahian man, ran a Web site that featured high-end *garotas de programa* (call girls). These *garotas* paid a fee of two hundred reais per month to have their pictures and contact information displayed to potential clients. João highlighted the class stratification of the sex industry in Salvador by referring to the *orla* as the *boca do luxo* (lap of luxury) and Praça da Sé and the Centro Histórico as the *boca do lixo* (trash heap). According to João, tourists seek high-end *garotas de programa* rather than the poor prostitutes of the Centro Histórico. Similarly, when I presented my research agenda to a group of feminist scholars at a university institute in

Salvador, they characterized members of Aprosba as poor, low-class, drug-addicted streetwalkers whom sex tourists would not seek out. Members of Aprosba, however, told a completely different story that involved innumerable experiences with European and North American male leisure tourists as well as *marinheiros* (ship workers) from around the world. When the ships docked, sex workers would take ferries out to meet the *marinheiros* on board, sometimes staying for up to a week.[6]

Despite the class differences in the various areas of the city, sex work—particularly tourist-oriented sex work—occupies a prominent place throughout. I encountered black sex workers in both the *boca do lixo* and the *boca do luxo*. Patrícia, a twenty-five-year-old black Brazilian woman who worked in Praça da Sé, had traveled to Italy, Chile, and Argentina with *gringos* with whom she was "namorando." Josefa, a thirty-nine-year-old *morena* (racially mixed and brown-skinned) sex worker whom I met in August 2007, had spent seventeen years "battling on the ships." *Batalhando* (battling) and *a batalha* (the battle) are colloquial terms for sex work: procuring clients, doing *programas*, and earning money. This term may reflect the harassment, violence, and persecution that sex workers confront on a daily basis.

The creation of Pelourinho as a World Heritage Site is a compelling manifestation of the sexual and racial geographies of Salvador's touristscape. The Bahian state attempted to rid the neighborhood not only of its poor black population but also of its sex workers. This case suggests that adopting an intersectional approach that considers gender and sexuality as part and parcel of the social exclusion of blackness can open up a plethora of analytical possibilities. Pelourinho's "renewal" thus involved not only a "racist project of 'whitening'" (Perry 2004) but also what I will call a *putaphobic* policing of sexuality. I am borrowing this term from Fabiana, the Aprosba leader who coined the phrase to signify a fear or hatred of *putas* (whores/prostitutes). Black women and sex workers (and black women sex workers) in Salvador have a queer relationship to the touristic landscape because they are always already seen as sexually deviant or somehow out of place. This argument draws inspiration from Cathy Cohen's (2005) provocative claim that "punks, bulldaggers, and welfare queens" have commonalities that are often overlooked by those who focus on gay as identity rather than queer as marginal. Despite police harassment and persecution, sex workers still solicit clients in Pelourinho, and black people who may have been "relocated" to distant neighborhoods still occupy the space of Pelourinho to partake in and perform Afro-Brazilian cultural practices. Black people and sex workers actively reclaim their agency and power by refusing to relinquish their rights to public space.

Political Economy and Tourism Development

Established as the first Portuguese colonial capital in 1549, Salvador went from being one of the world's leading sugar-producing regions to a rustic backwater by the end of the nineteenth century (Kim Butler 1998, 171). Rio de Janeiro replaced Salvador as the colonial capital in 1763, and São Paulo's coffee industry overtook Bahia's sugar and cacao production by the late nineteenth and early twentieth centuries (Hita and Gledhill 2009). Over the twentieth century and into the twenty-first, the major engines of Salvador's economic production evolved from commerce and public administration to oil extraction and refining operations and finally to tourism (Hita and Gledhill 2009).

Brazil has long been known as a "land of startling contradictions," with skyscrapers looming alongside slums and physical barriers dividing social classes (Arons 2004, 3). Brazil is often perceived as an "object of both fascination and sympathy," with the "exotic Brazil, of samba, sex and football prowess," and the "impoverished Brazil, of hunger, exploitation and violence" (McCann 2008, 7). In 1989, Brazil was the second-most-unequal country in the world, exceeded only by Sierra Leone (Francisco H. G. Ferreira, Leite, and Litchfield 2008). According to Brazilian economist Marcos Arruda, by the late 1990s, Brazil owed nearly US$250 billion to private banks, governments, and multilateral agencies such as World Bank and Inter-American Development Bank (1999, 1). Fifteen years later, however, Brazil is seen as an emerging megamarket, grouped with Russia, India, and China into what are known as the BRIC countries (O'Neill 2001).

Economists have predicted that growth in Brazil will outdistance economic growth in the United States and European Union in the near future (Roett 2010). Despite the relatively stable position of Brazil's growing economy, indexes of inequality remain high and the educational system remains poor compared to the other BRIC nations (McCann 2008, 8). Among Brazil's twenty-seven states and federal units, Bahia has the sixth-largest gross domestic product as well as the sixth-worst Human Development Index. In 2006, the Human Development Atlas stated that the distribution of wealth in the metropolitan region of Salvador is so bad that if the region were a country, it would have the second-worst level of income inequality in the world, after Namibia (Programa das Nações Unidas para o Desenvolvimento 2006). According to this report, income disparities are greater within the metropolitan region of Salvador than in Brazil as a whole: a resident in the richest area of Salvador earns twenty-five times what a resident in the poorest area earns. In Brazil as a whole, a resident in the richest area (the Federal District) earns five times what a resident in the poorest area (Maranhão state) earns.

Itaigara, the richest neighborhood in Salvador, has a Human Development Index equivalent to Norway, while the poorest neighborhood, Areia Branco in Lauro de Freitas, has a Human Development Index equivalent to South Africa (Programa das Nações Unidas para o Desenvolvimento 2006).

The Northeast may be considered Brazil's most underdeveloped region, but it is leading the nation in tourism development (Diegues 2001). In 2007, 74 percent of the country's tourism investments were located in the northeastern region (*Exame* 2007). Salvador is the largest tourism destination in the Northeast and the third-largest in Brazil. In 2007, six of the top ten new tourism investment projects were located in Bahia, and all of them were financed by foreign capital. Bahia's earliest state-sponsored tourism initiatives emerged in the late 1930s (Romo 2010, 152).[7] Different organs of the city's municipal government represented the incipient tourism industry in Bahia from the 1930s to the early 1960s (Queiroz 2002, 185). In the 1950s, the government of Salvador created a tourism tax and a tax exemption for hotels and became Brazil's first city to formulate a tourism plan (Queiroz 2002, 186). Despite these efforts, tourism was not yet understood as a "profitable economic activity" at this time (Queiroz 2002, 186). However, during the military regime (1964–85), the Brazilian government came to see tourism not only as a cost-effective way to generate employment opportunities and stimulate the economy but also as a way to preserve culture and patrimony (Teles dos Santos 2005).

In the 1970s, when the Bahian state focused almost exclusively on building its petrochemical industry, the tourism industry took a backseat to industrial expansion (Queiroz 2002, 115). However, tourism development gained momentum and support in the 1980s and 1990s as Bahiatursa, the state tourism agency, began to participate in fairs and expositions around the world with the goal of transforming Bahia into a major destination (Bahiatursa 1998). According to Anadelia A. Romo, this process exemplifies Bahia's skill at reinventing itself: "It began its life at the political center of Portugal's largest colony, languished on Brazil's margins for more than two hundred years, and then successfully refashioned itself as the cultural heartland of the nation" (2010, 6). Bahiatursa marketed Bahia to the world as the Terra da Felicidade (Land of Happiness). In the 1990s, tourist development in the Northeast became a federal priority and attracted international support with the launching of the Program for the Development of Tourism (Prodetur) (Tamar Diana Wilson 2008).[8] Seen as the region's most ambitious tourism development proposal, Prodetur-NE was designed to integrate the Northeast into the promising global tourism market (Soares do Bem 2005) by increasing tourist demand and generating employment and income through tourism sector activities.[9]

When the government created the Ministry of Tourism in 2003, the tourism sector became a top priority (Brazil 2007, 43). The ministry was charged with developing "tourism as a tool for transformation and a source of economic wealth and social development" (43). By 2007, revenue from tourism-related foreign exchange had "helped to enrich the country and make it more competitive internationally" (27). According to the *2007–2010 National Tourism Plan*, Brazil was competing well in the international tourism market.[10] While worldwide international arrivals grew approximately 56.5 percent from 1995 to 2006, the number of foreign tourists coming to Brazil grew by 150 percent over that period (Brazil 2007, table 3).[11] Marcelo Pedroso, director of international markets for Embratur, the Brazilian national tourism agency, expects six hundred thousand foreign visitors to come to Brazil for the World Cup in 2014, and the agency has launched an initiative encouraging tourists to seek out destinations beyond Rio de Janeiro and São Paulo ("Brazil Urges" 2012). In 2006, Brazil recorded US$4.32 billion in revenue from overseas tourists (Brazil 2007, 27).

Marketing the Black Mecca

Afro-Brazilian culture has certainly been a crucial factor in Bahia's emergence as a major tourist destination. But alongside celebratory affirmations of Afro-Brazilian cultural production coexist socioeconomic inequality, racism, and sexism. While the infrastructure in Salvador forces tourists to stay in their place, the same does not hold true for economically underprivileged Bahians. As integral members of the service economy, low-income Bahians—approximately 75–80 percent of them of African descent—make their daily commutes on crowded buses from peripheral neighborhoods to work in the tourist districts as waiters, maids, janitors, street vendors, and even stylized *baianas*. As tourism scholar Dennison Nash points out, "Others must serve while the tourist plays, rests, cures, or mentally enriches himself" (1989, 45).

As a place that has long been known as the Black Rome (Roma Negra) or Black Mecca, Bahia occupies an important space in global tourist imaginaries. These terms have been used to refer to Bahia because of its large population of African descent as well as the strong presence of Afro-Brazilian culture (Patricia de Santana Pinho 2004).[12] An estimated 4 million enslaved Africans were transported to Brazil between the mid-sixteenth and mid-nineteenth centuries, and 1.5 million of these people ended up in Bahia (Philip Curtin cited in Harding 2000, 3). Mãe Aninha, a famous Candomblé priestess and founder of one of the oldest Candomblé temples (*terreiros*) in Salvador, used the term *Roma Africana* (African Rome) to express the idea that "just as Rome was the center of Catholicism, Salvador would be the center of *Candomblé*" (Dunn 2007, 849). Black militants and cultural producers from other regions of the country later promoted the term *Black Mecca* because they saw Bahia as the principal source of African culture in Brazil despite centuries of miscegenation and cultural mixing (Agier and Cravo 2005 cited in Dunn 2007, 850). *Black Mecca*, then, speaks to a plethora of issues: the prominence of Candomblé, the legacies of enslaved Muslim Africans, the strong African influence on Bahian culture, and overwhelming number of people of African descent in Bahia (Patricia de Santana Pinho 2004).

Bahia has become a mecca not only for Afro-Brazilian culture but also for global signifiers of blackness and cultures of Africa and the African diaspora. Several souvenir shops in Pelourinho sell hats that have fake dreadlocks or beaded braids attached and that often feature the red, yellow, and green colors of the Ethiopian flag and Rastafarianism. Through such strategies, the Bahian tourism industry uses Afro-Brazilian cultural practices to market Bahia to the world. Bahian tourism scholar Acúrsio Pereira Esteves argues that this consumption of black culture is common in Salvador's tourism industry: "They sell even the very image of black people as eccentric, picturesque, or curious" (2004, 94). Keith, the African American tourist from Atlanta, told me, "If you want to get some culture, go to Salvador. People are exploiting black culture and black people. Everyone's making a little bit—prostitutes, *gringos*, hunters." Thus, the sexual economies of Salvador are a complex social scene in which the cultural and sexual realms intersect.

Salvador is unique in Brazil because it is the only destination that is situated unequivocally as a site of Afro-Brazilian cultural tourism. As Joceval, an Afro-Brazilian tour guide, put it, "Black culture is the great attraction that makes Bahia third in the national tourism ranking. If you take away African culture, Bahia has nothing." Brazilian scholar Jocélio Teles dos Santos notes that between 1971 and 1974, the Bahian state government published a magazine, *Turismo*, that used Afro-Bahian elements to define cultural and touristic policies (2005, 86). In 2002, Paulo Gaudenzi, former head of Bahia's Secretariat of Culture and Tourism, claimed that the "cultural uniqueness" of Bahia was its biggest claim to fame as a tourist destination (Queiroz 2002, 10).

Bahiatursa produced a tourist pamphlet with safety tips and pointers for navigating the city. The pamphlet imagines the "typical tourist" who visits Bahia as a blue-eyed white man interested in exploring Afro-Brazilian culture. The man is wearing a red, yellow, and green hat that has braids and features the Afro-Brazilian musical group Olodum. Thus, both Bahian and global signifiers of blackness are cultural goods that white tourists can consume and with which they can adorn themselves while on vacation in Bahia. The implicit gendered assumptions of the foreign tourist as male can also be seen in a guide for tourism professionals, *Brasil Sensacional!* (Bahiatursa and the Ministry of Culture and Tourism n.d.[b]), that gushes, "Whoever visits Brazil always comes back. And every time he comes back he will witness a different spectacle." In another tourist booklet, *Bahia, Brazil,* produced by Bahiatursa and the Ministry of Culture and Tourism of the Bahian state government, several vividly colored *berimbaus* (musical instruments used in capoeira) grace the cover and the text contends, "Bahia is a place whose praises are sung in popular Brazilian music—a mystical land where the people never tire of celebrating life, and nature sets an unhurried pace. But you need not rely on the words of poets and composers. Come to Bahia and see for yourself, and be prepared for this experience that awakens all the senses" (n.d.[a], 1). These words are accompanied by images of an *orixá* (Candomblé deity) statue, a church and skyline, the ocean, and *samba de roda,* a traditional style of samba danced in a circle. The pamphlet describes Bahia as an "Afro-American nation within Brazil" and presents romantic, exotic notions of Bahians steeped in a rich cultural heritage: in Salvador, "people walk like they are dancing and talk like they are singing" (2).

Such promotional materials illustrate Salvador's reputation as the site of blackness and cultural purity. As Christopher Dunn points out, the discourse of *baianidade* (Bahian-ness) "combines a celebratory affirmation of blackness and black culture with notions about cordial, non-confrontational race relations, sensuality, aesthetic beauty, and specific performative competencies" (2007, 850). Representations of Afro-Bahian culture emphasize its loyalty to African traditions, a sharp contrast to Rio de Janeiro. According to Livio Sansone (2003), the commodification of black culture in Rio de Janeiro revolves around samba and Carnaval, which celebrates mixture, borrowing, and cultural patchwork, while in Salvador, the emphasis is on roots or heritage tourism. Says Romo, "Bahia currently attracts millions of international and Brazilian tourists to a land portrayed as a living part of Brazil's past. The state's tourism board touts Bahia's claim as the 'birthplace of Brazil' and the cradle of Brazilian traditions" (2010, 7). Since as early as the 1970s, African American heritage tourism has been recognized as a target market for the Bahian tourism industry (Pinho 2008; Romo 2010).

Joceval connects this utilization of Afro-Brazilian culture in the tourist economy to racism: "Racism in Bahia and in Brazil is very perverse. . . . It's hidden. They like black culture but don't accept black people. Black culture is okay, but black people, no. This culture is sucked dry, but black people remain poor." Michael Hanchard similarly points out that racial democracy limits Afro-Brazilians to roles as "arbiters of expressive culture and sexuality" (1994, 74). Marcelo, an unlicensed tour guide who had worked in the industry for eight years, noted that he had no luck working with clients from other regions of Brazil or white Americans, whom he claimed were complicated, demanding, and racist: "They don't like black people, so they don't like Bahia."[13] Marcelo distinguished between white Americans, who do not like black people, and white Europeans, who formed an integral part of his client base.

Similarly, Fiúca, a white Brazilian woman tour guide, highlighted the irony of Afro-Brazilian culture's important role in the tourist industry: "Afro-Brazilian culture is utilized because it has vitality . . . but that which is used as an attraction doesn't benefit [everyone]. The majority of the black population is poor and suffers discrimination. Tourism [revenue] doesn't make it back to these populations." The crucial question to consider, then, is how marginalized Afro-Brazilian communities whose cultural heritage is being used to market their city to the rest of the world can enjoy some of the benefits of the transnational tourism industry in Salvador. This is the situation that *caça-gringas* and *pega-turistas* confront when they use their Afro-Brazilian cultural knowledge to approach and attract foreign tourists for intimate encounters. However, these individuals' attempts to remedy the inequality in wealth distribution in Bahia often do not benefit their communities.

Afro-Brazilian Culture in Bahia's Tourism Industry

One day at the beginning of Carnaval in February 2007, I was waiting to pick up someone at the airport in Salvador. Each time the sliding doors that led to the baggage claim area opened, I caught glimpses of *baianas estilizadas* (stylized *baianas*), with big-layered dresses, rows upon rows of shiny beads, and elaborate West African–style head wraps. The muffled sound of drums coming from inside the baggage claim became louder every time another happy tourist emerged. The *baianas* strolled around majestically, approaching visitors with warm, infectious smiles and offering gifts of *fitinhas do Bonfim*, thin strips of colored ribbon tied around the wrist three times to grant three wishes. This was not my first encounter with *baianas*, but the airport scene struck me because it is uncommon to encounter the stylized *baianas* outside of Pelourinho, where they pose for pictures with tourists—for a fee, of course. I wondered why the *baianas* were at the airport. When I returned home that day, I found my answers on the evening news. Bahiatursa had contracted the *baianas* to welcome tourists to Salvador during Carnaval. Another state tourism agency, Emtursa, also operated an information booth with a life-sized image of a *baiana*. However, although *baianas* smile and radiate the joy of the Terra da Felicidade, many of these women are poor and marginalized, commuting from the periphery of the city to sell *acarajé* (fritters made with ground black-eyed peas) in the tourist districts.

Baianas are iconic figures in Bahia, honored with plaques and exhibits that feature them in crisp, white lace and intricate head wraps. In Praça da Sé, the Memorial of the Baianas bears a sign: "The *baianas*, with their traditional outfits, are the icon of Bahia. . . . This memorial honors all the *baianas* in their diverse manifestations . . . who, with their art and tradition, became the muses of writers, composers, painters, photographers and all those who love the culture and people of Bahia." During my first summer research trip to Salvador in 2005, I was walking through Pelourinho when I noticed a black Brazilian woman calling out to passersby, "Come take a picture as a *baiana* and capoeirista!" She was standing in front of a tourist agency in the middle of Terreiro de Jesus, a popular plaza. Before long, I saw a white, English-speaking family of four strolling through the cobblestone streets. I turned away for an instant. When I looked back, the man was dressed like a capoeirista, wearing an Afro wig, and posing in front of a drum. His wife, dressed as a *baiana* with a turban on her head, joined him, while their two sons stood by, chuckling.

In Bahia, Afro-Brazilian culture has been transformed into a tourist commodity. It is an attraction that lures even white middle-aged leisure tourists from across the globe into its grasp, encouraging them to embrace, perform, and embody a previously foreign blackness. Walking through Pelourinho's winding cobblestone streets, one sees telephone booths shaped like coconuts, drums, and *berimbaus*. Given the state's long, sordid, and shifting relationship to Afro-Brazilian culture, what are the implications of the fact that foreign tourists can pay to dress up as Afro-Brazilian men and women? While obviously not all Afro-Brazilians are *baianas* or capoeiristas, the particular Afro-Brazilian identities that foreign tourists were invited to perform were explicitly linked to "traditional" Afro-Brazilian cultural practices. As Romo observes, "Capoeira and Candomblé, practices once earnestly repressed by Bahia's elite, are now promoted as cultural experiences to draw in visitors" (2010, 7).

The image of the *baiana* first garnered international attention through the body of a white Portuguese singer, Carmen Miranda, whose song, "O Quê É Que a Baiana Tem?" (What Is It That the Bahian Woman Has?), from the 1938 film *Banana da Terra*, became a hit. Although Miranda's performance repertoire drew generously from Afro-Bahian culture, she visited Bahia only once—for a month—after she was already famous (Ubaldo Marques Porto Filho 2006, 56). In Dunn's words, between 1930 and 1950, Bahia was constructed "in the national imagination as a place that was simultaneously exotic and paradigmatic vis-à-vis the nation" (2007, 854). Thus, the exoticized imagination of Bahia is not only transnational—circulating through tourism propaganda, for example—but also national. Consequently, domestic tourists from São Paulo or Rio Grande do Sul, for example, are just as likely to maintain ideas of black hypersexuality as are foreign tourists from Europe or North America.

Brazil as a whole and Bahia in particular have taken varying attitudes toward Afro-Brazilian culture. White elites in early nineteenth-century Bahia strongly opposed "Africanisms," and the legal system, government, and armed forces embarked on a zealous campaign to stamp out African cultural retentions that were believed to be running rampant in Bahian culture (Kim Butler 1998, 171). Bahia's earnest efforts to emulate the "order, progress, and modernity of Southern Brazil" illustrated a pervasive fear that Africanisms hindered progress (Kim Butler 1998, 17).[14] In the 1930s, under President Getúlio Vargas, the Brazilian state began gradually to incorporate certain aspects of black culture into the national image. Following Antonio Sérgio Alfredo Guimarães, this process can be seen as an aspect of the symbolic promises of racial democracy: Brazil prided itself on being a *mestiço* nation where "artistic, folkloric and symbolic manifestations of black Brazilians were recognized as *Afro-Brazilian culture*" (2006, 276). Thus, as Romo points out, "Bahia's African heritage moved from being viewed as a problem to becoming a treasured part of the state's traditions" (2010, 51). Before long, the state destigmatized black culture in urban Bahia and made it an integral part of the public image (Sansone 2003).

As Ubiratán Albino, a fifty-three-year-old Afro-Brazilian employee in the Secretariat of Tourism's special division for "Afro-ethnic tourism," told me in an interview, "O negro está na moda" (Black people are in fashion).[15] Thus, Afro-Brazilian culture has gone from being suppressed and criminalized to being transformed into romanticized and folklorized activities (MacLachlan 2003; Crook and Johnson 2000). As Dunn notes, Bahia's white elites and middle classes "have no problem with the idea that Salvador is a black city" (2007, 850). In fact, Bahiatursa has actively promoted this representation of *baianidade*. Yet the representation of Salvador as a "black city" has not diminished the "forms of racial exclusion and violence that have adversely affected the black community of Salvador" (Dunn 2007, 850). Furthermore, according to Edward Telles, the major contradiction of the predicament of black culture and black people in Salvador is that "blacks are granted free run of the cultural realm . . . and the culture of Africa is celebrated, apparently in exchange for relinquishing claims to economic and political power so that it can continue to be monopolized by a small white elite" (2004, 213).

Samba offers insight into the relationship between the Brazilian state and Afro-Brazilian cultural forms. Samba was an integral part of the larger project of institutionalizing national culture and providing a forum for black cultural expression (Darien Davis 1999; Vianna 1999). In the 1920s, when samba was restricted to black and poor populations in Rio de Janeiro, it was brutally repressed, and tambourines were considered weapons. However, in 1933, President Vargas officially recognized samba schools in Rio de Janeiro in an effort to win the loyalty of the urban working class and Afro-Brazilians (Meade 2003, 194). To garner popular support for his regime, Vargas created agencies designed to promote culture (Pravaz 2008a, 86).

Vargas's populist corporate dictatorship not only required all samba school themes to have national motifs but also regulated song themes and commissioned the production of hundreds of *sambas de exaltação* (laudatory songs) that praised the government (Darien Davis 1999). The lyrics often "formulated fables of Brazil as a happy people, living in a tropical paradise, and happily miscegenated, ideas usually expressed around the idea of the mulata or the 'brown' character of the Brazilian people" (Pravaz 2008a, 88). By the late 1940s, Rio de Janeiro's samba was presented as a national delicacy to illustrious foreign visitors, and Carnaval became a major tourist attraction and significant source of revenue (Vianna 1999; Meade 2003). At this critical moment in Brazilian history, "culture was invested with the task of homogenizing the nation through the appropriation of regional symbols" (Pravaz 2008a, 87).[16] At around this time, Brazilian popular music went global, propelled in part by Vargas's policies (Davis 2009). Darien Davis claims that blackness became "a mechanism through and by which Brazilians could celebrate 'authentic' national culture" (2009, 188).

Joceval

I first met Joceval, an Afro-Brazilian tour guide, at a cultural exchange event between a small group of African Americans and Afro-Brazilians at the Terreiro do Cobre in the neighborhood of Engenho Velho da Federação. Joceval is from a poor family in rural Bahia, and he migrated to Salvador in 2001. He worked as a waiter for ten years before becoming the first of his parents' twelve children to enter and graduate from college. He was inspired to study English in 1992 when he heard a song but did not understand the lyrics, and he was very proud of how far he had come from his poor rural childhood. He had spent nearly three weeks in Italy and had become proficient in English, Spanish, and Italian. While studying literature at the Catholic University of Bahia, he got a job working for Bahiatursa, which piqued his interest in tourism. Shortly thereafter, he took a six-month tour guide training course offered by the tour guides union. When he began working as a tour guide, he was in great demand because of his specialization in Afro-ethnic tourism.

Joceval's knowledge of Afro-Brazilian culture made him a popular tour guide for African Americans. One group of retired African American men ranging in age from fifty-five to sixty-two had been visiting Salvador every six months for the preceding three years. Three of the men had come on every trip, bringing along between two and four different friends each time. Joceval organizes excursions for them, including visits to the Chapada Diamantina, an ecotourist region of Bahia. However, he recognizes that "their major intention is girls. They aren't capable of getting girls like this in the United States." When they ask, Joceval shows them *casas* (houses of prostitution) located in middle-class residential neighborhoods along the coastline or in the Centro Histórico, where the men can encounter a variety of women—*morenas, negras*, white women with blond hair (a rarity in Bahia).

These *casas* are located predominantly in the neighborhoods of Rio Vermelho, Ipitanga, and Ondina. The men pay $R50 to the taxi driver plus R$150 to the *garota de programa*. In other *casas*, according to Joceval, a *programa* costs R$150, of which R$60 goes to the casa and R$90 goes to the *garota de programa*. Joceval sees his role as a facilitator, telling the men where to find the houses, but "I don't think I'm being a pimp." His "disidentification" (Esteban-Munoz 1999) with this term suggests that the sex tourism industry is a broad, far-reaching, diffuse institution that engulfs a variety of actors. In other words, it is part and parcel of the tourism industry itself, undergirded by both the erotic expectations of foreigners and the economic imperatives of tourism industry workers.

Jorginho

I met Jorginho, an Afro-Brazilian dancer, when I took his dance classes in Pelourinho. Growing up in a working-class, predominantly black neighborhood far removed from the tourist district, he rarely if ever saw tourists during his childhood and adolescence. Only when he began to work in the realm of Afro-Brazilian culture in 1997 did he begin to discover the ways in which foreigners were interested in that culture. Roughly half of the students in his classes were foreign tourists, students, and expatriates, a fact whose significance was not lost on Jorginho: "Tourism helps me a lot. I wouldn't have the quantity of students that I have [without tourism]. The Bahian doesn't value his own culture. I depend greatly on tourists. I have to know how to speak foreign languages."

Jorginho noted that Bahians often describe foreigners as cold, closed, and introverted. Conversely, the image of Bahians is "*gostoso* [sexy/tasty], attractive, extroverted." While on an international tour with the Balé Folclórico da Bahia, Jorginho dated women from Finland, Australia, Canada, Switzerland, the United States, Japan, Israel, and Puerto Rico and traveled to the United States, Australia, Canada, Argentina, and all over Brazil. According to Jorginho, although he loved dancing and performing, the Balé Folclórico only paid dancers adequately when they were on tour, and he realized that he could earn a better living as a dance teacher in Bahia than as a dancer/performer. However, he was dismayed to discover that being a dance teacher seemed to involve having foreign women and men see him as a sexual object. Jorginho's experience traveling abroad and interacting with foreign women taught him that the foreign, culturally different Other is simultaneously coveted and eroticized. In this early phase of his career as a performer, he reflected, "I was desired. I did shows at great theaters in New York City, Australia, and the women would go crazy. They knew we were Bahian, and they offered to show us around their cities. We would drink and make out. When I returned to Salvador . . . I could communicate in their languages, and I was coveted as a professor. 'Street dance' teachers were seen as sex objects. . . . It was a struggle. The foreign women would see me wiggling my hips and they would be attracted. After class, there would always be a foreign female student waiting for me. After a while, I created a consciousness that this wasn't what I wanted. I wanted my profession to be valued."

On one occasion, a foreign male tourist made assumptions not only about Jorginho's sexual availability but also about his sexual orientation: "Once I was drinking juice, and a tourist passed by me. He was trying to pick me up. He offered his phone number. The man told me I was very handsome and sexy. I told him that's not my sexual preference; I'm not a *garoto de programa* [male prostitute]. 'You should be careful to not offend people.' He asked, 'Then where can I find a *negão bonito* [big handsome black man] with a big—?'" Jorginho was frequently propositioned by both male and female foreigners: "I've already had some men asking me, 'Where can I get some girls here?' I responded, 'It's not like that. That's not with me.'" *Gringos* clearly thought that they understood Jorginho's role, although they did not.

Bahia has numerous Afro-Brazilians who have traveled to Europe as capoeiristas, dance instructors, and samba dancers, often as a result of their complex intimate transnational connections with foreign tourists. Jorginho explained, "Everyone has the desire to go beyond their borders. The Bahian is always in search of a tourist to travel with because here he isn't being valued. There, he will be valued much more." Jorginho is asserting that the skills and expertise of capoeiristas, dancers, and drummers are more in demand overseas than in Bahia because of the exoticness and foreignness of Afro-Brazilian culture. He credits a universal desire for transnational mobility as motivating Bahians to cultivate liaisons, friendships, business partnerships, and relationships with foreign tourists.

Jorginho's story reveals how the confluence of culture and sex plays out in the sexual economies of tourism, where black bodies and black culture are eroticized. The stories of Joceval and Jorginho illuminate how Bahian tourism industry workers are implicated in the intersections of culture and sex in Salvador's touristscape. Both men ultimately had to negotiate the politics of cultural consumption and assumptions of sexual licentiousness.

Candomblé: A Case Study in Afro-Brazilian Cultural Appropriation

One evening in January 2003, I saw wooden signs posted by a local tour agency advertising "Authentic Candomblé Tonight." I was traveling with an African American female friend who, like myself, was a practitioner of Santería, an Afro-Cuban religious tradition which, like Candomblé, derives from traditional Yoruba religious practices. We were surprised that sacred ceremonies could be transformed into moneymaking spectacles in the tourist economy. A few days later, a Bahian colleague invited us to a Candomblé *festa* (ritual celebration) for an acquaintance who had recently been initiated. At the *festa*, we saw a large group of tourists enter the sacred space. Dressed in casual clothes, they blocked the center aisle and doorway instead of moving to sit on the sides, which were segregated by gender. The tourists looked awkward and out of place, with expressions of shock on their faces as they witnessed *orixás* manifesting themselves in the bodies of their adherents. Long before the end of the *festa*, the group departed abruptly. Soon after they left, the *orixá* Iansã came and performed a fierce, energetic dance in the aisle and doorway, flailing her *iruke* (horsetail whip) as if she were clearing the space and the energy that the tourists had previously been blocking.

Three years later, at a meeting of Candomblé *terreiros*, Dr. Ordep Serra, an anthropologist, professor, and an *ogãn* (male religious leader) of Casa Branca, one of the oldest *terreiros* in Salvador, denounced the practice of tourist agencies charging exorbitant fees (up to one hundred reais per person) for tourists to attend Candomblé religious functions. In Serra's observations, the tourists often entered the sacred space with a profound lack of respect for what they were witnessing. They seemed to be under the impression that their payment entitled them to front-row seats, service, and food. To make matters worse, they often wore dark colors to a Festa de Oxalá, an act that is highly offensive to this *orixá*, whose preferred color is pure white. Most important, Serra complained that the tourists behaved as if they were witnessing a folkloric show or performance rather than a somber, serious, religious ceremony. Serra urged his fellow religious leaders to take the initiative and end this exploitative practice that allowed tourist agencies to profit from religion. He highlighted the sad irony that none of the profits from the "cover charge" ever made their way to the coffers of the Candomblé *terreiros.*[17] Danila, another tour guide, emphasized the fact that "Salvador is sought after because of Pelourinho, black culture, and history. For Italians, Afro-Brazilian religiosity is very mystical."

Salvador is home to some of the oldest and most famous *terreiros* in Bahia (Selka 2007, 73). The commodification, folklorization, and eroticization of Candomblé within the tourist economy reveals how the Bahian state has shifted over time in dealing with Afro-Brazilian cultural practices. Candomblé emerged as a collective Afro-Brazilian response to enslavement and resistance to dehumanization. It is a religion where blackness is marked with divinity, but it has now been integrated into the consumptive practices of globalized tourism (Harding 2000, 156).[18] The Bahian state and tourism industry have transformed Candomblé into a thing to be consumed, witnessed, and experienced by anyone who so desires. This is particularly nefarious in light of Cheryl Sterling's argument that Candomblé represents a space where Afro-Brazilian women can "gain personal power and agency in a social and political climate that continues to treat them as sub-citizens" (Romo 2010, 72).

The folklorization of Candomblé did not begin with the advent of the globalized tourism industry in Bahia. The three Afro-Brazilian Congresses that convened leading scholars to discuss the African contributions to Brazil in the 1930s polished Candomblé's image as the national folk institution (Romo 2010, 7). The first congress was held in Recife in 1934 and organized by noted Brazilian sociologist and anthropologist Gilberto Freyre, while the second congress was held in Salvador in 1937 and organized by Afro-Bahian ethnologist Edson Carneiro (51).[19] In the mid-1930s, it was not uncommon to read editorials in the Bahian press that "deplored the existence of Candomblé," and Carneiro organized a series of articles to educate the Bahian public about the religion in 1936 (65). The 1937 congress held in Salvador combined activism with scholarly work and involved both scholars and members of the Afro-Brazilian community, such as Candomblé leaders. Participants in this congress launched a formal petition for religious liberty (81). At the time, *terreiros* were required to purchase permits from the police department any time they wanted to celebrate a religious festival (82). According to Carneiro, the 1937 congress had a significant impact on Bahia: "It ended the image of terror that the Candomblés represented for the so-called superior classes of Bahia. . . . [T]hey ended up learning that blacks didn't eat people, nor did they practice indecencies during their religious ceremonies. The publicity of the congress, in the newspapers and radio, contributed to create a setting of greater tolerance for these slandered religions of people of color" (quoted in Romo 2010, 83–84). In 1967, the state governor of Bahia declared Candomblé a form of folklore rather than a religion. This act not only exempted Candomblé from certain constitutional protections but also placed it under police supervision. Since the 1970s, Candomblé priests have uniformly condemned the folklorization of their religion, which involves the display of ritual objects, music, and dances in Carnaval parades and nightclub shows to fascinate tourists and generate revenue for the state (Matory 2005, 182).

Stephen Selka points out that Candomblé is often featured prominently in tourist advertisements and that several of Bahia's politicians and entertainers are patrons of *terreiros*. Candomblé has been incorporated into daily life in Salvador, as can be seen in the ways in which shopping malls and apartment buildings are named after *orixás*. Similarly, Romo notes that "the tourist board itself distributes lists of *terreiros*, or temples of Candomblé, where travelers looking for an authentic vision of Afro-Brazilian culture may observe the continued force of the African heritage in Bahia" (2010, 7). Joceval, an adherent of Candomblé, previously took tourists to *festas* but he became offended by the behavior of tourists, who would "wear inappropriate clothes, come in groups of thirty to fifty people, and disrespect the people of the *terreiro*." By the time I spoke with him, he would "only take my clients who are genuinely interested . . . who have a profound respect for Candomblé," rather than tourists who would treat Candomblé like a show. He was particularly bothered by the fact that the *terreiro* often "doesn't get anything out of it" even though agencies charge between fifty and one hundred reais per person.

The extent to which foreign tourists are informed of appropriate dress code and behavioral expectations of Candomblé *festas* may vary depending on the tour guide or agency. Popular, well-known Candomblé *terreiros* often have public calendars of *festas*, and *festas* are usually open to the public, particularly members of the community in which the *terreiro* is located. All guests are served a plate of traditional Bahian food after the *festa* at no charge. In a sense, then, by charging tourists to see the *festa*, tour guides are capitalizing on this free community event. Moreover, many tourists may receive their first exposure to Candomblé at a folkloric performance such as the Balé Folclórico da Bahia, which offers a segment on *orixá* dances where the dancers mimic possession by the deities. Such presentations also influence the expectation that Candomblé *festas* will resemble performances.

After nearly two decades of the conservative right-wing state government of Antonio Carlos Magalhães, Bahia elected Jacques Wagner of the Workers' Party (PT) to office in October 2006. The new administration promptly launched the an "Afro-ethnic tourism" initiative with the goal of attracting African American heritage tourists and directing more of the financial gain from tourism into the hands of Salvador's Afro-Brazilian community. Billy Arquimimo of the Bahian state Secretariat of Tourism noted that "Afro-ethnic tourism is not new. What is new is the way the government is working with this tourism. . . . In the previous government, there was a lot of marketing, but there weren't any public policies for black people." Selling Bahia as a tourist destination, he said, requires increasing direct and charter flights from the United States and as well as the number of African American investors in Bahian hotels, companies, and products. The Afro-ethnic tourism initiative also planned to launch a program that would enable foreign tourists to stay in Candomblé houses and with cultural groups. Kátia, a black Brazilian woman who had worked with the initiative, described this as an effort to make sure that the *terreiro* and the community receive some of the income from tourism.

Kátia pointed out that whereas the previous government sold Bahia with Afro-Brazilian culture, the current government recognizes that black communities need economic development as well as cultural development. Now, black people who have experience in these communities will be working with the new state program, a benefit, she believes, because "what is the use of working in a majority black city where they're excluded?" This program is intended to change the current state of affairs, in which the privileges and resources that derive from tourism are "not found in the hands of black people." This proposed partnership with Candomblé *terreiros* represented a significant change from the way travel agencies and tour guides had been dealing with *terreiros*. Notes Kátia, "Candomblé *terreiros* have been treated only as a space of visitation, where the travel agencies and tour guides, not the *terreiros*, make the decisions. The state has a responsibility to intervene. . . . If the guide commodifies the *terreiro*, the *terreiros* have the right to complain." Afro-Brazilian religious leaders met with representatives of the secretariat of tourism and Bahiatursa to talk about ways to effect change. Group members agreed that the calendar of *festas* would be publicized only by the *terreiros* rather than by travel agencies or other third-party tourist-related organizations and that a trilingual pamphlet would be created to inform tourists about proper behavior inside *terreiros*.

Conclusion: Reclaiming Agency
in the Globalized Tourism Industry

On January 20, 2007, a Bahian friend invited me to attend a cultural exchange event at a *terreiro* in the neighborhood of Federação with a group of between ten and fifteen African Americans.[20] The event sought to promote dialogue between African American tourists and Afro-Brazilians. The group had met previously for other cultural exchanges, but I was recruited to help translate. The American participants included three women from Denver who were practitioners of Ifá religious tradition as well as a Methodist pastor and his family from Washington, D.C. The pastor spoke out against religious intolerance against Candomblé. One of the African American priestesses read a poem, "Dreaming Brazil," that was dedicated to the pastor and his family. While sitting on the floor listening to the poem, the pastor closed his eyes, and his body began shaking and jerking involuntarily. The *filhas de santo* (priestesses) looked at him with amazement. In their religious milieu, his movements were signs of an *orixá* coming to mount his or her "horse." Afterwards, one of the elder *filhas* joked, "I'm going to do his initiation because his place is here!"

African Americans and Afro-Brazilians alternated making presentations. One *ogãn* of the *terreiro* showed a local newspaper photograph of a military police officer stepping on a young black Brazilian man's face on the beach in the neighborhood of Pituba. The man had been falsely accused of stealing a white female tourist's purse. With his voice full of hope, the *ogãn* told the group, "You could be starting a new kind of tourism in Salvador, where our communities won't be exposed to . . . violence, prostitution, and so forth." The newspaper clipping raises anew a crucial question that Anani Dzidzienyo had asked nearly fifteen years earlier: "What have been the real rewards for Afro-Brazilians . . . now that the dominant society, including exclusive hotels, serves feijoada and the whitest Brazilians are practitioners of Candomble?" (Minority Rights Group 1995, 348). What benefits have Afro-Brazilians gained from the success of tourism in this Black Mecca where Afro-Brazilian cultural production is used to market Bahia to the rest of Brazil and the world? Afro-Brazilian culture rakes in millions of dollars every year, while police regularly beat (and even kill) Afro-Brazilian men and Afro-Brazilians are expelled/removed from their communities, their citizenship and rights denied in favor of the foreign tourist's comfort and safety (Sepúlveda dos Santos 1999). Apparently, as Romo astutely points out, "official interest in celebrating Bahia's African heritage has not resulted in reform that benefits blacks in Bahia" (2010, 158), nor has it altered the racial imbalance of power in Bahian society.

The spatial and racial dynamics of sex work in the tourist districts are bound up with processes of social exclusion. Notions of who belongs and who is out of place here are contingent on race, sexuality, and labor. Foreign leisure tourists and elites move about freely, the privileged occupants of tourist spaces that have been designed solely for occupants of these strata. Conversely, marginalized subjects such as black Brazilians and sex workers of various races are excluded and pushed out. Nonetheless, these marginalized subjects engage in practices and strategies to resist being exiled. Sex workers in Salvador, visible at sites heavily frequented by tourists, reveal how sexuality is public, politically contested, racialized, and economically charged.

Returning to the case of *caça-gringas* also gives us tools to think through the agency of marginalized subjects in attempting to reap some of the benefits of a tourism industry that largely excludes them. Bahian *caça-gringas* are constructed as "masterful culture bearers" who possess not only desired "techniques of bodily conduct" but also virile masculinity (Ness 2003, 96). They secure their masculinity through notions of conquest and physical prowess by relying on their Afro-Brazilian cultural expertise. Thus, they are attempting to intervene in the "puzzling coexistence of privileged Afro-Brazilian traditions with black economic and political marginality" that characterizes Salvador's contemporary touristscape (Romo 2010, 157).

When I was talking with Wilson, he told me that many *caçadores* pursue *gringas* out of necessity, while others do it for pleasure and leisure—to have fun. Wilson said that his friend, Sergio, a short, muscular, dark-skinned man with artificial dreadlocks, was "already getting sick of" the game of attracting foreign tourists because they had begun approaching him. In fact, he often had two or three *gringas* a day pursuing him. Sergio claimed, somewhat suspiciously, that one *gringa* had given him seven thousand reais even though he had not asked for it. While some *caçadores* were desperate enough to pick up seventy-year-old women, Sergio said that others find that idea horrifying. Wilson claimed that he pursues *gringas* not because he has to but because he likes to meet people of different cultures. These comments suggest that Bahian *caçadores* may pursue *gringas* or *gringos* out of necessity or a desire for cosmopolitanism. In this case, I conceptualize cosmopolitanism as the opportunity to expand one's network of friends, acquaintances, and lovers from all over the world, to enhance one's chances of traveling abroad, and simply to enjoy access to one's own city in a way that is usually reserved for tourists and Brazilian elites.

CHAPTER TWO

Racial Hierarchies of Desire
and the Specter of Sex Tourism

I met Becky, a twenty-nine-year-old schoolteacher from Portland, Oregon, at the bus stop in Barra when I saw a *caçador* (hunter) flirting with her. A blond, blue-eyed American woman, she looked visibly annoyed and uninterested. When the Praça da Sé bus came, she sat next to me, so we started a conversation. On her third trip to Bahia, Becky was renting a two-bedroom apartment in Barra with eight other people for a weeklong capoeira event. Before she left Portland, some of Becky's friends joked that she "would come back with a husband." "People thought I would have a harem," she said. However, she insisted that she came to Bahia solely to play capoeira, unlike her housemate, Annie, whom Becky described as a very friendly and outgoing woman who was constantly inviting Brazilians back to their apartment. "Being on vacation gave [Annie] license" to date freely and sleep with Brazilian men. In a sense, the liminality of the tourism experience enabled and empowered Annie to participate in practices in which she ordinarily would not engage at home.

Becky said that all of the women in the capoeira group have had experiences with aggressive Bahian men attempting to "pick them up." She has earned a reputation as "the Bitch" because she does not want to be bothered. Becky noted that in the Barra, "people know where we live and know our movements." In fact, a Bahian man followed one of her housemates to the apartment from the beach, and Becky's friend started crying because he would not leave. As a foreign white woman, Becky felt constantly harassed in the streets of Salvador by men who assumed she was seeking companionship. She occasionally frequented the Terça da Benção (Tuesday Night Parties) in Pelourinho but was overwhelmed by her constant negotiations with local men: "There's a lot of groping, and an overabundance of soliciting. I can't do this—it's so intense. . . . [I]t's like if you dance with them, you're saying much more." Becky reflected on the complicated sexual politics of the transnational space of capoeira in Salvador: "I've met people who are nice about helping with capoeira. I don't know what they want—if they're being nice because they're nice or because they see the dollar sign and passport." Becky's awareness of her economic and national privilege makes her question Brazilians' hospitality. The skepticism about ulterior motives that often underlies interracial liaisons and relationships—particularly cross-national ones—has also been described in Cuba and the Dominican Republic (Cabezas 2009; Fernandez 2010).

Furthermore, Becky's praise of Brazilian women as "gorgeous" and her recognition of the centrality of the butt in Brazilian aesthetics made her question why Brazilian men would want to hit on her: "It's usually the darker men who hit on me. I'm like, 'How could you choose this over Brazilian women?' I tell these guys, 'No, you're in love with me because you think I have a shit-load of money.'" Becky's reference to Brazil's "butt culture" reflects the fact that the country's popular cultural aesthetic valorizes *bundas* or *bum-bums* (backsides) rather than breasts, as is the case in the United States and other countries, although this aesthetic preference may also be differentiated along racial/ethnic lines in the United States. The popularity of "Brazil Butt Lift" infomercials on mainstream U.S. television channels is one indication of the renown that this Brazilian aesthetic has achieved.

Elisete, a middle-aged Afro-Brazilian tourism professional, had markedly different experiences from those that confronted Becky: "My own color draws attention in Pelourinho. I go to Pelourinho with no makeup, with jeans, tennis shoes, and clothes that cover my body. . . . Just by being a black woman, you become a tourist attraction. [The tourist] approaches you, thinking you're a sex worker—even the domestic tourist who comes on a business trip." Elisete's experiences reveal how black Brazilian women must engage in creative strategies and bodily practices to be treated with respect as they navigate through the touristic spaces of their native city. In this sense, they experience racism and sexism not only based on their identities and bodies but also as "spatial acts" (McKittrick 2006, xviii). Notions of the hypersexuality of blackness that circulate in the tourist imaginary create a racial hierarchy of desire in Salvador. While the standard of beauty still privileges whiteness, the standard of sensuality privileges women of African descent (Williams 2010).

These women's stories reveal the complexities of the racial hierarchies of desire in Salvador, where white foreign women and Afro-Brazilian women are situated in fundamentally different ways. Merely moving through the sexualized touristscape forces Afro-Brazilian women to negotiate propositions from foreign tourists, who assume that these women are sexually available. In some ways, Becky and other white foreign women are also presumed to be sexually available, but this assumption is not attributed to "innate" characteristics but rather is based on the assumption that white foreigners are seeking black eroticized bodies. Salvador's white Brazilian women are conscious that they are not foreign tourists' preferred objects of desire. One white Brazilian woman commented, "*Gringos* don't even look at me. They look at any black woman." Fabiana, the white cofounder and lead organizer of Aprosba, told me that at the age of forty, she no longer does *programas* with tourists because "they prefer younger women [and] black and *mestiça* women." She also said that when she used to go with groups of sex workers to the ships that were docked at the port, "there were around twenty *mestiças* and five white women," a ratio that indicates the preferred—though not exclusive—objects of desire for foreign ship workers.

This chapter articulates what I call the specter of sex tourism, an assemblage that encompasses the myriad ramifications and reverberations of sex tourism. The specter of sex tourism is a racialized discourse that profoundly affects the daily lives of Salvador's men and women—white and black, Bahian and foreign, sex workers and non–sex workers. This concept suggests that the reach of sex tourism extends beyond those who participate in commercial sexual transactions. In fact, it makes any and all transnational and cross-racial encounters seem suspect. One does not have to be a sex worker or a sex tourist to feel the effects of discourses regarding sex tourism. Becky's story illustrates the common expectation that foreign men and women who come to Bahia for cultural purposes will be eager and willing to engage in intimate encounters as well. This chapter reflects on the racial hierarchies of desire in the sexual economies of Salvador and the specter of sex tourism that consequently emerges. The chapter situates an ethnography of conversations with Afro-Brazilian women who were not sex workers but who were routinely mistaken for sex workers by foreign tourists in the historical context of discourses of black sexuality in Brazil. Furthermore, it engages important discussions of Brazilian racial discourses such as racial democracy, *mestiçagem*, and whitening and analyzes the ever-present role of these discourses in contemporary tourist propaganda used to market Bahia to the rest of the world as a site for erotic adventure.

Seduction in Tourist Propaganda: *Mulatas* and Racial Democracy

Brazil has been constructed as the "land of samba and sensuality" (Kingstone 2004). A 2002 print media advertisement created by Embratur, the national tourism agency, features exotic, round fruit and the words "Paradise exists.

And with no forbidden fruit. Come to Brasil and get away from your tensions." Tourists are encouraged to indulge their senses and abandon their inhibitions in a utopian escape from the world of worry, work, and weariness. The military government created Embratur in 1966 to reshape the "tarnished image of the country, caused by reports of torture and abuse by the dictatorship" (Bandyopadhyay and Nascimento 2010, 939). According to Patrick Larvie, "Brazil's tourist industry promotes the country as one which offers sexual attractions as part of the nation's natural and cultural resources" (1999, 163). Furthermore, anthropologist Angela Gilliam points out that the transformation of the northeastern region of Brazil into the "paradise of the tropics" relied on two clichés: "beautiful beaches with palms, and exotic, hot-blooded *mulatas* in provocative *tangas* [thongs]" (1994, 66).

Since the 1970s, Bahian state tourism agencies have utilized images of women as tourist products in pamphlets, videos, magazines, and other forms of advertising (Bandyopadhyay and Nascimento 2010). The images that Embratur has circulated position Brazil in the global tourist imaginary as a land of pristine beaches, nearly naked women with tan lines, *mulatas*, samba, and Carnaval (Bandyopadhyay and Nascimento 2010). Tourism advertisements have consistently represented Bahia as an exotic paradise of parties and promiscuity, beautiful women, magic, and sensuality—in short, as the most hedonistic part of Brazil. Afro-Brazilians are associated with physical prowess and nature through postcards that feature close-ups of the *bundas* of black women on the beach in miniscule bikinis, muscular black male bodies playing capoeira, and black women dancing samba. Countless such postcards are prominently displayed at newsstands in the tourist districts. Some postcards simply feature images of the backsides of black women; one shows a fly on a woman's backside with the caption, "The Fly with No Shame." Another postcard shows a black woman standing on an empty beach, her back turned to the camera and only the side of her face visible. The caption, "The North Coast of Bahia," does not even mention her presence.

A promotional video, *Ilhéus, a Terra da Gabriela* (Ilhéus, the Land of Gabriela), found in the Bahiatursa archives and sponsored by local and state governments, Bahiatursa, and an airline, also uses sexualized images of women of African descent to entice travelers. Ilhéus is a town in southern Bahia, a six-hour drive from Salvador. As the video shows a beautiful, unspoiled beach, a sensual female voice whispers to a (presumably male) audience, "You're going to fall in love, for sure." The video also shows scenes of a couple kissing, a man saying that he has "found paradise," and a close-up of a brown-skinned woman. The narrator refers to "the sensuality in the clove and cinnamon skin color" as one of many things the potential visitor will encounter and "fall in love with" in Ilhéus, a "house of your dreams" that is "ready to welcome you." Finally, the sensuous female voice says, "Now you have an obligation. But with no obligations. Come, come, and get to know me better. Live a romance with me. You won't be able to resist. It's a *pleasure* to meet you." The second *come* is whispered in an echo, and the tone of the narrator's voice emphasizes *prazer* (pleasure) in a way that gives its meaning a subliminal yet glaringly obvious sexual innuendo. The statement is accompanied by an image of a *mulata* wearing a sarong and a bikini top and walking away along the beach. Her unruly long black hair blows in the wind, and her hips sway from side to side. She enters the water and splashes, playfully throwing her hair back. The advertisement ends with the *mulata* embracing a white man—presumably a foreign tourist.[1]

Black women's sexuality in Brazil has historically been constructed as "available," "accessible" and less subject to the "honor" and respectability accorded to white female sexuality (Caldwell 2007, 40 ; Goldstein 2003, 114; Goldstein 1999, 567). Historically, the *mulata* has been figured as the national erotic icon. Since the 1930s, the figure of the *mulata* has served as the privileged representation of the mixed character of the Brazilian nation, beautiful, voluptuous, full of contagious energy, sensual, and possessing an inherent mastery of samba that is "in the blood" (Giacomini 1991, 222). The *mulata* "embodies the male sexual fantasy of uniting the white woman's respectability with the black woman's stereotypical lubricity and powerlessness" (Burdick 1998, 30). In the early twentieth century, when Brazil was consolidating its national identity, the federal government proclaimed that the best "product" that Brazil had to offer was its *mulatas*, a strategy that led to the emergence of a problematic phrase, *mulata tipo exportação* (exportation-type *mulata*). The fact that the *mulata* came to symbolize sensuality reflects how, as Alexander Edmonds points out, "physical beauty, along with samba and soccer, is a cliché of Brazil" that runs through five centuries of the country's history (2010, 24)

In the mid-1960s, Oswaldo Sargentelli, a white Carioca radio and television personality then in his forties, created what became world-famous *mulata* shows in Rio de Janeiro. Often described as a *mulatóloga* (mulattologist), or "the father of the Brazilian *mulata*," Sargentelli made a career marketing the exotic Otherness of the Brazilian *mulata*. These shows contributed to the international marketing of the *mulata* as the quintessential symbol of exotic Brazilianness and as a source of national pride and tourist revenue (Caldwell 2007, 60; Pravaz 2003). These shows positioned *mulatas* on stage as spectacle and entertainment for elite Brazilians and foreigners. At the shows' height, Sargentelli had up to forty *mulatas* working for him (Dalevi 2002). In 1985, he was accused of racism and of exploiting black women, but at the time of his death in 2002, he was again hailed as the father of the Brazilian *mulata* (Alves 2002). Thus, in these types of performances where samba is made to stand in for Brazilian culture, *mulatas'* bodies fulfill "the scopophilic desires of local (and international) audiences for 'authentic' tropical abandon and *mestiço* identity" (Pravaz 2008b, 109).[2]

The international tourism industry relies on the sexualized bodies of women to market tourism destinations as sites of pleasure and sexual possibility. For example, a poster for Pan Am airlines from around 1970 advertising flights to Rio features three brown-skinned women in tiny Brazilian-style bikinis with their backsides facing the camera. Their bodies are twisted in various elegant, sensual poses, and they all look over their shoulders at the camera. Text on the poster reads, "Oba-Oba dancers from Oswaldo Sargentelli's night-club in Rio de Janeiro, Brazil."[3] Such images are used to promote products in the national context as well. The Globeleza commercials, which announce the beginning of Carnaval season on Brazil's most popular television network, Globo, feature samba-dancing *mulatas* who are completely nude except for sparkles, body paint, and assorted accessories.[4] Valéria Valenssa, an Afro-Brazilian woman who made her name parading as queen of the drumming section of a large samba school in Rio de Janeiro while wearing only body paint (Pravaz 2008b), was the Globeleza model from 1993 until 2004.[5]

Stereotypes of black licentiousness and hypersexuality have circulated throughout the world since at least as far back as the European colonial conquest of Africa.[6] Hundreds of years later, these notions circulate within the Bahian tourist imaginary and create a racial hierarchy of desire in Salvador. As Kia Lilly Caldwell writes, the "term mulata has become synonymous with prostitute for many European men who travel to Brazil for the purposes of sexual tourism" (2007, 60). Thus, national imaginations of black women's sexual accessibility have profoundly affected tourist assumptions and expectations. An old Brazilian adage cited by renowned sociologist Gilberto Freyre highlights the racial hierarchy of Brazilian women: "Branca para casar, mulata para fornicar, negra para trabalhar" (White women to marry, *mulata* to fornicate with, black women to work) (Freyre 1963 quoted in Caldwell 2007, 50). In the context of sex tourism, the notion of *mulata para fornicar* is catapulted into the international arena. A crucial aspect of the myth of the *mulata* is that she makes the white man fall victim to the heightened powers of black female sexuality. She is the seducer, while he is the seduced.

Freyre asserted that "the brown-skinned woman was preferred by the Portuguese for purposes . . . of physical love" and praised "the mulatto girl" who gave white Brazilian elite men "our first complete sensation of being a man" (1956, 13, 278). He further claimed that the Portuguese were "always inclined to a voluptuous contact with the exotic woman" (185). Scholars such as Natasha Pravaz (2003) have argued that *mulata* has shifted over time from a racial category to more of a performative, even occupational category. In other words, the *mulata* category is more about what one does (that is, dances samba) than about what one is. Nonetheless, the shift from a racial to an occupational or performance-related category does not mean that the term *mulata* has completely lost its racial connotation. It is still very much linked to a particular racialized female body, even if the meaning has been extended.

Performing what Pravaz calls *mulatice* (*mulata*-ness) does not foreclose also identifying as black or Afro-Brazilian. Even Valenssa, who is known for being the Globeleza *mulata*, also identifies as a *negra* (black) (Pravaz 2003, 131).[7] Thus, rather than being opposed or mutually exclusive, *mulata* and *negra* are situated on a continuum of Brazilian color categories that are shifting, overlapping, and flexible. When I discuss notions of "black hypersexuality," I am making a political choice to include the *mulata* in that configuration. In so doing, I draw from the scholarship and activism of Brazilian women of African descent who have situated the *mulata* under the umbrella of blackness. In July 1975, a group of Afro-Brazilians gathered at the Congress of Brazilian Women to draft the Manifesto of Black Women, which states, in part, "Black Brazilian women have received a cruel heritage: to be the objects of pleasure of the colonizers. The fruit of this cowardly crossing of blood is what is now acclaimed and proclaimed as the only national product that deserves to be exported: the Brazilian mulatta. But if the quality of the product is said to be so high, the treatment that she receives is extremely degrading, dirty, and disrespectful" (quoted in Caldwell 2007, 152).

Pioneer black Brazilian feminist scholar-activists Sueli Carneiro and Lélia Gonzalez corroborate the idea that the *mulata* is included under the rubric of black Brazilian or Afro-Brazilian women. According to Carneiro, "Yesterday we were in the service of frail mistresses and rapacious plantation owners; today we are domestic workers for 'liberated' women and housewives or mulattas-for-export" (1999, 218). Gonzalez highlights how images of black women have shifted depending on their relationship to space. While black women in public space have been associated with entertainment, leisure, and the Carnaval atmosphere (the "mythical exaltation of the mulata"), black women in the domestic space of the home have been associated with the drudgery of domestic work (the *mucama* of the colonial period) (Ratts 2011, 4). The black domestic worker is "the drudge who carries her family and other people's families on her back"; she is "the opposite of exaltation, since she is the everyday" (Gonzalez 1980, 230). As Bernd Reiter points out, domestic work not only provides a mechanism for exploiting and controlling the poor but also enables their patrons to be fully self-realized as citizens by freeing themselves from housework (2009, 80).

Afro-Brazilian is a term that can encompass women of African descent who may have various descriptors (for example, *morena*, *mulata*) for their skin colors, hair textures, and facial features. As Alma Guillermoprieto states, "The *mulata* serves to perpetuate one of the myths that Brazilians hold most dear, that there is no racism in Brazil, that miscegenation has been natural and pleasant for both parties, that white people really, sincerely, do like black people. In fact, the aesthetic superiority accorded to light-skinned black women—*mulatas*—underlines the perceived ugliness of blacks before they have been 'improved' with white blood" (1990, 180). Freyre also distinguishes between the *mulata* as a sexualized figure and the enslaved black woman as a desexualized wet nurse (Pravaz 2009, 87).

Understanding how the *mulata* has been figured as Brazil's national erotic icon offers a compelling case study in the eroticization of women of African descent in general. But this is not the only expression or example of Brazilian hypersexuality. In fact, to argue that it is would privilege a Rio de Janeiro–focused center of analysis that excludes more peripheral Brazilian cities such as Salvador. Regional hierarchies have long valorized the South and Southeast, where the major metropolitan centers of Rio de Janeiro and São Paulo are located, while other regions have been relegated to the status of backwaters. The racial dynamics of Salvador are distinct from other major cities in Brazil. In Salvador, the *mulata* is not alone in being perceived as hypersexual. In fact, *mulata* is no longer a salient category or popular term of identification in the local context as a consequence of the black movement and the area's rich Afro-Brazilian heritage. As Edmonds points out, black social movements see *morena* (brown) and *mulata* as terms that show racial alienation (2010, 126). In Salvador, the *negra* and *morena* are also sexualized and imbued with heightened erotic powers in much the same way as the *mulata* has been historically.

What are we to make of all these color terms? As Anani Dzidzienyo points out, "What makes Brazil 'Brazil' is the possibility it offers its residents to define themselves in multiple ways" (2005, 149). Reviewing some of the Brazilianist scholarship on race relations can help us parse out the various color categories of women of African descent, which include *negra*, *morena*, *mulata*, *parda* (brown), *preta* (black), or *escura* (dark), and others. John Burdick discovered that *negra* often refers directly to the unchangeable essence of a person (that is, blood), while *preta* (black) and *escura* (dark) refer specifically to skin color (1998, 19). Until the 1980s, *negra* was avoided as a self-referential term, but black social movements have led *negra* to overtake *preta* in popularity. In Salvador, I often heard black movement activists say that *preto* should be used to describe the color of one's shoes or bag, not a person. Burdick also mentions that the *preta* is often described as having hair the texture of steel wool (32). In fact, some songs describe the nappiness of *pretas'* hair and even their distasteful odor.[8] However, despite her hair's socially defined ugliness, the *preta's* body is regarded as the "seat of primitive, uncontrollable sexuality" (38). Burdick interviewed one dark-skinned woman who said, "I won't go out with a white boy because all he wants is sex. And if he gets angry, he'll throw your color right at you, calling you *nega* [pejorative term for *negra*], insulting you" (39). Burdick also describes how *pretas* were destined to be "the last ones chosen and the ones first abandoned" in the "awful calculus of the heterosexual romantic economy," in which even black men would rather pursue relationships with *morenas* or *brancas* (27). Moreover, young black women "have fantasies about being accepted by handsome light-skinned men"—what one woman called her "white Prince Charming"—and some entertain the fantasy of cleansing/purifying the womb (39). In this context, it may be understandable why black and mixed-race Brazilian women might see an advantage in pursuing *programas* and *namoros* with foreign men.

Although blackness is in some ways devalued in Brazil, brownness (*morenidade*) is nonetheless seen as the preferred social type. Russell G. Hamilton points out that the term *moreno/a* can cover a broad range of phenotypes, ranging "from a lightly tanned brunette to a dark-toned *mulata*" (2007, 187). Similarly, Pravaz says that for Freyre, "morenidade encompasses everyone from the fair-skinned brunet to brown-skinned mestizos of every hue from light to dark, and even blacks" (2009, 89). Edmonds contends that *moreno/a* "leaves one open . . . to the question of racial origin" (2010, 132). Brazilians also sometimes use the term *moreno* to refer to blacks as a way to "avoid the 'impolite' connotations of assuming that one has African descent" (Pravaz 2009, 90). Pravaz points out that *morenidade* is one aspect of the idealized perfect body, which in Rio de Janeiro takes the form of the tanned white woman. The ideal Brazilian body type for a woman is small breasts and large buttocks, and many observers link this preference to the large population of African descent (92). Ironically, while white women aspire to have tanned bodies with large buttocks, women of color are pressured to have long straight or wavy hair in conformity with Eurocentric standards of beauty. In this context, as Edmonds points out, the culture of beauty is also significant, as can be seen by the fact that "Brazil has some of the world's highest per capita rates of cosmetic surgery" (2010, 187). In addition to being associated with beauty, whiteness has long been associated with notions of civilization, elevated social status, education, employment, and the middle class (Reiter 2009, 43). The eroticization of the *mulata* fits within the context of racial democracy, *mestiçagem*, and Lusotropicalism.

Racial Democracy, *Mestiçagem*, and Lusotropicalism

The national exaltation of the *mulata* reflects narratives of racial democracy and *mestiçagem* (racial and cultural mixing) that have been central elements in Brazil's definition of itself since at least the early twentieth century. Perhaps no other aspect of Brazilian history and culture has been more highly contested and widely debated than racial democracy.[9] As the official doctrine of the Getúlio Vargas regime (1930–45, 1951–54), racial democracy served as the ideological glue that held together the Brazilian nation. It played a fundamental role in Brazil's projected image as an inclusive, nonracist nation-state (Darien Davis 1999). Brazilian scholar of race relations Carlos Hasenbalg refers to whitening and the myth of racial democracy as "the primary ideological weapons of 'racial subordination' in Brazil" (Hasenbalg 1979 quoted in Denise Ferreira da Silva 2004, 726). Denise Ferreira da Silva understands whitening and racial democracy as "hegemonic constructions of the Brazilian nation" (2004, 727), while Pravaz sees *mestiçagem* as "the dominant way of thinking about race relations in Brazil" since the 1930s (2009, 88). Freyre's theory of Lusotropicalism, which holds that the Portuguese were more racially tolerant, open to miscegenation, and immune to prejudice than were other Europeans, underlies Brazilian notions of *mestiçagem*.

Racial democracy propagates the idea that all Brazilians are mixed, a situation that is thought to preclude the existence of racism.[10] Freyre describes Brazil as "hybrid from the beginning" and as the American society that was "most harmoniously constituted so far as racial relations are concerned" (1986, 83).[11] For him, mixed-race people were the pride of Brazil rather than degenerates, and he saw miscegenation as Brazil's salvation rather than its damnation. Freyre celebrates female beauty as a natural product of miscegenation, and as Edmonds points out, this approach "was then part of a nation-building project that transformed mestiçagem into a potent symbol of Brazilian identity" (2010, 131). The myth of racial democracy quickly spread to international scholars such as American anthropologist Charles Wagley, who asserted in a 1952 UNESCO-sponsored study that Brazil was "renowned in the world for its racial democracy" (Guimarães 2005, 120). The image of Brazil as a nonracial paradise reached the United States, where many African

Americans entertained the idea of immigrating to Brazil to escape white supremacy (Hellwig 1992).

Proponents of racial democracy have argued that slavery was more benign in Brazil than elsewhere in the Americas, that class is a more significant marker of inequality than race in Brazil, that the "mulatto escape hatch" created opportunities for economic and social mobility and racial transcendence in Brazil, and that "race" is an (Afro)–North American imposition on Brazil (Bourdieu and Wacquant 1999; Degler 1971, 178; Landes 1947; Pierson 1942). Sociologist Donald Pierson was the first U.S. social scientist to conduct extensive research in Bahia and the first scholar of any nationality to study race relations, rather than African survival, there (Romo 2010, 114, 118). He ultimately concluded that "Bahia was a supremely well-adjusted society in terms of race relations" (Romo 2010, 115). Burdick (1998) and Robin Sheriff (2001) have sought to discover how the idea of racial democracy operates in Brazilians' daily lives, with Burdick asserting that racial democracy must derive some of its power from being partly true and Sheriff describing racial democracy as a dream of what Brazil ought to be rather than what it actually is.

Opponents of racial democracy, conversely, have understood it as a myth that has been fundamental to the maintenance of white supremacy in Brazil. These scholars have revealed that while racism may differ in Brazil, it is still pernicious. As Robert Stam points out, "Brazilian racism is a racism that dares not say its name: its most distinctive feature is its nondistinctiveness" (1997, 54). Scholars of the Escola Paulista (São Paulo School) such as former president Fernando Henrique Cardoso, Florestan Fernandes, and Roger Bastide drew on Marxist thought, quantitative research, and the sociology of race relations to reject the assumption of the primacy of class over race inequality and to situate race or color prejudice as "expressions of the persistence of *traditional* strongholds in the 'yet to be modernized' Brazilian social space" (Denise Ferreira da Silva 2004, 720; Fontaine 1985). Cardoso's research in Porto Alegre in southern Brazil affirmed that racial prejudice indeed existed and that "Negroes" were deemed inferior because of their color, not their class (Cardoso 1965 cited in Domínguez 1994). Likewise, Fernandes understood racism as an archaic survival from the precapitalist slavery past, and he anticipated that racism would disappear as the competitive social order became well established (Domínguez 1994; Telles 2004).

In the 1970s, research on race in Brazil was deeply influenced by the country's burgeoning black movement (Fontaine 1985). Research in this period highlighted race as a central feature of Brazilian society and analyzed how the Brazilian social order maintained racial inequalities without encountering significant opposition and conflict (Hasenbalg and Huntington 1982; Winant 1992). According to Denise Ferreira da Silva, the Escola Carioca (Carioca School) of race relations emerged in the 1970s and has "now become the dominant paradigm in studies of racial subjection in Brazil," challenging the Escola Paulista's notion that racial prejudice was a holdover of "traditional Brazil" by gathering ample evidence of ongoing racial exclusion (2004, 725). The Escola Carioca wrestles with the central questions of "How can an 'anti-racist racial ideology,' *racial democracy*, co-exist with high levels of 'racial [socioeconomic] inequalities?' Why don't these inequalities lead to the emergence of 'race consciousness' among black Brazilians?" (Denise Ferreira da Silva 2004, 725). Furthermore, in her attention to the ways in which racial ideologies have shifted and transformed over time in the particular context of Bahia, Anadelia Romo presents a fundamental dilemma: "How did Afro-Brazilian culture become so valued while Afro-Brazilians themselves remain excluded from participation in public schools, and indeed, from Brazilian democracy itself?" (2010, 8). Pointing out that race "is both a social and historical construct, but it is not necessarily a national one," she critiques the way that studies of race in Brazil have claimed to provide a national overview even though their conclusions are largely based on São Paulo and Rio de Janeiro (12).

After the fall of the military regime in 1985, foreign scholars returned to studying race in Brazil. Political scientist Michael Hanchard (1994) argues that Brazilian "racial hegemony" neutralized racial identification among non-whites, thereby preventing widespread racial mobilization. This hegemony promotes discrimination by reproducing stereotypes that denigrate blacks and valorize whites while simultaneously denying the existence of racial discrimination (6). Other observers critique racial democracy for depriving Afro-Brazilians of any "legally explicit cause for their subordination against which they might mobilize" as a consequence of the absence of official or legal barriers to their absorption into society (Marx 1998, 169).

As Anani Dzidzienyo points out, "Today, unlike twenty-five years ago, very few people would assert with any confidence that Brazil has no racial problem" (2005, 138). In 1995, Cardoso became the first Brazilian president to officially recognize the existence of racism in the country, and with President Luíz Inácio Lula da Silva's creation of the Secretariat for the Promotion of Racial Equality in 2003, Brazil became the first country to have a cabinet-level government organization to focus on racial issues (Caldwell 2009). However, despite the fact that scholars since the 1950s have endlessly critiqued and challenged the myth of racial democracy, it still rears its head, particularly in contemporary discussions of affirmative action and sexual/romantic relationships (Dzidzienyo 2005; Guimarães 2006). Dzidzienyo describes the persistence of a sector of the Brazilian academy that has come to Freyre's defense by positing racial democracy as "symbolic of Brazilian race relations" and as an ideal that can "serve as a guide for social conduct" (2005, 138). Racism in Brazil today clearly manifests itself in subtle forms (Sodré 1999) such as disguised practices, hierarchical differentiations, and a general acknowledgment of inequality (Guimarães 2001) as well as in evaluations of beauty and attractiveness and sexual desire. The discourse of racial democracy has important implications for how black culture has been eroticized in the Bahian tourism industry.

Historical Legacies: The Eroticization of Black Culture in Brazil

Bahia's tourism industry is built on the enduring legacy of the myth of racial democracy. On the one hand, Brazil has accepted and valorized the African past, particularly in terms of cultural heritage (for example, samba, capoeira, Candomblé, and food).[12] Yet on the other hand, this cultural acceptance has failed to improve the contemporary realities of Afro-Brazilians (Patricia de Santana Pinho 2008, 82; Romo 2010, 8). The great irony of racial democracy is that the co-optation of Afro-Brazilian culture occurs alongside the persistence of racist attitudes toward Afro-Brazilians. As early as the 1960s, French anthropologist Roger Bastide suggested that "Afro-Brazilian culture was treated as a source of aesthetic enjoyment for whites . . . and manipulated in order to create a cultural nationalism which might compensate blacks for the whites' simultaneous push to maintain the country's colonial economy" (1967, 112). Although Freyre celebrated the African influence on Brazilian society and claimed that the "mark of the African" was present in Brazilians of all races, he did not necessarily accept these cultures as equal (Romo 2010, 51). Moreover, these celebrations of culture do not change the fact that disproportionate numbers of Afro-Brazilians still reside in favelas, are excluded from access to public higher education, are killed by police, and experience other manifestations of racial discrimination (Perry 2004; Smith 2008; Vargas 2004).

The eroticization of Afro-Brazilian cultural practices has a long history that can be traced back to foreigners who visited Brazil during slavery. As early as the 1650s, one visitor to Brazil was convinced that the "lascivious movements" of enslaved Africans "threatened the mental health of white people" (Fryer 2000, 87). An American who visited Rio de Janeiro in 1852, the Reverend Charles Samuel Stewart, also commented that the "native, heathen dances" of enslaved Africans "surpassed in revolting licentiousness anything I recollect to have witnessed" (91). In the mid-1870s, "black dancing" was galvanized as a form of entertainment for foreign visitors (93). In the 1940s, a wealthy white Bahian man described Candomblé priestesses who "dance into a frenzy, then strip themselves naked in the woods and dance some more" (Landes 1947, 139).

The realm of the sacred is not left unscathed in the transnational tour- istscape of Salvador, where an eroticized blackness is situated as the valued ideal. In her classic monograph, *The City of Women*, anthropologist Ruth Landes describes the numerous "male admirers" of women in Candomblé: white Bahian medical school students "found it more exciting to go to a priestess than to a commercial prostitute . . . because the priestess was a definite personality, and . . . there was always the chance that she would not accept the lover . . . and often she would not accept any money" (1947, 144). A 2005 Salvador guidebook written by Paulista authors replicates the racialized foreign/local paradigm in sex tourism in the national context with the southern/northern regional divide in Brazil (Crepaldi and Maciel 2005). Elisete and several of my other Afro-Brazilian interlocutors told me that they felt sexualized and objectified by white Brazilians from the South in much the same way as they did by foreign tourists from the Global North.

In the Salvador guidebook, Iara Crepaldi and Guilherme Maciel use the image of the *orixá* Iansã to discuss sexual freedom: "Sex in Salvador follows the style of the *orixá* Iansã, who walked around with her straw mat and spread it out on the ground without ceremony whenever she wanted to have sex with someone. In the Bahian capital, it is best to have sex under the light of the moon, in the middle of the forest, in beach sands" (2005, 139). These authors thus use the sacred to naturalize the hypersexuality of Afro-Brazilians, which is significant in this context where discourses of black hypersexuality abound. In Yoruba mythology, Iansã is known as the temperamental goddess of the wind, a fierce warrior who could compete with the male warriors, Ogum and Xangô, and a deity who could transform herself into a buffalo.

Representations of Afro-Brazilian religion in guidebooks and ethnogra- phies have material implications in people's lives. I met several Afro-Brazil- ians involved in Candomblé who denounced sexual tourism seeping into their religious communities. Arturo, a thirty-eight-year-old black gay activist and priest of Iansã, denounced sex tourism in Candomblé *terreiros*, including his own place of worship. Furthermore, he had met many gay foreign tourists who were interested in exploring Candomblé not for spiritual reasons but rather because they identified it as a "black space" where they could encounter their "objects of desire"—black men. Arturo discussed Bahian "boys" who brought *gringos* home to meet their families because "it's a thing of pride to date a white European with money. But after [the tourist] goes back to his country, the connection is lost. Or maybe he sends a little money, but it doesn't take the family out of poverty."

While the *mulata* can be seen as a quintessential case of the eroticization of black sexuality in Brazil, this phenomenon does not apply exclusively to women. The eroticization and marketing of Afro-Brazilian culture has affected the daily life of Jorginho, a dance teacher. Having already received several offers and opportunities to travel abroad, Jorginho decided to put his cultural expertise and professional transnational connections to work to travel to Germany, where he "perceived that there was a coveting of my body. . . . There was a woman who did class with me [in Salvador] for one to two months. . . . She left here and said that she would bring me there. One year later, she contacted me via email, with an intermediary to translate. We closed the deal. She sent money here; I bought cold-weather clothes and the plane ticket. In January, I traveled to Germany. I taught [dance] classes in the school where her Brazilian friend taught. . . . I didn't know I was going to stay in the house alone with her. She tried to seduce me—she walked around naked, in her panties. She said she liked me and asked me to marry her. She got down on her knees. I'm married; I'm not here for this type of thing."

After a few weeks, Jorginho returned to Brazil, and he looked back on this experience with disdain and regret, as it confirmed what he had felt all along: foreign tourists often create stereotypes of Bahians. "Me, as a teacher of dance and culture, it's very difficult because people come with those stereotypes [of] the dancer as a prostitute, *negão gostoso*, and *negona gostosa* [sexy/tasty black man/woman]." Despite Jorginho's professional expertise, he could not go to Germany strictly as a professional. Rather, his former student's gift of transnational mobility had strings attached. According to M. Jacqui Alexander (2005), sex tourism requires the existence of "fetishized natives," who are presumably waiting for the tourists to come and rescue them from the drudgery of their daily lives. "Fetishized natives" are rendered silent "to be appropriately consumed" within the context of sex tourism, and they "cannot live and breathe . . . for purposes other than the foreign or the sexual" and are not "permitted to travel" (70). Jamaica Kincaid's novel *A Small Place* also highlights this immobility on the part of the "native": "Every native of every place is a potential tourist, and every tourist is a native of somewhere. . . . But some natives—most natives in the world—cannot go anywhere. . . . They are too poor to go anywhere. They are too poor to escape the reality of their lives; and they are too poor to live properly in the place where they live, which is the very place you, the tourist, want to go" (1988, 18–19).

Jorginho's story illuminates how intimacy pervades relations of transactional sex and ambiguous relationships as well as the realms of Afro-Brazilian cultural production and performance. His experience also reveals the anxieties regarding how one is perceived and the need to constantly negotiate a sense of selfhood in light of a plethora of assumptions and perceptions that attempt to fix one in a narrow category (for example, *negão gostoso*). Jorginho's experience lends credence to Livio Sansone's claim that black bodies "have become omnipresent commodities in tourist brochures" and have been utilized as commodities, particularly in "explicit black spaces" of cultural production such as *blocos afros* (Afro-Brazilian Carnaval groups), capoeira, and Candomblé houses (2003, 57). However, Sansone overlooks the crucial point that the black body that has become a tourist commodity is also highly eroticized. The specter of sex tourism in Brazil creates a situation in which any black Brazilian woman may be mistaken for a prostitute and any interracial relationship may be seen as suspect.

The Specter of Sex Tourism

Notions of black hypersexuality have historical roots in Brazil but have also circulated transnationally in tourism propaganda. As Jorginho's story illustrates, these notions have concrete material effects on people's daily lives in the touristscape of Salvador. The specter of sex tourism extends far beyond those who are directly involved in sex-for-money transactions between foreign tourists and Bahian men and women. Kátia, a thirty-five-year-old black educator and employee of the Secretariat of Tourism, has had more unpleasant experiences with tourists mistaking her for a prostitute than she can count. In her view, "The black woman is seen as an extension of the equipment of pleasure in this city." In much the same way that tourist postcards and propaganda represent black women as extensions of lush, natural landscapes and secluded beaches, Kátia believes, black women are also an extension of the music, dance, bars, beaches, parties, and other things that give Salvador its reputation as a party capital and the Land of Happiness. Katia discovered that she needed to carry herself differently in the streets of the tourist district—she had to be more serious and establish physical distance and formality around foreign men. On one occasion, when a tourist asked her if she was working, she responded, "Yes," because she was, in fact, working for a band that was about to perform. However, he then asked her how much she charged, demonstrating that he was referring to a different kind of work. She was offended, and he apologized profusely for having assumed that she was a prostitute.

According to Débora, a tour guide, an Angolan woman and her Italian husband on vacation were having breakfast at their hotel when a group of young Italians at a neighboring table commented loudly, "Let's go to the beach to try to get a prostitute, because he already got his." The tourists had racialized assumptions about the nature of the couple's interracial relationship. The specter of sex tourism and its widely circulating notions of black hypersexuality extends even to visiting black women. Much like the *mulata* dance shows, sex tourism represents one of the few social spaces where black women are preferred over white (Caldwell 2007, 59).

A perhaps unintended consequence of sex tourism is that it perpetuates a situation in which all transnational relationships are suspect. People are concerned with determining whether a relationship is "real" or is a case of sex tourism. People in interracial, cross-national relationships feel pressured to prove the authenticity of their relationships and suffer because other people assume that such relationships are "fake." Maristela, a middle-class Afro-Brazilian college-educated woman, had an older sister who was married to an Italian man whom she had met on the beach. In talking about the pairing, Maristela relied on certain tropes to counter the automatic suspicions that accompany any relationship that began at such a prime site of sex tourist interactions: her sister's class status and education, the length of time that she and the Italian had dated, and the fact that they married. Maristela explained that although her brother-in-law may have started out in search of an erotic adventure with an exotic black Brazilian woman, the relationship ended up as something different, more *real*.

Thirty-five-year-old Cristina came from a black middle-class family of lawyers. She operated a travel agency from her home and was a part-time law student. When she wanted to go to Germany to visit her German boyfriend, she made a point of paying for the trip with her own money so that she would not feel purchased. She lived in Germany for several years and married the boyfriend, although they later divorced, in large part because of other people's adverse reactions to the union of a white German man and a black Brazilian woman. In 2007, she began offering online Portuguese classes to foreigners. One of her students was Mathew, an African American man from Atlanta, and he began boldly flirting with her. At one point, he asked if she was a *travesti*,[13] saying that he had heard there were a lot of *travestis* in Salvador and that his friend "got played" by one. Though annoyed and a bit offended by his question, she responded that she was, in fact, a cis-gender woman.[14] Mathew was planning a trip to Rio de Janeiro and decided to visit her in Salvador as well. As a favor, she looked up the flight and hotel information without charging him the twenty dollars that she usually charged as part of her job. But she was shocked when he asked if he could stay at her house because, he explained, he would rather give money to her than to a hotel. She described him as a "cara de pau," a colloquial Portuguese phrase that means "shameless." Although they had established a rapport over the internet, his impropriety made her question his character and his intentions, wondering if he was merely seeking an erotic adventure with a Brazilian woman. The specter of sex tourism thus affects how people interact with each other—what they think about each other, their motivations, and their intentions.

Simone, a twenty-nine-year-old Afro-Brazilian secretary, met her German boyfriend while spending three months in his country. A family friend gave her the gift of the plane ticket and a place to stay, but she had to do domestic work for spending money. She met Günther when she and a group of Brazilian friends went to his restaurant. They were still together five months later, after she returned to Salvador. He was planning to visit for three weeks, and if all went well, she would move to Germany to be with him. Nonetheless, Simone was afraid of being mistaken for a prostitute when she was with Günther during his visit, saying, "Maybe I'll never take him to my neighborhood." She felt that the key to avoiding this assumption would be for her to speak German fluently, which was difficult since she worked and had little time to study the language. Moreover, Simone reflected, "I'm going to be seen in a negative light not only by people who don't know me but also by people who do know me, because people are going to judge me. . . . This prejudice exists, and I think that even if I come back [to Bahia] speaking German marvelously well, even if I'm well dressed and have a nice car, people are always going to look at me like, 'Ah! The Bahian woman got lucky to snag a *gringo* to improve her life!'" Although she could not avoid these perceptions, Simone believed that that she could control her behavior and the way she dressed as a means of minimizing the problem. She emphasized the importance of dressing "appropriately" when out in the streets with Günther rather than wearing a skimpy top or short-shorts. In other words, like Elisete, Simone was aware of how her body would be read when she walked through Salvador on the arm of a *gringo*, and she strategically sought ways to counter negative perceptions. This is the weight of the specter of sex tourism that Afro-Brazilian women must carry on their shoulders—being perceived as sex workers by virtue of their race and their connections to foreign men.

These women's stories of being mistaken for prostitutes show how black Brazilian women are, in the words of black feminist geographer Katherine

McKittrick, "seemingly in place by being out of place" in the touristscape of Salvador (2006, xv). Placelessness is a common feature of black women's experiences throughout the African diaspora, so the proper place for black women is "out of place." Many of the women I interviewed expressed a sense of anxiety about distancing themselves from the image of black hypersexuality and attaining a standard of respectability.[15]

Conclusion

An intersectional, transnational (black) feminist approach enables an understanding of how the mutual imbrications of race, class, gender, nationality, and sexuality play an integral role in how black Brazilian women are interpellated as prostitutes on an almost daily basis in the touristscape of Salvador. These women's stories challenge claims by proponents of racial democracy that class trumps race in Brazil. To some extent, the assumption of hypersexuality has been attached to all Brazilian women as a consequence of Embratur's marketing of eroticized images of Brazilian women in miniscule bikinis, samba, and Carnaval. However, the idea also arises from a particular, historically rooted, diasporic framework that specifically links blackness and hypersexuality. In the Brazilian context, this blackness shows up in a way that accounts for the history and prevalence of interracial mixing. Thus, *morenas*, *mulatas*, and other people of African descent are affected by the myth of black hypersexuality because, as Freyre's work has illustrated, the *mulata*'s hypersexuality is attributed to her "black blood."

Furthermore, these women's stories refute the notion of Brazil as what Donna Goldstein calls a "color-blind erotic democracy" (2003, 133). This phrase calls attention to the sexualized aspects of the myth of racial democracy—that is, to the notion that sexual liaisons across color lines offer proof of Brazil's racial democracy. As Goldstein points out, the "patterned forms of inequality" are often "embedded in or enacted through racialized eroticism" (1999, 567). In other words, desiring the racial/erotic Other does not constitute proof that one has overcome racist beliefs and tendencies, as some might assume; rather, this desire may in fact confirm and affirm racism. The "politics of interracial sexuality are fundamental to racial formation" in Brazil (Sexton 2008, 15). As Jared Sexton contends, "White supremacy and antiblackness are obsessed with interracial sexuality" (2008, 32). In the sexual economies of tourism in Salvador, the mere act of a black Brazilian woman walking hand in hand with a foreign tourist can be read as what Christen Smith calls a "moment of racialized encounter" that "makes blackness legible" (2008, 1). Even if this black woman is not a sex worker, even if she has a "real" relationship with a foreigner instead of a fleeting liaison, society often reads her as a sex worker. There are always already racial and sexual meanings mapped onto her body. Evelyn Hammonds criticizes black feminist scholars for focusing exclusively on the "restrictive, repressive, and dangerous aspects of black female sexuality" to the detriment of issues of "pleasure, exploration, and agency" (1997, 177). How can we as black feminist scholars recognize this painful history while ensuring that we are attentive to black women's agency, power, erotic autonomy, and freedom (Miller-Young 2008, 2010)?

CHAPTER THREE

Working-Class Kings in Paradise

Coming to Terms with Sex Tourism

In Pelourinho, there is a graffiti image of an old, overweight, bald, and bearded European man standing with his arms stretched wide. Wearing a yellow shirt and green shorts (the colors of the Brazilian flag), he holds the Italian flag in one hand and gives the thumbs-up sign with the other. A banner over his head reads, "Benvenuti a Salvador" (Welcome to Salvador), and a comment bubble features his greeting: "Ciao!" That the character is Italian is significant because Italians are ubiquitous in discourses of sex tourism in Salvador, where the term *Italian* has become synonymous with *sex tourist*. More than three hundred thousand Italians visit Brazil each year, and they are the leading foreign tourists to visit Bahia (*Exame* 2007, 104). Although Salvador usually follows Rio de Janeiro and São Paulo as a major Brazilian tourism destination, it attracts the largest number of Italian tourists—approximately 121,000 each year (*Exame* 2007, 104).

The image of this Italian tourist fits with the hegemonic depictions of sex tourists in various countries of the Global South as well as in the scholarly literature. As Martin Opperman points out, "the term sex tourism invariably evokes the image of (white) men, usually older and in less than perfect shape, traveling to developing countries . . . for sexual pleasures generally not available, at least not for the same price, in their home country" (1998, 1). Various people—from Bahian tourism industry workers to journalists and politicians engaged in campaigns to eradicate sex tourism—construct a caricature of Italians as the prototypical sex tourists. In a news report on sex tourism at the Aeroclube, a shopping center in Boca do Rio, a coastal Salvador neighborhood, a black sex worker told reporters, "Bahia would go hungry if it weren't for the Italians who spend [money]. The Bahian man comes and spends the whole night with one beer, but the Italian *spends*." In fact, according to the report, Italians paid up to R$250 to spend an entire night with sex workers (*Hoje em Dia* 2007). The Bahian imagination of Italian men serves as a figure against which Bahian men may position themselves, particularly in terms of morality, sexuality, and mobility. Italian tourists were commonly described as men from lower-class backgrounds who took advantage of the privileges of their foreign currency (*Exame* 2007). In March 2007, Marta Suplicy, the Brazilian minister of tourism, said that combating sex tourism was one of her priorities: "We don't want this type of visitor in our country" (Cavalcante 2007).

However, other characterizations of sex tourism also exist. A group of African American gay men at Barra Beach focus on another black man lying on the beach, sizing him up and commenting on his chiseled body, his coppery skin tone, and his curly brown hair. In their loud and brazen English, they situate him as a perfect example of an exotic Bahian man—the kind of man they are seeking. They did not realize that this man was a fellow American, and he was listening attentively as they talked about him. Having spent a great deal of time in Salvador over the preceding ten years, nearly fluent in Portuguese, and with deep personal and spiritual ties to Bahia, Sean found the situation very amusing. He had heard about a particular group of gay African Americans who travel to São Paulo and Salvador every year and considered them merely a black gay version of sex tourism. This sentiment was echoed by Travis, a black gay man from New York who was invited to join the tour group but refused because he was uncomfortable with the idea of traveling to Brazil for sex.

This gay African American tour group has a blog that features travel information for participants, flyers for Brazilian parties organized on their behalf, and photos of anonymous Brazilian men, some with captions describing them as the "flavor of the day." Part of the goal of the trip is to participate in Bahia's Gay Pride celebrations and Brazil's Independence Day festivities. The group made a food donation to an orphanage and clinic for people living with AIDS. The organizer describes Salvador as a place with "more men than you can count," including, in one case, a "lair of men." He tells readers, "Like I always say when in Brazil, do a Brazilian. And, I intend on doing a few! Remember what goes on in Brazil stays in Brazil." Even while exoticizing black Brazilian men, the African American blogger still demonstrates a sense of diasporic connection. He mentions that most of the Afro-Brazilians live in the lower part of the city, near the favelas: "What can I say our people are poor all over the world!" He also advises the participants to "come [to strip clubs] ready to tip and you will be treated like a king. They were just not use [*sic*] to receiving anything like that so it took them by surprise. Remember many people . . . are very poor so they really appreciated it. Trust me." Among the Portuguese phrases he suggests that travelers learn is "Quanto custa?" (How much?).

Some scholars have argued that sex tourism offers white heterosexual northern men a way to access gendered power that they feel they lack in their home countries as a consequence of the demands of "liberated" Western women (Brennan 2004; Kempadoo 2004). In this sense, traveling abroad and encountering racialized erotic Others who supposedly embody more "traditional" aspects of femininity and domesticity revives sexist notions and ideologies. But what happens to the idea that sex tourism is intrinsically about escaping gender constraints and based on underlying tenets of racism and exoticism when those traveling in search of sex and erotic adventure are African American men (straight and queer), women (white and women of color), and less wealthy (as opposed to moneyed) foreigners? In other words, how do our understandings of power and exoticization shift when traveling subjects do not fit into hegemonic representations of sex tourists? The understanding of sex tourism as involving presumably heterosexual imperial encounters with "exoticized, Third World Others" is clearly troubled when, for example, the sex tourist is an Italian man seeking a *travesti* (male-to-female transgender) sex worker, when a black lesbian sex worker starts a "relationship" with an elderly Dutch male tourist with the knowledge of her wife, or when a tour group of African American gay men descends on Salvador each year with the underlying intention of engaging in casual sex with exotic Afro-Brazilian men—the straighter, the better. A comprehensive definition of sex tourism thus must encompass a broad range of sexual and intimate encounters.

Despite the prominence of heterosexual sex tourism in media and scholarship, Brazil is a popular destination for gay and lesbian tourists from around the world (Howard L. Hughes 2006).[1] In a 2011 research survey, Out Now Global LGBT2020, Brazil was named the tenth-most-popular country for lesbian/gay/bisexual/transgender (LGBT) tourism.[2] Brazil was featured in a cover story in the winter 2006 issue of *The Out Traveler* magazine: the headline read, "Brazil Heats Up: Two Boys, Ten Beaches, and One Sexy Summer in South America." Ernesto Camacho, vice president of Prime Travel in Chicago, stated, "Bahia is ready as a destination for the gay, lesbian, bisexual, and ally public" (Cerqueira 2009). João de Sales, a tourism professional who brings LGBT tourists to Brazil, said that "Salvador has continued to grow as an interesting option for GLS tourism in Brazil" (Cerqueira 2009).[3] The Brazilian government's May 2011 approval of gay marriage is likely to only increase the country's popularity as a gay tourism destination, and the International Gay and Lesbian Travel Association held its 2012 convention in Brazil. However, the Grupo Gay da Bahia reported that 272 gay people were murdered in Brazil in 2011 and 75 were murdered in the first ten weeks of 2012 (Petenbrink 2012). Brazil is thus simultaneously striving to situate itself as a progressive gay tourism destination and wrestling with underlying homophobic sentiments.

This chapter helps to provide a better understanding of the complexities of tourism, race, and sexuality in Salvador by integrating theoretical approaches from both tourism and sexuality studies. I begin by delving further into the question of Italians as the quintessential sex tourists and the accompanying issues of class. I then describe the various ways in which sex tourism has been defined and understood in academic scholarship, in the popular media, in government anti–sex tourism campaigns, and by my informants. I also highlight how the Brazilian government defines sex tourism as a manifestation of child sexual exploitation. Next, I explore the often-neglected perspectives of tour guides and tourism industry workers, who articulate how sex tourism operates in Salvador.[4] The chapter ends with a case study of Tiago, a black gay Bahian tour guide who specializes in gay African American clients. Tiago's story brings to light many of the issues and concepts explored in this chapter, including the question of class privilege, connections between cultural and sexual tourism, and tour guides' roles as expected facilitators of sexual adventure for tourists.

Italians and the Question of Class

Several people working in the tourist sector said that Italians visited Bahia with the sole objective of having sex with black Brazilian women. Caetano, an employee in a beachfront apartment-hotel, pointed out that while his place of employment had "faithful clients" (mostly Italians and Americans) who came every year during the winter, the majority of the tenants were Brazilians, including many families. He consistently received complaints from residents about Italians who "only come to Bahia for sex tourism." "Italians like sex a lot," he stated. Caetano recounted his daily encounters with Italian tourists and black Bahian women who either were (or were assumed to be) sex workers: "Those who work the night shift (10:00 P.M. –7:00 A.M.) like I do see many things," among them "tourists who have a different woman every day." Caetano suggested that perhaps working-class Italian tourists were willing to spend money on black sex workers because in Italy "they are *nobody*, but

here they want to show off." He noted that most of the Italians he encountered were blue-collar workers such as security guards or factory laborers.

Similarly, Marcelo, a thirty-four-year-old unlicensed tour guide who works
primarily with African American and European clients, described Italians as
poor and dishonest tourists who "don't bring anything of interest to the country. They fight a lot with women, they curse out black prostitutes, they are low
quality. . . . Italians have the vision that all Brazilian women are prostitutes."
Débora, a tour guide of Brazilian and Italian descent, told me about a time
when she referred a group of Italian tourists to middle-class nightclubs that
were not heavily frequented by prostitutes. Unhappy with their experience,
the tourists asked her, "Why are you giving us places where the women are
nuns?" She quipped that they must be "afraid of hearing a woman tell them
'No.'" The tourists were seeking—and expecting—easy sex and did not want
to endure the negotiations and risks of rejection that dating usually entails.

Several of my tour guide informants contended that Italians were of a lower
class status than more preferred tourists. Fernando pointed out that the image of Bahia as a sexual place "attracts the profile of tourists that don't bring
much money into the state. It's different from ecotourists, for example, who
have a higher purchasing power." One contributor to *Exame* magazine's 2007
annual review of the Brazilian tourism industry maintained that Brazil "runs
the risk of attracting only the international public of the second class, formed
by low-income Europeans who land here in charter flights" (Cavalcante 2007).
These "second class" visitors are also referred to as "C and D class foreigners," "*turistas* McDonalds," and "*duristas*" (a combination of the Portuguese
words *duro* [broke] and *turistas* [tourists]). Similarly, anthropologist Adriana
Piscitelli notes that magazine articles tend to characterize sex tourists as "low-
level people who spend little and provoke problems" (1996, 16).

Débora confirmed the idea that Italian men "feel like kings" in Salvador,
where "an expensive steakhouse restaurant . . . is the price of bread and coffee
in Italy." Similarly, João, a white Bahian man who runs a Web site featuring
profiles of Bahian sex workers, asserted that several Italians in Barra hotels
are waiters in Italy—"the middle class there is king here." In addition to being
depicted as "less moneyed" foreigners, Italians were also described as "miserly
men": according to Caetano, sex workers often said that Italians were "more
aggressive" and tried to avoid paying for *programas*. This idea stands in stark
opposition not only to scholarly literature's dominant representations of sex
tourists as affluent businessmen but also to African American men's newly
generated reputation as "big spenders" inspired by hip-hop video fantasies
of freely flowing money and beautiful women (Cobb 2006; Jewel Woods and
Hunter 2008).

Clyde, a Belgian man who had lived in Salvador for sixteen years, positioned Italians in a disparaging way. On his third visit to Bahia as a tourist, Clyde met a Bahian woman, fell in love, got married, and decided to remain permanently in Salvador. Unable to find adequate employment in his field of computer engineering, Clyde capitalized on his knowledge of Dutch, French, English, and Portuguese to work in the tourism industry. He took a six-month tour guide course sponsored by the Serviço Nacional de Aprendizagem Comercial (National Service of Commercial Learning) and began working as a tour guide four years before I interviewed him.[5] Clyde took pride in his status as one of only two tour guides in Salvador who spoke Dutch, and he estimated that approximately 99 percent of his client base consisted of Europeans. He also stated that sex tourists came primarily from lower-middle-class or working-class backgrounds. In 2007, when Clyde and I spoke, the Turismo Étnico-Afro division of Bahia's Secretariat of Tourism was undertaking a major initiative to increase the number of direct and charter flights to Salvador from the United States in an effort to increase the already burgeoning number of African American tourists. He worried that a similar effort to increase the number of charter flights from Europe directly to Salvador could increase sex tourism, because their low prices attract people with less purchasing power: "We guides are afraid that we will have more sex tourism with more charters, and our clients that come in search of culture and history will decrease."

Although the popular media and government discourses characterize foreign sex tourists as members of the lower class, tourism studies scholarship has tended to focus on the upper class. In her classic work, *Bananas, Beaches, and Bases: Making Feminist Sense of International Politics*, Cynthia Enloe (1990) characterizes sex tourism as involving men from affluent countries who imagine certain women (usually women of color of a lower economic status) as more available and submissive than the women in their home countries and who are willing to invest in sexualized travel or adventure. While the fact that Italians are from an affluent country is consistent with this dominant image of sex tourists, the presence of these members of the working classes simultaneously challenges representations of sex tourists as elite, upper-class businessmen.

Coming to Terms with Sex Tourism

Two of my Bahian interlocutors offered statements that reflected the range of class backgrounds of tourists who come to Bahia in search of erotic adventures. Arturo, a black gay activist, quipped, "I've met sex tourists from bakers to businessmen," and Naiara, a black lesbian dancer and emcee, said that sex tourists range from "suit and tie to flip-flops." Fabiana, the president of Aprosba, expressed the pervasiveness of "sex tourism" when she remarked that all foreign tourists "really come to have sex, even if they come to work. . . . They take advantage of the opportunity and meet pretty Brazilian women who are charming and seductive, can move and have curves. . . . Everyone ends up doing sex tourism." Similarly, Jacqueline Leite of the Humanitarian Center for the Support of Women (CHAME) said that tourists who come to Brazil for sex range from university professors, doctors, and architects to factory workers and bus drivers (José Antônio Gomes de Pinho et al. 2008, 146). In other words, while the phrase *sex tourism* often evokes images of red-light districts, prostitution, and exploitation, it also encompasses much more ambiguous situations (Clift and Carter 2000, 24).

A 2003 article in a popular Brazilian magazine, *Veja*, quotes a forty-three-year-old male tourist from France as saying, "I'm not interested in tourist attractions or beaches. I come to meet people. I adore Brazilian women. There's no better reason to visit Brazil" (Schelp 2003). In the same magazine two years earlier, journalist Adriana Negreiros described the prevalence of sex tourism by saying that "never before have so many men decided to search in the Brazilian Northeast for the queen of the home that they want to construct on the other side of the ocean" (2001). Local media sources thus link sex tourism not just to erotic adventures that take place while on vacation, but also to possibilities of domesticity, marriage, and migration. Similarly, CHAME asserts that sex tourists are "attracted by the image of supposed submission of women of the Third World, they come in search of a docile wife, tamed, and at the same time, sensual" (n.d.[b], n.p.).

Sex tourism developed as a subfield of tourism studies in the late 1970s, and much of the scholarship has focused on Southeast Asia and the Caribbean.[6] Sex tourism began to appear in Brazil in the 1970s, though it did not emerge as a major issue until the 1990s (Bandyopadhyay and Nascimento 2010). For Piscitelli, sex tourism can be defined as "any travel experience in which the furnishings of sexual services by the local population in exchange for monetary and non-monetary reward is a crucial element for the success of the trip" (2001, 4). She sets the stage for understanding sex tourism as going beyond commercial sex or sex-for-money exchanges by pointing out that exchanges of gifts instead of money often occur.

Adriana Piscitelli, Glaucia de Oliveira Assis, and José Miguel Nieto Olivar's recent edited volume, *Gênero, Sexo, Amor, e Dinheiro: Mobilidades Transnacionais Envolvendo o Brasil* (Gender, Sex, Love, and Money: Transnational Mobilities Involving Brazil) (2011), also highlights the diversity and complexity of sexual tourism in Brazil. Essays in this volume address such topics as *caça-gringas* in the northeastern state of Natal (Cantalice 2011), representations of prostitution in the Brazilian media (Beleli and Olivar 2011), masculinity and sex tourism in Rio de Janeiro (Blanchette 2011), and international sex tourism in São Paulo (Ana Paula da Silva 2011). Piscitelli's chapter describes how the Brazilian concept of *ajuda* (financial assistance) complicates a clear-cut understanding of sexual and intimate encounters between foreign tourists and local women as strictly commercial: "If the *programa* evokes a contract of services, *ajuda*, placed within a tradition of hierarchical exchanges, refers to notions of support, care and affection that are expressed in terms of a contribution for economic survival and consumption" (2011, 550). Moreover, sexual exchanges for *ajuda* are not stigmatized the way *programas* are (445).

In the broader Caribbean context, Jafari Sinclaire Allen articulates "tourist sex labor" as "romantic excursions and the cultivation of relationships with the implicit or explicit promise of sexual contact, for a foreigner's implicit or explicit promise to give monetary or other material support, or a promise of emigration" (2007, 186). This definition closely parallels my own. Its emphasis on implicit and explicit promises highlights the ambiguity that is a central feature of the sexual economies of tourism in Salvador. This definition speaks to the particularities of the Bahian context because it encompasses a broad range of relationships that are cultivated in this process and recognizes that motivations and expectations may be explicit or implicit, spoken or unspoken. For my purposes, these ambiguous encounters characterize sex tourism in Salvador.

Other scholars emphasize sex as the primary factor motivating tourists' desire to travel to particular countries, an understanding that elides the ambiguities of sex tourism (Soares do Bem 2005). Many tourists travel for leisure, cultural, business, or political reasons but may find themselves, perhaps unexpectedly, engaging in sexual/romantic encounters while abroad. As Martin Opperman points out, tourists who spontaneously experience sexual encounters abroad when the opportunity presents itself would generally not consider themselves "sex tourists" (1998, 11). Furthermore, gauging a tourist's primary motivation for travel may be challenging for researchers and journalists attempting to understand this phenomenon. In Salvador, this primary motivation is particularly difficult to determine because of the dual attraction of culture and eroticized blackness. Whatever their motivations, tourists play a significant role in constructing Salvador's sexual economies of tourism.

The World Tourism Organization defines sexual tourism as "trips organized within or outside the tourism sector, with the use of its structures and networks, with the primary purpose of permitting commercial sexual relations of the tourist with local residents of the destination" (Roseno 2006, 299). However, what sensationalist media accounts consider "sex tourism" may often resemble interracial dating with broader differences of class and nationality. Marcelo had older female clients from Finland, the Netherlands, Spain, and other countries who over time became girlfriends. He noted, "I don't seek it out, but it happens. It's a thing of the moment. They ask me for a tour, then invite me for a beer, and ask if I have a girlfriend. It wasn't sexual tourism." Similarly, Fernando, a forty-one-year-old white Bahian tour guide who had previously lived in Hawaii, Puerto Rico, and California, claimed that sex tourists "have it in their heads to search for sex, whether it be paid or not." He elaborated on the various ways to find sex in Salvador, which included passively awaiting the approach of a sex worker in a public place, going to pornographic Web sites or clubs, or consulting taxi drivers. This expansive definition of sex tourism accurately captures the scope and scale of what occurs in the sexual economies of transnational tourism in Salvador. As an assemblage, sex tourism in Salvador is diffuse, involving a variety of actors and settings, nodes and shifting features.

Bahians also had specific ways of identifying participants in sex tourism. Afro-Brazilian tour guide Joceval said that Italian tourists were the "principal clients of sex tourism in Bahia," generally preferring "*negras* and *morenas* and sometimes suntanned white women with dark hair." According to Keith, an African American tourist from Atlanta, sex tourists are generally middle- or upper-class men between twenty-five and forty years old of various ethnic backgrounds who work in corporate America. Keith claims that the Bahian women who have sex with tourists are dark-skinned black women between the ages of seventeen and thirty, many of them poor or even homeless; they have children and migrate from rural areas to Salvador to increase their earning possibilities. One CHAME publication notes the cross-racial nature of these liaisons: "What one observes in the discourse of foreign tourists is that this supposed preference for women of African descent is supported by the image of the hot, fiery, easy, and available Brazilian woman that was constructed during the colonial era and slavery in Brazil" (n.d.[b], 18). Furthermore, according to Reginaldo Serra, a white Brazilian police officer with the Delegation for the Protection of Tourists (Deltur), what is most salient is the role of "difference": "Everything here is a novelty for Europeans. If they see a house in ruins, they think it's a beautiful thing. If they see black people here, it attracts their attention." Thus, Serra sees the eroticization of racial and cultural difference as playing a pivotal role.

Brazilian governmental and nongovernmental agencies mobilize these various understandings in attempts to deal with sex tourism. Several of my informants felt that the government was not doing enough to eliminate the problem. Danila blamed the "hypocrisy of the government": "Oversight is lacking—it's a big contradiction. Barra is a point of prostitution. Everyone knows it. The informality of Brazilians results in a lack of protest against things that are wrong. We are all enforcers of the law." In this view, all Brazilians should take it upon themselves to act against this "crime," even if the police turn a blind eye. If everyone were to become an enforcer of the law, what would it mean for sex workers' rights and for people engaged in cross-racial, transnational relationships? Because it is constantly shifting, sex tourism is often difficult to identify without falling into the trap of perpetuating stereotypes. Also, by mentioning that Barra is a point of prostitution, Danila contributes to the criminalization of sex work despite the fact that adult prostitution is not a crime under the Brazilian law.

Naiara, a young black feminist activist, student, and member of the burgeoning local hip-hop movement, took a similar position in claiming that the government does little about sex tourism: "I don't see the state as being very alert about this. They put the advertisement 'Sexual exploitation is a crime,' and [yet] you see fourteen-year-old girls in bikinis drinking Coca-Cola [with tourists]. . . . If the state were to think about this, it would stop receiving money from *gringos*." Naiara thus points out the contradictions between the state's anti–sex tourism discourse and its acceptance of the foreign currency that tourists bring to Brazilian coffers. Therein lies the great contradiction of the sexual economies of tourism: the state would like to earn much needed foreign currency from tourism, but it does so on the backs of women of color whose bodies are positioned as tourist attractions. *Sex tourism* is a nebulous and sometimes problematic term with no clear boundaries and definitions, yet it has nonetheless been incorporated into governmental and nongovernmental debates and policies.

Sex Tourism as Child Sexual Exploitation

Although Embratur, the Brazilian national tourism agency, has largely been responsible for circulating the sexualized images of Brazilian women that have contributed to the global tourist imaginary of Brazil as a racial-sexual paradise, Embratur began to be criticized for marketing Brazil in this way in the early 2000s (Bandyopadhyay and Nascimento 2010). Consequently, Embratur shifted its strategy by launching a nationwide campaign with the tag line, "Beware! Brazil is watching you!" and removing images of nearly nude women from its tourist propaganda (Bandyopadhyay and Nascimento 2010). While sexualized images of adult women created the portrait of Brazil as a sexual paradise, most Brazilian governmental campaigns against sexual tourism have situated it as something involving solely children and adolescents. The federal government's Sustainable Tourism and Childhood program produced a brochure that referred to sexual tourism as a type of violence that violates not only the principles of the World Code of Ethics in Tourism but also human rights. In so doing, this campaign situates sexual tourism exclusively as a crime against children and adolescents.

The 2009 Trafficking in Persons (TIP) Report published by the U.S. Department of State claims that "child sex tourism remains a serious problem, particularly in resort and coastal areas in Brazil's Northeast" (U.S. Department of State 2009).[7] Maria do Rosário, a representative of the Workers' Party from the state of Rio Grande do Sul, explicitly defines sex tourism as a crime involving children and adolescents: "Sexual tourism is intolerable for social, legal, and economic reasons, as it constitutes a crime to negate the right of healthy development of children and adolescents, create a degrading image of the destination and its citizens, and take away the opportunity to develop a model of sustainable tourism" (*Tarde* 2005). However, my research as well as that of other Brazil-based scholars suggests that the majority of sex tourism occurs among consenting adults, both sex workers and non–sex workers (Blanchette 2011; Blanchette and Da Silva 2011; Mitchell 2011b; Piscitelli 2007).

The federal government announced the National Plan for Confronting Commercial Sexual Exploitation of Children and Adolescents in Tourism at the World Social Forum in 2005 (*A Tarde* 2005).[8] In reference to the campaign against the sexual exploitation of minors during Carnaval, Carmen Ines Garcia, representative of the National Confederation of Commerce, noted, "The foreign tourist, as soon as he arrives, will be warned that exploiting children and adolescents is a crime in this country" (*A Tarde* 2005). Launched during Carnaval in Rio de Janeiro, Salvador, Recife, and Fortaleza, these campaigns included the distribution of flyers, T-shirts, and trash bags with messages warning against the sexual exploitation of minors. During Carnaval 2004, young people wearing shirts reading "Sexual exploitation is a crime" distributed pamphlets to tourists and explained that "sex with a person under fourteen could land them in jail for up to ten years" ("Brazil to Fight" 2004). Another campaign slogan urged people to "Conscientize. Mobilize. Impeça a exploração sexual infantil. Brasil. Quem ama, protege" (Become aware. Mobilize. Impede child sexual exploitation. Brazil. One who loves, protects)" ("TAM" 2005). In 2007, the campaign's slogan was "Exploração Sexual Infanto-Juvenil: Não Brinque neste Bloco!" (Child and Youth Sexual Exploitation: Don't Play in this Carnaval Group!) (D'Eça 2007).

In 2005, the Ministry of Tourism launched an action plan that consisted of a code of conduct that outlined proper behavior for tourism professionals to help prevent the exploitation of minors (*A Tarde* 2005). The campaign produced materials targeted at a broad range of industry workers, such as waiters, managers, hotel receptionists, street vendors, and bartenders. It placed signs at hotels and internet cafés in Barra and other neighborhoods in the tourist districts that read, "Exploração Sexual Infanto-Juvenil e Crime" (Sexual Exploitation of Children and Youth Is a Crime).

On January 30, 2007, I attended the launch event for a campaign organized by the Committee to Confront Sexual Violence against Children and Adolescents in Bahia. The meeting, which took place at a popular hotel in downtown Salvador, included dozens of illustrious participants who represented agencies such as UNICEF and Bahiatursa, the state and municipal governments, various nongovernmental organizations, the police force, and television crews.[9] Waldemar Oliveira of the Committee to Confront Sexual Violence against Children and Adolescents in Bahia opened the plenary with the statement, "We haven't advanced as much as we would have liked." However, the presence of so many people was a sign of the campaign's success over the preceding ten years. Oliveira described the goal of the campaign as to "identify and punish those who exploit our children," and he considered it a success since more complaints were being lodged than had previously been the case. Edna Sena, president of the Brazilian Association of the Hotel Industry, spoke proudly of her association's work with the Public Ministry and the state government to require that all affiliated hotels post signs announcing that "Sexual Exploitation of Children and Adolescents Is a Crime." A representative of Bahiatursa said that in representing Bahia abroad, the organization was seeking the kind of tourism that "can bring together families" in an effort to combat the sexual exploitation of children and adolescents.

Another representative emphasized the need to focus on poverty to prevent child sex tourism: "If we reduce inequality, then they won't need to sell their bodies." In this view, prevention involved educating tourists so that "when they come, they know that our children and adolescents are not tourist attractions." Deltur's Officer Serra echoed such sentiments, noting that in an impoverished place such as Bahia where street children ask passersby for twenty cents, almost anything could happen "if a tourist offers them fifty reais to do a sexual act." However, Serra also highlighted the important and often-overlooked point that "sex tourism isn't just with children; it's with adult women as well."

One particular case of (possible) child sex tourism that circulated throughout Brazilian society during 2007 highlights some of the complexities of the sexual economies of tourism in Bahia, particularly with regard to the contentious category of age. On January 25, 2007, the *Correio da Bahia* newspaper ran a story about a sixty-five-year-old American sex tourist who was caught

in Pelourinho (Lyrio 2007). According to journalist Alexandre Lyrio, Stuart
Livnyi was arrested with "Viagra and his passport in hand" for allegedly having sex with a sixteen-year-old Bahian girl. Mônica Mendonsa, a thirty-six-
year-old woman from Rio de Janeiro who was Livnyi's ex-girlfriend, reported
Livnyi to the Disque Denúncia hotline of the Special Unit of Childhood and
Adolescence. Livnyi and Mendonsa had reportedly lived together for five
months but had separated a week before this incident occurred. Mendonsa
said that she broke up with Livnyi because he had physically assaulted her
and attempted to rape her. According to the article,

> For $R150, which would be paid soon after the *programa*, the foreigner had
> taken the girl to one of the rooms of the hotel. The negotiation was done quickly
> in a meeting in the Cruzeiro de São Francisco, near Deltur, in Pelourinho. Upon
> catching the two of them in the sexual act in her hotel, . . . Mônica Mendonsa
> decided to notify the police. "I called because I saw that it was with a minor. She
> started yelling that she was sixteen and would only leave there with the money.
> I won't allow an old man to abuse a child like that," Mendonsa affirmed, deny-
> ing that her ex-boyfriend had done something similar before. The adolescent
> confirms that she consummated the sexual act with the tourist and became
> irate when he refused to pay the amount previously agreed upon. "In addition
> to not paying me, he offended me in front of everyone. That's why I made a
> scene," she explained. The foreigner denied all of the accusations and defended
> himself, saying that he just called the girl to talk in the room, where they slept
> separately. Livyni says he's the victim of his ex-girlfriend. (Lyrio 2007)

In a documentary, *Cinderelas, Lobos, e um Principe Encantado* (Cinderellas,
Wolves, and a Prince Charming) (Joel Zito Araújo 2009), television journalist
Eduardo Bocão gives a slightly different version of the story: Livnyi, the owner
of a *pousada* (cheap hotel) in Pelourinho, was charged with sexually abusing
a child between six and nine years old. He spent ten days in jail before his
attorney freed him. How did the girl go from a teenager in the newspaper
article to a young child in the documentary? Danila had yet another version
of the story: Livnyi got involved with Mendonsa and invested in a small hotel
in Pelourinho. One day they had an argument, and she set him up with the
minor. Livnyi was arrested for pedophilia and "lost everything." But the girl
"wasn't innocent. She had already been doing *programas*." Thus, Danila seems
to consider Livnyi an innocent victim of both an unscrupulous and bitter
Brazilian woman and a depraved underage girl for whom sex with older,
foreign men presumably was not a novelty.

The illegality and reprehensibility of sex with minors is unquestionable, but
it is important to question to what extent youth is used as a sensationalist tool

to evoke certain emotions. Journalists tell lurid stories of "shockingly young" girls lined up along the street, "flagging down drivers for sex," and of mothers prostituting their daughters (Kingstone 2004). People unhesitatingly mobilize and rally around "victims" and fight to secure the rights of children and adolescents. The girl child in particular is constructed as the "ideal victim," the embodiment of innocence—powerless, feminine, young, and seemingly passive.[10] In *Children and the Politics of Culture*, Sharon Stephens asserts that children have often been portrayed as "innocent and vulnerable victims of adult mistreatment, greed, and neglect" (1995, 9). In the context of modernity, the "deviant childhoods of Third World children" are interpreted as "local particularities and instances of backwardness and underdevelopment," Stephens claims (19). However, the dynamic of sex tourism adds one crucial dimension to this global nexus, because the perpetrators are foreign, privileged Others from the "developed" world. Similarly, Heather Montgomery contends in her ethnography of child prostitution in Thailand that although child prostitution is morally reprehensible, it is important to understand morality not as a "a single, uncontested category which precludes all further discussions" but rather as a notion that is informed by circumstances such as the economic situation and family background of a child (2001, 3).

Brazilian campaigns against sex tourism that focus exclusively on children and adolescents miss a crucial point. Several scholars and journalists have pointed out that in Brazil, children and adolescents are more likely to be sexually exploited by members of their own families and communities than by foreign tourists. At a July 2005 seminar organized by the Interdisciplinary Institute for Women's Studies of the Federal University of Bahia, Debora Cohim of Projeto Viver, an organization that offers services to victims of sexual violence, said that she receives between ninety and one hundred accusations of sexual violence each month. In her experience, an estimated 72 percent of the sexual aggressors in these cases are people who close to the victims, such as family members or neighbors. This sentiment was echoed by Jô Costa of CEDECA, a Salvador-based nongovernmental organization that works specifically on issues of sexual exploitation of and violence against children and adolescents.[11] Costa asserted that the three major categories of people who commit sexual violence against minors are fathers, stepfathers, and neighbors.[12] A lot of work has been done in the Bahian interior (countryside) regarding the sexual exploitation of youth by truck drivers, who offer rides and seek sexual favors in return. A 2002–3 CEDECA study showed that truck drivers bore most of the responsibility for the dislocation of girls from small rural towns to Salvador's sexual markets (José Antônio Gomes de Pinho et al. 2008, 135).

Efforts to combat sex tourism in Brazil have important social and cultural implications. By narrowly defining sex tourism as the sexual exploitation of children and adolescents, government campaigns construct sex tourism as a problem to be eradicated—an unequivocally unethical violation of human rights. According to Jacqueline Leite, addressing the question of youth is simpler because "when you work with youth, there are laws, and distinct methodologies." Rio de Janeiro–based anthropologists Thaddeus Blanchette and Ana Paula da Silva point out that technically under Brazilian law, a "*sexual tourist* is any foreigner involved in sex crimes," and since "contracting an adult, self-employed prostitute for the provision of sexual services is not a crime in Brazil [this practice] should not be considered sexual tourism" (2011, 144). What characteristics would a government campaign to eradicate sex tourism with consenting adults have? Would it result in the increased criminalization and stigmatization of sex workers? How would this affect women of African descent, who are always already hypervisible as sex workers, even when they are not actually sex workers? And if the government were to further criminalize sex workers, what effects would that action have on the tour guides and other tourism industry workers whose clients often seek sexual and intimate encounters as part and parcel of the gendered tourism experience?

The Structure of Sex Tourism

Tour guides, as well as other locals who work closely with tourists, are often called on to act as intermediaries or brokers, facilitating intimate encounters between foreign tourists and Bahians. Danila has created a niche for herself in the tourism industry by specializing in Italian clients and has frequently been asked about where and how to find women: "I tell them I'm not the person, I don't know. . . . I've had people who didn't want to experience anything about Bahia, only women. . . . An Israeli man said 'I need a *mulata*.' As a female guide, I don't have this type of information. . . . Two Italian travel agents told me they were bringing a group of sixty men and therefore they needed to know about the nightlife and women. I said that I would transfer them to a man to do the nightlife part." For Danila, the major barrier separating her from her foreign clients was gender, not nationality, race, or other axes of difference. In her perception, a Brazilian man would have no problem facilitating a client's sexual encounters. She also had several foreign clients who attempted to flirt with her and treated her like a potential sexual conquest.

Fiúca, another tour guide, came from a white middle-class family of doctors. After studying philosophy in college, she spent five months in England and more than two years in France. When she returned to Brazil in 1986, her mother secured her a job with Bahiatursa. She had worked in tourism propaganda and marketing in São Paulo for six years before becoming a freelance guide in Salvador, and at the time of our interview, she had a total of twenty years of experience in the tourism industry. Fiúca actively resisted clients' attempts to place her in the role of facilitator of sexual encounters. Once, when she was called to pick up two Spanish male tourists at a luxurious hotel on the coastline, she was surprised to see them come downstairs with four *garotas de programa* (call girls) on their arms. Fiúca told them that she was paid to take two people, so if they wanted to bring four more along for the ride, they would have to pay extra, and they agreed. Fiúca told this story as an example of her disapproval of sex tourism, but her resistance merely resulted in extra money for her.

Caetano, the twenty-two-year-old man who worked in a beachfront apartment-hotel, told me that several hotels in Salvador have a book that they provide to tourists who request it.[13] This book contains pictures and contact information for various women. Caetano was quick to add that his place of employment had for the past three years displayed a sign saying that it did not tolerate sex tourism and did not have a book; nevertheless, many Bahians and foreigners referred to this establishment as a major site of sex tourism. As someone who mostly worked the night shift, Caetano was quite knowledgeable about how visitors entered guests' rooms. Visitors, including sex workers, filled out forms with their names, professions, addresses, and phone numbers; left their national identity cards at the front desk; and paid fees of thirty-five reais per person. According to Caetano, Italians did not like to fill out the forms. Danila said that "some [hotels] don't let prostitutes enter before midnight, but after midnight they enter with registration and payment."

Black Gay Tourism

Tiago, a thirty-year-old gay Afro-Brazilian tour guide who specializes in the GLS niche, capitalizes on foreigners' perceptions of Bahians as sensual and hospitable. Tiago's Web site describes Salvador as the "land of rhythm and samba-reggae music," perfect for tourists who are "interested in music and parties." Utilizing a common trope, the site describes Salvador as a "magical place": "You can feel it in the air when you arrive. It is one of those unique places with its own culture, music, history and traditions, while also blessed with great weather year-round, incredible beaches, wonderful people and awesome food!" The pleasures of a visit to Salvador include "incredible beaches where you can relax, get a tan, drink beer or Caipirinha . . . and meet the most gorgeous local girls or guys. By the way, we *baianos* and *baianas* are one of the most warm, sensual, hospitable people you'll find anywhere." Thus,

Tiago strategically uses stereotypes of Bahians as sensual and hospitable to highlight their unique appeal to foreigners.

Tiago had spent nearly a year in in England and Germany and was fluent in English, was proficient in German, and also spoke some Spanish and French. Most of his clients were gay, lesbian, bisexual, or transgender African American men from New York, Washington, D.C., Atlanta, and other major metropolitan areas. In four years of working with this community, he had only three lesbian clients. He shows his foreign clients around gay/lesbian places of interest (bars, clubs, and gay-oriented events) and helps them "make contact with local gays." He also provides airport transfers; directs clients toward gay-friendly hotels, flats, guesthouses, saunas, restaurants, and art galleries; and helps tourists "connect with quality massage and escort services." Upon request, Tiago will also organize welcome parties on the beach with what his Web site describes as "great local food, drinks, a fantastic samba band, and lots of hot locals."

Tiago's clients were between thirty-five and fifty years old and were highly educated—doctors, lawyers, engineers, doctoral students, government workers, and university professors. According to Tiago, although some people think that more educated people are more likely to be able to control their desires, his experience indicates that the opposite may actually be true. He knew a lawyer from New England who lived a very "limited life" but came to Salvador three times a year and "organizes a harem." Becky, the white American woman who traveled to Salvador with her capoeira group, mentioned that her friends in the United States expected her to return with a "harem," indicating that this word may circulate widely in Salvador's touristscape and routinely be applied to people of diverse genders and sexual orientations. Regardless of whether the term reflects actual activities in Salvador, the idea of "organizing a harem" persists in expectations about what one is supposed to do while on vacation in Brazil.

Tiago noted that most of his clients were interested in Afro-Brazilian culture and wanted to learn about music, culture, and religion. Similarly, Gregory Mitchell described the case of Derryl, a fifty-year-old gay African American software engineer who visited Salvador and hired local men such as beach vendors to serve as his guides/companions. For him, "sex was just another way to experience local culture in Bahia" (2011b, 11). Derryl saw his trip to Bahia as a pilgrimage and understood his participation in the sex industry as part of a larger project of black gay pride—for example, by taking Carlinhos, a local *michê* whose time and services Derryl had purchased, to visit museum exhibits on slavery, Candomblé, and capoeira (671). According to Mitchell, African American gay tourists relied "on essentialist notions of a shared blackness with Brazilians even while casting the black *michês* as sexually voracious Others" (12). Consequently, the Bahian *michês* internalized the essentialist idea that their blackness enhanced their sexual appetites.[14]

While many African American gay tourists are drawn to Bahia because of its cultural heritage, Tiago also noted that approximately three in ten of his clients "don't want to know anything about culture or history—they're only interested in sex tourism. The rest are a mix—they want a little history and also sex." Between 60 and 70 percent of his clients engage in sexual liaisons while in Salvador: "It's rare that someone comes here and doesn't want easy sex," he said, and "I can't say 'You can't do sex tourism!' I must orient them about the risks." He also warned his foreign clients to avoid putting themselves in dangerous situations. In the gay saunas, he said, the "boys" charge fifty reais for a *programa* that lasts from one to two hours, while on the streets, *michês* may charge only thirty reais for sex. Despite the higher cost, Tiago preferred to send his clients to the saunas because the male sex workers there were registered and more professional and the security was better than in the streets. He also claimed that the *michês* who solicited clients in the streets were not as strict about condom use. Tiago felt a great sense of responsibility to protect his clients and feared that if he did not give them information, they would try to find sex on their own, placing them in riskier situations: "They would go to Barra, where they would find someone working with sex on every corner, but they could also be working with other things like robbery and drugs."

According to Tiago, his clients generally preferred heterosexual men over gay men or *travestis*. More specifically, the tourists wanted men who exuded dominant notions of masculinity. He also claimed that while 60 percent of his clients were openly gay, most of them lived semicloseted lives in the United States, pretending that they were "eternal bachelors" rather than being fully out. Tiago distinguished between the sexual politics of the United States and Europe and that of Brazil: "Our [GLS] community is more liberal. Men here are open to bi or gay sexual relations. What I hear about the U.S. and Europe is that gays get with gays and heteros get with heteros. Sex tourism increases when men come here, have a good experience, and return to their countries and tell everyone about it." In this sense, Tiago echoed a commonly held sentiment in studies of gay tourism: gay travel provides an opportunity to seek out a gay space and escape the heteronormative constraints that confront them in their home communities (Howard L. Hughes 2006, 51). Likewise, some scholars have viewed gay tourists as "pilgrims" in search of community and identity (Howe 2001). However, Jasbir K. Puar complicates the liberatory potential of gay tourism by arguing that "the claiming of queer space" does not necessarily disrupt heterosexual space (2002b, 936). The claiming of any space—including queer space—is a process that is "informed by histories of colonization" (936). Furthermore, she argues that gay tourism simultaneously disrupts "racialized, gendered and classed spaces" and claims "class, gender, and racial privilege" (936).

In much the same way that the economic privilege of (presumably) hetero-sexual Italian tourists enabled them to feel like kings in Salvador, gay African American tourists also claimed certain privileges in this touristscape despite their racial marginalization. This is reminiscent of M. Jacqui Alexander's (1997) claim that white gay capital follows the path of white heterosexual capital. Perhaps the same could be said about black gay and heterosexual capital. Gay tourists are sometimes welcomed because they are characterized as having higher disposable incomes and educational levels than other tourists (Luciano Amaral Oliveira 2002). Puar makes the similar point that gay and lesbian tour-ism is "an ironic marker of an elitist cosmopolitan mobility" in which a "group is momentarily decriminalized through its purchasing power" (2002b, 942). Despite having misgivings about creating a niche market for gay tourists, a nation's leaders may realize that doing so is a wise economic choice. However, homophobia and fears of sex tourism sometimes motivate actions against gay tourism. Fernando, a forty-one-year-old white Bahian tour guide, thought that gay men were promiscuous and less likely to enter into long-lasting relation-ships and that "homosexuality is also closer to prostitution than heterosexual-ity." Consequently, he believed that increasing gay tourism would also increase sexual tourism in Salvador. In this sense, as Chris Ryan and Colin Michael Hall point out, stereotypes of gay people as single and perpetually seeking casual sex are reinscribed into a homophobic discourse of sex tourism (2001, 104).

Sex tourism is a "global assemblage" (Collier and Ong 2005) with shifting definitions and understandings in Brazilian society. It is a phenomenon that occurs in various parts of the world but has local particularities depending on historical and cultural context (Padilla 2007). According to Stephen J. Collier and Aihwa Ong, an assemblage is "the product of multiple determinations that are not reducible to a single logic" (2005, 12). Sex tourism is a constel-lation of contradictory desires, practices, and beliefs that are perpetually shifting and transforming depending on the complex configuration of local circumstances and transnational imaginations. Assemblages involve forms "that are shifting, in formation, or at stake" and are contingent, unstable, partial, and situated (12). Most important, the study of assemblages reveals "a specific historical, political, and economic conjuncture in which an issue becomes a problem" (14). In Brazil, sex tourism is articulated as a problem and an object of intervention by the state and civil society in diverse and often contradictory ways. The complexity of this phenomenon is illuminated by juxtaposing discourses about sex tourism in the public arena with those articulated not only by scholars, but also by tour guides and other tourism industry workers.

CHAPTER FOUR

Tourist Tales and Erotic Adventures

In the summer of 2005, I interviewed Joe, a twenty-eight-year-old white public school teacher from New York City. We met at a party in a working-class neighborhood, Vasco da Gama. Certain cues suggested to me that he was American: his pale skin, his style of dress, his hip-hop-inflected dance movements, and his expression of sheer ecstasy at being at a crowded, sweaty, party with a live band and very few foreigners. When I approached him to strike up a conversation, I discovered that he was, in fact, American. He was very friendly and gregarious as we discussed what had brought us to Salvador. When I told him about the topic of my research, he chuckled and volunteered to participate in an interview. We exchanged phone numbers and scheduled an appointment for the following week.

On a breezy day, Joe and I sat on the rocks overlooking Barra beach after he had just finished his guitar lesson. Joe was well traveled, having spent time in Europe, Morocco, and Mexico. When I asked him what originally brought him to Bahia, he enthusiastically exclaimed, "The women and the music!" He had enjoyed his first trip to Brazil so much that he had vowed to return regularly, and this was his third visit. He found life in Brazil easier and less stressful than in the United States, and he made a point of visiting Salvador at least once a year: "After spending two months here, I have a good sense of what it's like for wealthy men in America. The women think I'm rich, and the sex comes easy." His whiteness, American nationality, and foreign currency led locals to perceive Joe as "rich," even though his salary as a public school teacher would hardly qualify him as such in the United States. In this way, his story challenges scholarship and media coverage on sex tourism that tends to depict sex tourists as older, upper-middle-class businessmen (Enloe 1990). Furthermore, as Nancy A. Wonders and Raymond Michalowski argue, sex tourism provides an opportunity for men from the developed world "to experience—in their bodies—their own privilege" (2001, 550). This privilege goes beyond white privilege to encompass gender, national, and class privilege as well.

Joe admitted that Brazil was the first country to which he had traveled where the possibility of sex was a key motivating factor. While he boasted that he "turned down more sex in Brazil in one month" than he was "offered in NYC in a year," he also emphasized that he was "not coming to Brazil for two months just to get pussy!" He portrayed himself as a connoisseur of all things Brazilian, a fact that was reflected in his busy schedule of guitar, Portuguese, drumming, and dance lessons. Joe engaged in certain strategies to establish himself as a "traveler" or "temporary resident" rather than a "typical" tourist, including immersing himself in Brazil's language, music, and culture; attending parties in peripheral, working-class neighborhoods such as García and Vasco da Gama, where the presence of tourists was not common; and renting a furnished apartment in the neighborhood of Federação, which was outside of (though still relatively close to) the tourist district. I somewhat identified with Joe in this regard, a fact that reflects long-standing tensions between tourists and ethnographers, travelers, or sojourners, all of whom desire to move beyond the facade or "front stage" of tourism (Goffman 1959, 22).

This chapter sheds light on the motivations, experiences, and subjectivities of sex tourists. How do sex tourists understand and articulate their racialized desires? How is the tourist experience characterized by liminality? Finally, how does the desire for "touristic intimacy" (Frohlick 2007, 152) play out in Salvador's touristscape? Drawing inspiration from Julia Harrison (2003), Susan Frohlick uses this concept to describe how tourists seek intimacy to justify "international travel as a means to gain cross-cultural understanding" (2007, 152). Erotic desires, she argues, are inseparable from the desire for "touristic intimacy" (154). As a concept that evokes the diffuse nature of sexualized tourist practices, "touristic intimacy" can be applied to the touristscape of Salvador because it blurs the boundaries between the cultural and the sexual.

Joe elaborated on issues of fantasy, exoticism, and racialized desires when he said, "I've had a thing for Latin, brown-skinned women since my early twenties. I'm from [a place] where there are a lot of blond white girls. Whatever you have, you like the opposite—they're exotic, intriguing." Here he constructs his racialized desire for brown-skinned "Latin" women through the specter of difference. Scholarship in tourism studies has illustrated the important role that difference plays in foreigners' imaginations of exotic sites and the presumably erotic people that inhabit tourist destinations. Orvar Lofgren describes vacationing as a "cultural laboratory" in which fantasy becomes "an important social practice" (1999, 7). The fantasies that emerge in this "cultural laboratory" usually involve a racial erotic Other. As Steven Gregory points out, the tourist experience is constructed in "gendered and racialized terms—as an encounter with a docile, obliging, and feminized other" (2007, 137). Joe continued, "It's common knowledge that Brazilian women are hot. After the Snoop Dogg video, a lot of guys said, 'I gotta go!'" He is referring to "Beautiful," a collaboration between Snoop Dogg and Pharell filmed in Rio de Janeiro in 2003. As T. Denean Sharpley-Whiting (2007) notes in her chapter on video vixens and diasporic sex tourism, hip-hop videos filmed on the beaches of Brazil perpetuate eroticized images of Latin American women to the mostly African American audiences that consume them.

Joe drew interesting distinctions between women from Rio de Janeiro and those from Salvador, with both race (that is, blackness) and class playing roles in his stereotypical notions of "authentic" Bahian women. He preferred Salvador because "in Rio it's harder to meet girls because of the stigma of being with a *gringo*. They all think you're rich. Poor girls are easier to meet. Rich girls don't need you. You're exotic to them." Once again, class emerges as an important social distinction. However, he also contended that "Rio has more beautiful women" than Salvador, though he also pointed out that those who prefer southern Brazil generally do so "because they like white girls." Despite's Joe's preference for brown skin, his statement that Rio has more beautiful women than Salvador seems to conflate "beautiful women" with white women. In so doing, he reinforces the distinction between black and mixed-race women, who are seen as hypersexual, and white women, who remain the standard of beauty and respectability. Though his racialized desire for Brazilian women of African descent may be read as a problematic case of exoticizing the Other, Joe uses it to construct a subjectivity of heightened racial tolerances vis-à-vis those who travel to southern Brazil because they prefer "white girls."

Joe relied on constructed notions of what Chandra Talpade Mohanty calls "third world difference" (1991, 53–54) by attributing particular cultural differences to geopolitical and economic disparities between "advanced" and "less advanced" countries: "In advanced countries, . . . everybody thinks so much before doing things. Here, women are primitive, primal, they show raw emotion, and they're crazy and impulsive. They don't go by what's reasonable. They're not calculating. Here people go on feeling. They do anything at any time. People here are more free because they don't have shit, they're not as programmed. It's the same with Brazilian women who are born here but live in the U.S. Women here are very up-front and honest—there's less games. . . . Here, I can be a little more aggressive and still not be as bad as Brazilian men. People are more willing to talk to each other in general. They're not afraid of each other." According to Joe's logic, the fact that Brazil is characterized by a lack of economic resources results in people being less "rational" and "logical" and more "free." The juxtaposition is clear: in First World countries, people overthink things and consequently hinder their freedom; in Third World countries, people (particularly people of color with lower incomes), rely on feeling alone and are therefore less inhibited in their sexuality and their emotions.

In referring to Brazilian women as "primitive" and "primal," Joe explicitly participates in what Kamala Kempadoo and Jo Doezema refer to as the "exoticization of the Third World 'Other'" (1998, 10). Kempadoo also notes that for Westerners, black women in the Caribbean represent the "primitive, barbarous Other" (1999, 26). Denise Brennan (2004) underscores how sex tourists' fantasies about women in particular places are deeply rooted in colonial racist discourses and fueled by media and Internet depictions. For example, Western sex tourists perceive Dominican women as poor, uneducated, dependent, hot, sensual women who genuinely enjoy sex with older white men: in the words of one German sex tourist, Dominican women "like to fuck [and] have fiery blood" (195). Similarly, another sex tourist posted in an online newsletter that "Dominican women love sex and they love American men" (Gregory 2007, 163).

Joe saw Brazilian women—including those residing in the United States— as closer to nature, both in terms of the "primitive" physical landscape and in terms of their "raw emotions." Thus, he does not need to travel to Brazil to encounter women with the qualities he desires. Joe naturalized Brazilian women as having an "essence" that is maintained even if they are raised and socialized in the United States, a belief that may also explain why he preferred to date Latin American women of color at home in New York. In this sense, Joe's racialized desires challenged how scholars have traditionally used the concept of liminality to understand how tourists engage in certain practices, behavior, and desires that they would not ordinarily indulge at home (Lofgren 1999; Pratt 1992; Turner 1969). Rather than emerging in the liminal phase of a trip to Bahia, Joe's desires were present at home as well. Joe also distinguished among nationalities: "Colombians have beautiful faces, but Brazilians have better bodies." This comment highlights how transnational constructions of Latin American femininities are connected among those who travel—physically or virtually—for sex, romance, or marriage in Latin America.[1]

Joe's description of one particular encounter with a Bahian woman illustrates the terms of approach and negotiation in sex tourism as well as the ambiguity present in these encounters. He met thirty-year-old Carminha at the internet café where she worked in a beachfront touristic neighborhood: "We made eye contact and smiled. She kept looking, so I blew her a kiss. [Later], she came to look for me at the bus stop." He was clearly flattered by her initiative, which helped consolidate his idea that in Brazil, he could hit on women without them thinking he was a creep. Being in Bahia liberated him to express his sexual assertiveness. After exchanging telephone numbers, Carminha called him first. When they made plans to meet, she suggested going to his apartment "to talk." He promptly obliged, enjoying her "take-charge" attitude: "She attacked me [sexually]! . . . The girls here are aggressive. She was crazy—she could have had sex ten times!" Interestingly, he quickly transitioned from talking about one particular woman to generalizing about "the girls here." Part of the attraction of sexual experiences in Bahia for Joe was the fact he felt that he did not have to work as hard to sleep with women. Rather than seeking to dominate Third World women, Joe took pleasure in what he perceived as Bahian women's sexual aggressiveness. Similarly, Luis, a Peruvian American tourist who lived in Brasília, also expressed the idea that Brazilian women were more sexually assertive: he was with a Bahian woman who "took charge of the situation. . . . Let's say she almost raped me."

In describing his sexual encounter with Carminha, Joe tacked back and forth between describing her and using the experience to generalize about Bahian women. "They're nuts, the Bahian women. They'll kiss your armpit. They like to be hit in the face and on the ass. They'll spit [on you]. They want to be called *putas* [whores] and *cachorras* [dogs]. They try to slap [you]. They're primal, primitive, and animalistic. Maybe it's because the men are so rough with women here." Joe found these sexual practices strange, but they also excited him and reinforced his notions of Bahians as uninhibited, wild, and free. However, Carminha's uninhibited sexuality had strings attached: "She told me she didn't want me to be with any other girls. . . . I'm not looking for a girlfriend here. I had to kick her out of my house. She was crazy—calling three times a day."

This situation brings up the concept of reciprocity, which is crucial to understanding the power-laden interactions of the contact zone of sex tourism. Mary Louise Pratt (1992) describes reciprocity as a desired object of travel in which efforts are made to establish equilibrium through exchange. One might think of reciprocity as stories sex tourists tell about themselves.

In dismissing Bahian men as overly aggressive and rough, Joe establishes himself—a white American heterosexual man—as superior to local men. The concept of reciprocity provides the analytical tools to interrogate the passing desires of actors involved in transnational sexual/romantic liaisons. It offers a language for asking what people seek in the pursuit of these relationships as well as a way of understanding the possibility that those hopes and aspirations are often contradictory and incompatible. Carminha's and Joe's desires ultimately were incompatible. While he expected to find a commitment-free sexual encounter, she hoped for something more—perhaps a potential boyfriend or a husband who could give her opportunities for upward and maybe even transnational mobility.

Joe's testimony also demonstrated a tension between dating and commercial sexual transactions, a distinction that reiterates the ambiguity of transnational sexual/romantic encounters in Salvador. He pointed out that Carminha had previously been married to an Italian man with whom she had children, and he noted, "Here, it's hard to say if she's a prostitute or a normal girl." Notwithstanding the problematic way that Joe constructed prostitutes as something other than "normal" women, he also refused to pay for sex with professional sex workers. Instead, he preferred to "date" working-class women of African descent and distanced himself from men who sought out commercial sex. While Joe claimed that he had never been with a prostitute in Salvador, he had been with a sex worker at a *termas* (spa/brothel) in Rio de Janeiro. He had learned about these spas from a friend in New York City who "loves Latin women too" and "became an addict" while doing online research on the sex scene in Rio de Janeiro. Joe and his friend's shared desire for Latin American women created a bond of male sociality.

Knowledge about sexual commerce in Brazil thus circulates through various sources, including internet Web sites and by word of mouth from others who have firsthand experience in these places (see also Brennan 2004; Constable 2007; Gregory 2007; Schaeffer-Grabiel 2006). This phenomenon highlights Dean MacCannell's (1999, 110) claim that a tourist's first contact with a destination is actually with a representation of the site through accounts from other tourists, travel books, travel programs, films, or lectures. As an Embratur publication put it, "The foreign tourist, besides bringing dollars, is our best propaganda abroad. For this reason, he receives special attention" (Beatriz Oliveira and Kaizer 2002, 23). Thinking of foreign tourists as the "best propaganda abroad" is a double-edged sword, however. On the one hand, this form of advertisement can encourage more visitors by highlighting the country's natural wonders. On the other hand, it can perpetuate the transnational circulation of ideas about the hypersexuality and availability of Brazilian women and men of African descent.

Joe went to one *termas* in Rio de Janeiro five times. After so many visits, he "knew all the girls there" and thought they were all so "sweet" that "you wouldn't believe they're prostitutes." He described the experience as "clean and classy": "You got a robe and a bracelet with a number. There was a Jacuzzi, a dance club part, and a strip club. There were thirty beautiful girls. In a *termas*, the girls are mostly white and *morena*, nineteen- to twenty-five-year-old girls putting themselves through college. They have [sexually transmitted disease] tests every week. . . . It was $R250 for a room, girl, entrance, and drinks in the *termas*." The racial distinction here is significant. The more protected, safe, elite, private establishment had mostly white or *morena* women, whereas women who solicit clients on the streets, particularly in Bahia, are disproportionately of African descent. After paying for the same woman three times at the *termas*, he spent an entire week with her, during which time they "hung out like boyfriend and girlfriend." According to Joe, this woman, who was studying psychology in college, "looked black but had straight hair." Joe did not pay her during this time, and she would not allow him to pay for anything; on one occasion, she bought him some of the drug ecstasy. "She had money, . . . was smart, and could converse." Joe had never been with a prostitute in New York City, and he swore that he would never tell people back home about this experience.

The encounter between Joe and the woman who worked in a *termas* can be seen as an example of what Elizabeth Bernstein calls the "girlfriend experience," which she defines as an exchange that resembles a nonpaid encounter between lovers (2007b). Unlike the "quick, impersonal sexual release associated with the street sex trade," the girlfriend experience generally involves a lengthy period of foreplay, mutual stimulation, and postcoital cuddling (2007a, 194). This new variety of sexual labor provides what Bernstein refers to as "bounded authenticity" (2007b, 6), or the sale and purchase of "authentic" emotional and physical connections. Sex workers fulfill clients' fantasies of sensuous reciprocity through a simulation of desire, pleasure, and erotic interest and make clients feel "desired, esteemed, and loved" (2007a, 192). Joe felt liberated to purchase sex in Brazil because he positioned the women as somehow different—as not really prostitutes (Kempadoo 2004, 123).

Joe's racialized desires did not translate into heightened racial tolerance or an absence of racial prejudice. On the contrary, he was clearly invested in privileging the foreign (Brazilian) blackness that he encountered on vacation as superior to the domestic (U.S.) blackness he encountered every day at home. He claimed that black Brazilians did not have "the same hatred of white people" as African Americans and that "it feels safer [in Brazil] in black neighborhoods. I don't know if there's been a real civil rights movement here. Here, there are better family values in black communities. Poor black girls in the U.S. are hard; here they're sweet, nice, and soft. Black people in the U.S. are much harder in general; here, they're kinder and more helpful. Poor people here are very nice. The African American community is twisted up in their morals, in what's given priority and importance. I don't see any improvement happening anytime soon. There's no good black leadership in America. City schools are shit. Kids learn too early about sex and drugs. Here, you'll see a girl who doesn't smoke or drink and has an 11:00 P.M. curfew but is an animal at sex." Joe also failed to consider how his perception of these presumably cultural differences were shaped by his positionality as a foreigner in a tourist destination.

Joe's attention always returned to sex—to establishing black Brazilian women (and girls) as sexually exceptional. While proponents of racial democracy may have interpreted interracial mixing as proof of nonracism, the transracial erotic desires at play in the context of sex tourism are often deeply embedded in racist discourses. In other words, racisms can be as much about xenophilia as xenophobia. Elisa Lucinda's poem "*Mulata Exportação*" (Mulata Exportation) offers a critical response to the discourses that situate *mulatas* and black women as erotic objects that prove that Brazil is nonracist. Interracial flings are not necessarily antiracist. In fact, depending on one's motivations, these encounters are often laden with racist stereotypes and ideas.

Joe's experiences reveal how the privileges of whiteness are often exacerbated on vacation, particularly in Brazil and other societies that have entrenched racial hierarchies and where whiteness is implicitly valued as superior to other races and ethnicities. Sociologist Jonathan Warren describes Brazil as "a racial paradise for whites" where they can "enjoy an incredible degree of uncontested white privilege" (2000, 160). He goes on to point out that "whites can more easily indulge in racial privilege without guilt because white privilege is naturalized and unmarked in nonwhite spaces" (160). Instead of recognizing how his subjectivity as a white, male U.S. citizen in Brazil shapes the way Bahians interact with him, Joe interpreted these qualities as intrinsic to the black Bahians' nature. Furthermore, Joe positioned "Latin women" and "African American women" as two mutually exclusive categories when he said, "There's something with Latin women. . . . They have a power that African American women don't have. They celebrate their sexuality and beauty." Thus, even though most of the "Latin women" he pursued were of African descent, he considered these Brazilian women to be marked most

significantly by their Latin American culture, with all of its attendant connotations in his imaginary. Felicity Schaeffer-Grabiel has described the ways
in which transnational marriage Web sites depict Latin American women
as docile, feminine, "overly sexualized," yet "untainted by modern capitalist
relations" (2004; 2005, 332–34). While Joe is an unabashedly self-proclaimed
sex tourist, other foreign tourists would not consider themselves as such.
Nonetheless, their stories illustrate the ways in which sexual possibilities
underlie the tourist experience in Brazil.

The Possibilities of Sex and Transnational Male Sociality

Keith

Recent scholarship and journalism has focused on the prevalence of African
American male sex tourism to Rio de Janeiro (Cobb 2006; Sharpley-Whiting
2007; Jewel Woods and Hunter 2008). Keith, an African American man from
Atlanta who worked in the pharmaceutical industry, had been to Bahia three
times since 2002, but had never been to Rio de Janeiro, even though he had
heard rumors about the "girls in Rio" before his first trip to Brazil. Keith
first came to Bahia with his capoeira group, and he felt so "at home" that he
has returned repeatedly. He voiced his displeasure at discovering the racial
dynamics of sexual tourism during his first trip to Salvador: "I saw a lot of
beautiful black women with old white men."

Only on subsequent trips did Keith learn more about the situation of
garotas de programa. Leonardo, a black Bahian tour guide, quipped to Keith
that the literal translation of *garotas de programa* meant that you could "program them to do whatever you want." This was Keith's first hint that procuring "girls" for foreign clients was an integral part of Leonardo's tour guide
responsibilities. Keith distanced himself from Leonardo after hearing that
he had raped a young Brazilian woman who worked for him. Regarding
the question of sex tourism, he said: "I have some values that I don't depart
from—no exploiting children and no sex with prostitutes." Reflecting on his
experiences as a tourist in the sexual economies of Bahia, Keith revealed,
"I meet sex tourists every day. I've met guys who come up to me and ask,
'Where de girls at? Do they have clubs like in Rio?' There's Casquinha de Siri
on Monday, Wednesday, Friday, or Saturday. All the prostitutes go. There's
Aeroclube on Tuesday, where the prostitutes go. I've never told tourists that
because I don't want to promote this." Keith was well versed in the sex work
scene, though he never admitted to participating in these sexual economies.
Gossip, rumors, and hearsay thus play a central role in studying sex tourism

(Brennan 2004; Frohlick 2007). In dealing with taboo subjects pertaining to sexuality, people are often more comfortable talking about other people's sexual practices. Keith told me about a friend with whom he shared an apartment in Salvador. By day, the friend ran a project to help poor communities in Salvador, "but by night, he was on the prowl trying to sleep with Bahian women." He also told me about another acquaintance who allegedly went to Rio for the sole purpose of staying in his hotel room and having sex with Brazilian women.

Ahmad

Ahmad, an African American tourist from a predominantly black, working-class community in New York, traveled to Bahia to visit two American female friends who were residing there. As a graduate student in a monogamous relationship in the United States, Ahmad was not interested in pursuing sexual encounters in Salvador. Nonetheless, Brazil still represented the possibility of sex in his imagination and had an indelible influence on him. One day, Ahmad went to a beach in Salvador. "I was there to see women. I spent a whole day taking pictures of asses, and my fingers are crossed that the pictures come out good." He explained this pursuit as "strictly Brazil" and "thirty-five-year-old peer pressure": "I wanted to go home and show the fellas that what we thought was true, because all my men back home think the same [about Brazil]: chicks with thongs who are ready and willing to have sex."

Ahmad told me that everything he had ever heard or seen about Brazil suggested that it was a place full of "loose women who are ready for sex." One of the places he was exposed to this idea was through pornography: "There's a whole section of porn just for Brazilian women. . . . I had one tape of Brazilian women and it spread around the neighborhood—that tape is revered. . . . There's one Brazilian woman [porn star] with a huge ass and tattoo of a spider on it. . . . It's legendary. That's what we think of Brazilian women: tan lines, cocoa brown skin, big asses, and ready to fuck." In this sense, Ahmad's "tourist tale" falls into what Edward M. Bruner describes as the "pre-tour narrative" stage, which consists of preconceptions about the destination gathered from various sources such as tourist advertisements and media representations (2005, 22). Several of my informants' stories indicate that the media played a significant role in contributing to the circulation of images and stereotypes about the hypersexuality and accessibility of Brazilian women of African descent. Although the "touristic practices" (Urry 2002, 2) in which Ahmad engaged were continuous with his desires and male-bonding practices at home, the liminality of the tourist experience still provided him with more license to express those desires.[2] Myths of hypersexuality fueled his "touristic practice" of taking pictures of anonymous women's bodies. However, for heterosexual African American men, the notions of hyper-sexuality of Brazilian women of African descent may have more to do with connotations of Brazilianness than with connotations of blackness than may be the case for European and American men.

However, Ahmad pointed out that this idea of Brazilian women did not hold true in his experiences there:

> Although the bikinis were small, everybody was covered and comfortable. . . . It didn't seem like the small bikinis were meant to attract dudes; it was more what they're used to wearing, what they go to the beach in. For me, it's some-thing exotic, but for them it's just what they wear to the beach—for fat people, skinny people, old people. . . . You come with the idea that there's *gonna* be single women all over the place, as if Brazilian dudes don't exist. . . . You enter a running and working social system where women wear small bikinis, very short denim skirts, tight clothes. That's what they do here. . . . They probably know it's sexy, but it seems like these women were doing their thing, whether going to work or having boyfriends. This culture is moving and working and not just waiting for me to jump in and enjoy. Before you come here, that's what you think—like it's a candy store waiting to be used and exploited. I think it might even be reversed: it's a candy store waiting to pull fools in and exploit them. The candy ain't as sweet.

Ahmad's testimony reveals how the idea of Brazil as a "sexscape" (Brennan 2004, 15) carries a great deal of currency, even when these fantasies and desires are not accompanied by actual sexual encounters. It also shows that processes of exoticization of Brazilian women of African descent are not the exclusive domains of white European and North American men. Despite claims of diasporic solidarity with black people in other parts of the world, heterosexual African American men also exoticize Brazilian women of Afri-can descent, though perhaps in slightly different ways than their white coun-terparts. African American men seem particularly interested in an aesthetic that privileges race mixture, light skin tones, and curly/wavy hair (Jewel Woods and Hunter 2008, 159–60; Cobb 2006; Sharpley-Whiting 2007). Ah-mad's statement emphasizes the role of cultural differences and imaginaries, a viewpoint that fits with what Bruner calls the "post-tour telling" stage of "tourist tales" (2005, 23–24), in which Ahmad's actual experiences in Bahia reshaped his preexisting ideas.

Ahmad and Ronaldo, a black Bahian man, bonded across language barriers in part through their shared interest in Brazilian women's bodies. Ronaldo helped Ahmad take photos of women's backsides ("booty shots"). Ahmad said that Brazilian men were "more than willing" to help him take pictures of women, using hand gestures to communicate the presence of a woman to photograph. Ahmad reflected on the complicity of Bahian men in a process that could be seen as exoticizing and objectifying Brazilian women: "It's dude shit that we do in the States, too. When cats come to town, we go to a strip club, show them women. . . . It's something I've seen me and my fellas do at home as well. [Brazilian men] know I like taking pics of women, and they like women. . . . It just felt like dudes kickin' it. . . . They didn't have ready access to easy women. We don't either at home. . . . It seemed like dudes hangin' out and doing what they normally do. They know they have a lot of good-looking women around here. It seemed like they felt that Brazilian women were beautiful—almost like they were proud of them." The camaraderie between Ahmad and Ronaldo is a form of "male sociality" that traverses national borders to unite them in their common expressions of heterosexual desire and fantasy (even when the participants know that these fantasies will not be fulfilled).

According to Gregory, male sociality is an important component of "imperial masculinity" among male sex tourists (2007, 133). It revolves around "a set of ritualized spectacles through which men fantasize the nonbeing of women and, in turn, imagine themselves to be all-powerful subjects" (149). Ahmad and Ronaldo demonstrate a form of transnational male sociality in which men of different nationalities bond over their heterosexual desires for women. Men participate collectively in actions such as gawking at and commenting on women's bodies and taking photographs. Through practices and performances of male sociality and heterosexual masculinity, male sex tourists cultivate adventure, risk, and competition. For Gregory, "imperial masculinity" is a "normative ideal and social practice" that encompasses what heterosexual men believe themselves to be, possess, and represent (133). Thus, masculinity is something that one does rather than a quality that one possesses (Gutterman 2001; Whitehead and Barrett 2001).

Read in the context of male sociality, erotic encounters with "native" women serve as a rite of passage that consolidates white male economic privilege in the patriarchal global order. But what kinds of privilege do heterosexual African American men consolidate in this process? While some observers assert the significance of global black solidarity in African American tourism in the African diaspora, African Americans nonetheless constantly carry "American privilege" in their travels. In fact, several of the African American male sex tourists interviewed by Jewel Woods and Karen Hunter noted feeling "like white men" while in Rio de Janeiro (2008, 199).

In *Don't Blame It on Rio: The Real Deal behind Why Men Go to Brazil for Sex*, Woods and Hunter sought to "expose" sex tourism as a harmful practice that is "ruining the black family" (2008, 19). However, failing to problematize their informants' statements ends up leaving negative stereotypes of African American women unchallenged. Brazilian women are "sisters" but are not considered "black women," a term used specifically to refer to African American women. Woods and Hunter privilege mixture as a signifier of the unique beauty of Brazilian women, and they have a flawed understanding of the country's racial hierarchies. They say that whitening meant limiting the number of black babies, which is historically inaccurate (2008, 178). Whitening in Brazil involved purposeful encouragement of racial mixing, including incentives for European settlement as a means of whitening the population. Woods and Hunter refer to Brazil as "Black Womb" that nurtures black men (181), a statement that has numerous dangerous implications. It erases the existence of the very real effects of racial inequalities in Brazil, where black men often suffer from police violence and discrimination. Woods and Hunter's statement clearly refers to black American men, because black Brazilian men are completely excluded from their depiction of Rio de Janeiro.

The fact that Ahmad could not fathom the thought of returning home without booty shots to show his friends reveals how Brazil is constructed as a sexual paradise in which "sex is understood as a necessary component of a successful visit" to the country (Blanchette and Silva 2005, 262). Ahmad did not need to have sex for the possibilities of sex to form an integral part of his tourist experience. Thaddeus G. Blanchette and Ana Paula da Silva's work on sex tourism in Rio de Janeiro highlights the fact that sex is seen as a "typical souvenir of Rio" (2005, 262). One foreign tourist traveled to Rio after a friend told him that visiting Rio was like "living a pornographic film twenty-four hours a day" (Blanchette and Silva 2005, 263). However, when the man actually traveled to Rio, he found it difficult to meet women who were not professional sex workers. While he initially resisted engaging commercial sex workers, near the end of his trip, he changed his mind: "How can I go back to the office and say that I went to Brazil and didn't have sex with anyone?" (263).

Conclusion

The (imagined) hypersexuality of Brazilian women of African descent played a pivotal role in the experiences of both Joe and Ahmad, regardless of whether or not they actually had sex with Brazilian women. As Frohlick points out, "intimacy beyond sex acts" is central to "ethnosexual tourism" (Frohlick 2007, 142), which Joane Nagel defines as crossing boundaries of convergence between ethnicity and sexuality (2000, 159).

While scholarly definitions of sex tourism often consider it to be travel exclusively in search of sex—often with prepurchased packages that include the services or companionship of a local woman, Joe's story reveals how the lure of both culture and sex plays an important role in constructing Bahia as the land of erotic adventures in the global tourist imaginary. This connection between seeking culture and sex was a common theme among foreign tourists. Another American tourist, Richard, called Brazil a "land of mysteries" and emphasized the power he perceived within capoeira, which had motivated him to travel to Brazil. Richard described Brazilians as "warmer and more open to human communication" than Americans. Brazilian women "aren't closed off to men" even when not particularly interested in talking to those men. Richard "didn't go to Brazil to date," but he "hoped for it. It wasn't my first intention to go for the women, like a lot of people. I really got fed up with a lot of tourists." In much the same way that Joe sought to differentiate himself from the image of the typical tourist, Richard also distanced himself from foreign tourists who only wanted to drink beer, dance, and date by staying in a working-class community rather than in a tourist district. He "wanted to know the real Brazil . . . to live where people are real."

Joe, Ahmad, and Richard had different backgrounds, motivations, and practices yet shared a desire to perceive themselves and have others perceive them as not like other foreign tourists. Such "touristic intimacy" is, according to Frohlick, "a kind of sociability" in which tourists "connect with and essentially become part of the body/landscape of the Other" through their encounters with local people (2007, 152). For Joe and Richard in particular, living among ordinary, working-class Bahians rather than remaining cloistered in the tourist districts was one strategy for fully immersing themselves in Brazilian ways of living; other strategies included taking music lessons and Portuguese classes and having intimate encounters with Bahian women.

The experiences and subjectivities of foreign tourists must be taken seriously. Embracing an intersectional perspective that attends to the multiple and sometimes contested ways in which foreign tourists seek to perform touristic intimacy offers a challenge to the notion of Brazil as a racial democracy. Foreign tourists' motivations for traveling to Bahia and desires and hopes for their tourist experience illustrate the intersecting realms of culture and sex that characterize the touristscape of Salvador. More specifically, the stories of Joe and others refute the perception of Brazil as a "color-blind erotic democracy" where interracial desires, liaisons, and relationships are considered proof of the absence of racism (Goldstein 2003, 133). Joe's tourist tale shows how discourses of black hypersexuality circulate both within Brazil and transnationally. Foreign men who travel to Brazil in search of the mythologized sexuality of black and brown women appropriate the notion of the *mulata tipo exportação* (exportation-type *mulata*).

CHAPTER FIVE

Aprosba

The Politics of Race, Sexual Labor, and Identification

In November 2006, I was invited to attend my first meeting of the Association of Prostitutes of Bahia (Aprosba). When I walked into the group's small headquarters, located near the Praça da Sé bus stop, I encountered a group of seventeen women and three small children. As soon as I entered, Fabiana, the group's cofounder and lead organizer, stood up and greeted me with a warm smile and the customary two kisses on each cheek. A white Brazilian woman in her early forties from the state of Paraíba, Fabiana allowed me to introduce myself and discuss my research with the members. Aprosba had weekly meetings every Tuesday afternoon at 3:00. These meetings served as a space for politicization, empowerment, and the sharing of knowledge and experiences regarding issues of sex workers' rights, working conditions, and health. At the end of the meeting, each woman in attendance would receive between fifteen and thirty free condoms, provided by the Ministry of Health.[1] Women were encouraged to arrive on time: anyone who arrived after 3:15 would not be allowed to enter and consequently would not receive condoms.

Aprosba meetings were a space to share traumatic experiences with empathetic, understanding listeners. I regularly attended the meetings throughout the course of my fieldwork. The meetings featured speakers leading workshops on a range of issues, including dental health, sexually transmitted infections (STIs), contraception, and the proper use and disposal of condoms. At a particularly intense December 2006 meeting when the lead organizers were away running a workshop in a rural part of Bahia, three women shared their experiences of sexual assault by the men who were supposed to serve and protect them—police officers. Two of the rapes occurred when the women were minors, and at least one of the officers did not use a condom, leaving his victim afraid of contracting HIV from this incident. All of the women present offered words of encouragement and support, even volunteering to accompany her to get an HIV test. The therapeutic act of "confession" helped them to realize that they were not alone in their struggles and that they could overcome hardships. By encouraging the rape survivor to get tested for HIV when she was immobilized by fear, the women attempted to empower her with the idea that she could take control of her life and her health. Furthermore, awareness of one's HIV status is particularly important in a country with one of the world's leading programs for distributing antiretroviral drugs. At another Aprosba meeting, members discussed issues of unity and the role of the police in their lives. Marisa told the women, "We need more unity. We shouldn't be envious of other *putas*. . . . We shouldn't talk about our problems with the police because the police don't help. . . . [T]hey . . . beat women." Here, Marisa challenges the assumption that the police "protect and serve."

In laying out Aprosba's history and activities, this chapter analyzes the group's place in state, regional, and transnational networks of sex workers' associations. Aprosba operates at the epicenter of mechanisms of state control and regulation while simultaneously challenging the state by mobilizing for sex workers' rights. This chapter brings ethnography of Aprosba members into dialogue with the theoretical and political distinctions related to terms such as *prostitute* and *sex worker* as well as into the debate regarding whether sex work can be understood as a practice or an identity. In highlighting the important activism and organizing efforts of grassroots Brazilian sex workers on the local, national, and transnational scenes (Desai 2002), my work contributes to scholarship on transnational feminism, women and development, and discussions of the "NGO-ization" of women's movements (Alvarez 1990; Thayer 2010).

This chapter embraces an intersectional framework that pays close attention to the racial and class dynamics of the organization and follows Kamala Kempadoo's (2001b) call for more women of color scholars to use a transnational feminist and postcolonial framework for studying sex work. For Kempadoo, a transnational feminist approach would "explore histories and contemporary meanings of Black and Brown women's sexuality" in light of racism, colonialism, gendered relations of power, and globalization (2001b, 42). Furthermore, a transnational feminist approach to sex work also includes "a rethinking of practical strategies and programs to address the specific situations for women of color in the global sex trade" (Kempadoo 2001b, 43). A detailed description of Aprosba offers an interesting ethnographic site of analysis to highlight these issues.

Background

Aprosba was founded in 1997 by a group of prostitutes in Salvador who felt the need to combat the violence that they confronted and raise awareness about safer sex practices in their community. At the time, prostitutes in Salvador were plagued by discrimination, unwanted pregnancies, and sexual and physical assault by both clients and police officers as well as a lack of knowledge about the prevention of pregnancy and HIV/AIDS and other STIs. Aprosba is the only organization in Bahia run by and for prostitutes. Conversely, many Brazilian civil society organizations are dominated by privileged people Bernd Reiter calls "the included," who make decisions for their excluded clients, rather than with them (2009, 89). Aprosba works to improve the living conditions of prostitutes rather than convince them to stop doing sex work. Its mission is to "fight for the education of female sex workers in Bahia, valuing them as citizens who are conscious of their rights and responsibilities and investing in the capacity-building and organization of this group for their inclusion in society."[2]

The emphasis on citizenship is significant in the context of social movements and civil society organizations in Brazil, particularly given the history of the military dictatorship (1964–85). In *Negotiating Democracy in Brazil: The Politics of Exclusion*, Reiter (2009) argues that the persisting inequalities in Brazilian society undermine democracy. Becoming a full citizen requires that the state recognize one as an autonomous individual able to make his or her own decisions. Problems arise when "the included" are perceived as having rights that must be protected while "the excluded" (poor, marginalized people) are perceived as relying on favors (2009, 146). As low-income, marginalized women who suffer from stigmatization, Brazilian sex workers have been excluded from the benefits of full citizenship despite the fact that adult prostitution is legal.[3]

Prostitution is recognized as a professional activity in the *Classificação Brasileira de Ocupações* (Brazilian Classification of Occupations). In the Code 5198, *profissional do sexo* (sex professional) includes various names: *garota de programa, garoto de programa, meretriz, messalina, michê, mulher da vida, prostituta*, and *trabalhador do sexo*. The job description of a sex worker is defined as someone who "seeks sexual *programas*; attends and accompanies clients; and participates in educational actions in the field of sexuality. The activities are exercised following norms and procedures that minimize the vulnerabilities of the profession" (*Classificação* n.d.).[4] Gregory Mitchell (2011a, 159) points out that in 2005 the Brazilian government rejected forty million dollars from the U.S. Agency for International Development that was contingent on Brazil publicly condemning prostitution. Furthermore, he notes that Pedro Chequer, director of Brazil's National HIV/AIDS Commission, called prostitutes the government's "partners" and condemned President George W. Bush's mandate as theological and fundamentalist (160).

Fabiana stated that one of Aprosba's goals is "to show that prostitutes are also dignified people who exercise a profession like any other" (Francisco 2006). Aprosba has approximately three thousand affiliated members, but the group estimates that Salvador has between four thousand and five thousand sex workers. The process of affiliating with Aprosba involved calling, filling out a brief form on the Web site, visiting the office, or attending meetings. Attendance at the weekly meetings ranged between five and thirty women. This lack of participation could be attributed to the location of the Aprosba office. According to Fabiana, women who work in Barra or other locations outside of the Centro often do not come to meetings, while those who work closer to the Centro are more likely to attend. Most of the sex workers who worked in the Praça da Sé and Barra were of African descent, but many did not actively or regularly participate in Aprosba.

Bárbara, an active member of Aprosba, said that sex workers whose *pontos* were located on the *orla* (coastline) might not attend Aprosba meetings because of their grueling work schedule. During my fieldwork, Bárbara worked nights on the *orla* between the beach of Patamares and a nightclub, Casquinha de Siri, as well as during the day at motels and movie theaters in the Centro Histórico. She said that the "girls" begin to arrive at Patamares between 2:00 and 5:00 in the afternoon and at Casquinha de Siri around 10:00 at night, especially on Mondays, Thursdays, and Fridays. "They don't seek out Aprosba because they work at night and sleep during the day," she said. Furthermore, the women would have to pay bus fare to travel from the *orla* to the Praça da Sé. Bárbara also pointed out that girls who work the *orla* must contend with constant persecution—they are often beaten by police officers, filmed with hidden cameras, and raped: "They're afraid to be there."

The police violence that sex workers in Salvador experience resembles what occurs in other countries. Amalia Cabezas asserts that sex workers in Cuba and the Dominican Republic "bear the brunt of state-inflicted violence against women" and rarely receive police protection when they are victims of sexual and physical violence at the hands of clients, husbands, or intermediaries (2009, 140). In the Dominican Republic, police demand bribes, rape sex workers, and conduct mass arrests to prevent sex workers from "bothering" tourists (146). Moreover, women of African descent are more likely to be read as sex workers and arrested, while white sex workers often pass under the radar, undetected (Fernandez 2010, 132).

In addition to holding meetings, safer sex workshops, and group activities and distributing condoms, Aprosba representatives periodically visit areas of prostitution to distribute educational materials. Furthermore, the organization does theatrical presentations, conducts workshops at universities, and trains prostitutes to be *multiplicadores* (multiplying agents) who can pass information along to their peers. Aprosba also refers members to lawyers and health clinics, offers support in cases of sexual or physical abuse, contacts local media outlets, and organizes protests when the need arises. Whenever clients refused to pay for *programas*, sex workers called police, and they found that emphasizing their affiliation with Aprosba seemed to encourage the police to intervene and force clients to pay. To prevent this problem from arising, Aprosba taught members to ask for money before the sexual act.

The Difference That Aprosba Has Made

Members of Aprosba seemed grateful for the difference that the group had made in their lives. Several members spoke of "before Aprosba" as a time when they were uninformed about preventing pregnancies and STIs, when a few of them were addicted to drugs, and when they had no way to combat the violence of their daily lives. When she was a teenager, Bárbara was a substance abuser, but Aprosba helped her overcome her addiction and enabled her to finish high school and complete ten minicourses that taught her such skills as giving manicures, sewing, telemarketing, and working with computers.[5] Aprosba's educational efforts had also resulted in a decrease in unwanted pregnancies among sex workers. According to Fabiana, in 1998, it was common to see at least five pregnant women at the meetings. But by 2007, safer sex workshops at Aprosba meetings had led the women to become more conscientious about taking measures to prevent unwanted pregnancies. Fabiana also believed that Aprosba's work had also led to a reduction in the violence that sex workers faced.

One female police officer was extremely tough on prostitution in the Praça da Sé, harassing sex workers and trying to prevent them from gathering. With the help of Aprosba, the sex workers in the area filed a complaint against the officer. She received a reprimand, and her superiors obliged her to greet the sex workers in the Praça when she saw them each day. After a few months, the situation improved, and the prostitutes returned to the police station, this time, to bestow praise on the officer, whose perspective on prostitution had changed significantly. Reflecting on this experience, Fabiana believed that the women needed to "toe the line" to guarantee their rights as prostitutes. They had to strike a balance and avoid being too confrontational in their encounters with politicians, police officers, and other people in positions of power. Aprosba had also gone to the Delegacía da Mulher (Women's Police Station) when there were instances of violence against prostitutes and conducted workshops to help doctors learn to treat prostitutes without judgment or trying to persuade them to "get out of the life."[6]

Sex workers who worked in the Praça da Sé saw it as a *ponto* that had certain benefits over other places they could procure clients, such as bars and brothels. Gilmara, a young black woman with braids, commented women working in the Praça did not "have to drink or listen to loud music." And whenever police officers gave sex workers a hard time by trying to kick them out of the Praça, they could count on Aprosba for support. Denise, who had worked in the Praça for ten years, described how the commercial sex industry functions in the Praça. There are *pousadas* (cheap motels that rent rooms by the hour) that charge prostitutes fees of between one and three reais to bring clients into the rooms. Some of the *pousadas* provide condoms to sex workers for free, while others sell them to make a profit. Despite the risks associated with being in an open, public place, women who worked in the Praça generally kept all of the money they earned rather than giving a portion to a third party. Although prices vary in brothels [*bregas*], sex workers customarily charge clients fifty reais, of which fifteen reais goes to the house. Brothel owners charge departure fees of forty-five reais to clients who want to take women outside the brothels.

Aprosba's visibility seemed to have made an impact on clients in the Centro Histórico. According to Gilmara, violence from clients had disappeared from the Praça da Sé because "clients are very aware [and] ask us if we're associated with Aprosba." Zita, who was from Salvador but had migrated to the neighboring town of Camaçari, noted the difference in men from the Centro and those on the *orla* and in other cities: "The men in the Centro are well trained. They know about prevention. But on the *orla*, they think they're clean." She also emphasized that the men on the *orla* often do not see the need to use condoms for oral sex. Here, Zita contends that Aprosba's efforts to educate sex workers about safer sex have been passed on to clients in the Centro, who have become more aware of the importance of prevention measures, while men in areas where the presence of Aprosba is not as strong may still uphold outdated ideas about how STIs are spread. The ideas that look or smell can determine whether people are "clean" and that STIs cannot be transmitted through oral sex are just a few of the popular misconceptions that Aprosba is striving to change through its peer health education efforts. In this way, Aprosba is fulfilling the CBO requirement that sex workers must participate in safer sex workshops.

Feminist Debates: Abolitionist and Sex Worker Rights Perspectives

I first encountered Fabiana in August 2005 at a labor conference in Salvador on "Transforming the Relationship between Work and Citizenship: Production, Reproduction, and Sexuality." She was sitting in the audience when Gabriela Leite, a prominent sex workers' rights activist from Rio de Janeiro, spontaneously invited her to stand and address the group. The first words that Fabiana uttered before the audience full of feminist academics were "Eu não gosto de feministas, e feministas não gostam de mim!" (I don't like feminists, and feminists don't like me!). Her bold words, spoken with a smile, nonetheless hinted at the long-standing tensions between feminists and sex workers.

Scholarly studies on prostitution often depict sex workers either as exploited "sex slaves" who are commodified and forced to sell their bodies against their will or as cosmopolitan heroines who brazenly choose to use their sexuality as a means of advancement.[7] As Marjolein van der Veen puts it, "What is enslaved, exploited, and degraded within one discourse is held up in the other as free, self-sufficient, and engaged in self-realization" (2000, 122). Abolitionist perspectives have defined the parameters of international discourse on prostitution for over a century (Doezema 1998). This approach considers prostitution by nature to be exploitative, even likening it to rape. For abolitionists, "exploitation" is a morally loaded category in which prostitution is naturalized as "wrong" and "immoral." Jo Doezema says that for Kathleen Barry, cofounder of the Coalition against Trafficking of Women, "the existence of a "prostitute who is unharmed by her experience is an ontological impossibility" (2001, 27). In seeing prostitutes as victims, radical and Marxist feminists tend to support the criminalization and/or eradication of prostitution, which can render sex workers more vulnerable to agents and traffickers and deny them legal and political rights (van der Veen 2000; Dewey and Kelly 2011). Abolitionist perspectives lament the oppression of prostitutes yet offer few substantial alternatives for women who engage in sex work to make a living. They attack the exploitative aspects of sex work yet do little to change the exploitative conditions under which many prostitutes labor. Consequently, Aprosba plays an extremely important role because it is run by and for prostitutes and strives to improve their working and living conditions and ensure their rights.

Aprosba leaders and members argue that legitimizing sex work would guarantee them important protections and improve their working conditions. In Fabiana's words, "As much money as you earn [from prostitution], you lose because of illegality." Although adult prostitution is legal in Brazil, sex workers are still criminalized and stigmatized in many ways, which has a profound impact on their working conditions. For example, sex workers were forbidden from embarking on the ships that docked in the port of Salvador, but they would go anyway, risking arrest. In particular, prostitutes who work at night and sleep during the day are exploited by various people, including taxi drivers who charge them exorbitant rates or demand free sex in exchange for transportation and traveling saleswomen who charge higher prices for clothes than stores charge. Perhaps this constant hustle is one reason that sex workers in Salvador colloquially referred to their work as *batalhando* (battling). According to Gabriela Leite, four days after her second child was born, she had to return to work in a São Paulo brothel. Her employer offered no maternity leave or vacation, and she had to pay a *diária* (daily rate) where she was living. Abolitionists may take this as evidence that prostitution should be abolished, but Leite highlighted this story to demand better working conditions and rights for sex workers.

In addition to Aprosba, other social and religious organizations work with prostitutes in Salvador, but these groups are often engaged in moralizing missions to "rescue, rehabilitate, improve, discipline, control, or police" sex workers (Altman 2001, 101). According to Fabiana, "There are several organizations that say that they work with prostitutes, but they only want to take us out of prostitution. Only we know ourselves. We are searching for a better quality of life." Fabiana's understanding that these organizations usually have abolitionist ulterior motives has caused her to see prostitutes as most qualified to advocate for themselves.

In opposition to the abolitionist approach, the sex worker rights approach calls for the decriminalization of prostitution and rejects the assumption that sex work is morally reprehensible. This perspective highlights the potential empowerment and benefits of women in the sex industry, emphasizes the entrepreneurial aspects of prostitution, and rearticulates sex work as a laboring activity (Kempadoo 2001a, 43; Kempadoo and Doezema 1998; Dewey and Kelly 2011; van der Veen 2000). In researching and writing about sex work, I draw inspiration from this approach as well as Dennis Altman's warning to avoid embracing stereotypes of prostitutes as "necessarily marginalized and self-hating" (2001, 113). Ethnographers must take seriously sex workers' articulations about their lives, loves, and labor instead of assuming that they are exploited based solely on their occupation.[8]

Salvador's structural, political, and economic conditions as well as the limited opportunities available to women based on their educational level, socioeconomic status, race, and color certainly play roles in making sexual labor a viable option for women. However, it is also important to consider agency, pleasure, and benefits over other available types of labor. Steven Gregory (2007) makes this point clearly in the context of women's labor in the Dominican Republic, where the low wages, exploitative working conditions, sexual harassment, and abuse women experienced working in export-processing zones made the autonomy and higher pay of sex work more appealing. As of March 2012, Brazil's minimum wage was R$622 per month. While export-processing zones are not common in Bahia, domestic work offers a parallel: it is seen as an exploitative form of labor that is often the only option available for low-skilled women, particularly those of African descent. *Cinderelas, Lobos, e um Principe Encantado* (Cinderellas, Wolves, and a Prince Charming), a documentary by Afro-Brazilian filmmaker Joel Zito Araújo, features a black woman sex worker in Salvador who explains that while she can easily bring home R$1,200 a month from sex work, she would only earn between R$380 and R$460 as a domestic worker. She repeatedly tells the filmmaker, "One would go hungry."

The precarious position of sex work in the broader context of informal labor makes it difficult to guarantee access to necessities such as state-sponsored retirement benefits. In Brazil, workers have a *carteira de trabalho* (work card), which employers are supposed to sign to document each person's jobs. According to Fabiana, this is yet another way that prostitutes are "workers whom the law does not protect." She elaborates, "I'm a professional. I want the regulation of prostitution so that it can be recognized as a profession. I'm forty years old, and it's already difficult for me. I fight so that prostitutes can receive retirement . . . earlier. . . . A woman can work her whole life as a prostitute and when she gets too old, she has to work as a street vendor" because she has not accrued social security benefits. Thus, sex workers are part of a broader network of people who work in the informal economy in Bahia, without a *carteira assinada* (signed card), which means that their work experiences do not enable them to earn the benefits of Social Services. And engaging in much less lucrative domestic work would not solve this problem for prostitutes. In 2008, domestic workers—90 percent of whom were black women—constituted more than three-quarters of the workers who lacked signed cards (Craide 2008; Sterling 2010). In 2006, black women earned 66.4 percent of the salaries of white men in Brazil, an increase from the 55.4

percent women earned in 1995 (Craide 2008). The number of sex workers with unsigned work cards is difficult to estimate. As M. Jacqui Alexander writes of the Bahamas, sex workers serve the tourism industry by making the destination a "better place for the tourist" while simultaneously inhabiting the "boundaries of (im)morality and (il)legality" (2005, 60). Salvador, like the Bahamas, features a "contradictorily ironic state reliance on women who do sex work" (59). In this light, it is important to situate Aprosba in the context of municipal, state, and federal government entities as well as regional, national, and transnational networks of sex workers' organizations.

Aprosba on the National and International Stages

Aprosba is a part of an intricate network of regional, national, and international sex workers' associations. Aprosba was a member of the Rede Brasileira de Prostitutas (Brazilian Network of Prostitutes), which was established in 1987 during the First National Meeting of Prostitutes in Rio de Janeiro. The Rede promotes prostitutes' political empowerment and strengthens their professional identity with the goal of gaining them full citizenship rights, reducing the stigma and discrimination they face, and improving their quality of life.[9] An integral part of the articulation of prostitutes' rights and empowerment comes from the idea that they have access to a freedom of travel and mobility in a way that other women may not. The Rede's logo states, "Good women go to Heaven. Bad women go anywhere they want." In some sense, then, the popular imagination sees prostitutes as free agents who have escaped the surveillance and domination of oppressive male patriarchs (fathers or husbands).

The Rede's Fourth Annual Meeting, held in December 2008, featured approximately fifty prostitutes representing twenty different associations from seventeen Brazilian states ("Daspu Faz Encontro" 2008). Organized by a Rio de Janeiro nongovernmental organization (NGO), Dávida, the meeting also drew participants from the United Nations as well as international prostitutes' networks. The topics of discussion included the regulation of prostitution, health programs, and prejudice against prostitutes. Leite presented research that revealed human rights violations of prostitutes in eleven Brazilian capitals. One of the tangible results of this meeting was a Statement of Principles that the Rede created and distributed and that were adopted by the groups and associations represented at the meeting. The principles included:

1. Adult prostitution is a profession.
2. Prostitution should be regulated and formalized.
3. We are against the commercial sexual exploitation of children and adolescents.

4. We are against the creation of limited and confined zones for prostitution, sanitary control, and those who associate prostitutes with criminality and the trafficking of human beings.
5. We defend the right of migration for legal work.
6. We defend the right of adults to participate in sexual tourism—being solicited and doing a *programa* with a foreigner is not a crime. We are against the criminalization of clients of sex tourism.
7. We repudiate victimization, discrimination, prejudice, and stigma against prostitutes.
8. We promote the self-organization of prostitutes. (Lenz 2008)

These principles suggest that Brazil's prostitutes are actively fighting for their rights as citizens. They assert their right to engage in sexual labor while simultaneously taking a stand against underage prostitution. They distinguish between prostitution and trafficking and problematize the characterization of sexual tourism as immoral and illegal. An online article in *Beijo da Rua*, the Rede's newspaper, concludes, "Once again, with objectivity and clarity, the organized *putas* decree: we do not sell our bodies, we sell sexual services; sexual labor is a sexual right" (Lenz 2008).

The Rede also played a role in founding Daspu, a popular clothing line launched by Rio prostitutes affiliated with Dávida. Daspu fashion shows have been held in Rio de Janeiro, São Paulo, Salvador, and Mexico City, among other locales. An August 2007 Daspu fashion show in Salvador attracted activists, artists, prostitutes, journalists, socialites, and fashionistas ("Daspu Faz Sucesso" 2007). Women and men, professional models and prostitutes, youth from poor communities, NGO activists, and artists walked the runway wearing the latest Daspu collection. One of Daspu's goals is to bring visibility to the movement for prostitutes' rights. According to Leite, "The fashion of Daspu is a way to draw attention to the social issues—that is, the right of prostitutes to citizenship—as well as a way to generate income for the members" ("Daspu Faz Sucesso" 2007).

In May 2007, Aprosba's leaders were eagerly awaiting the completion of a new studio for the association's radio station. The new studio was beautiful, featuring top-of-the-line equipment, air-conditioning, and padded walls. The previous year, Aprosba had become the first sex workers' association in the world to launch a radio station, Radio Zona, funded by a grant from the Ministry of Culture (Francisco 2006). Fabiana also explained the significance of the radio station: "We exercise our profession with dignity, but we aren't respected by society. We have always had very little space in the media, except when there crimes occur involving prostitutes. We are going to use the radio to circulate programs tailored basically to our profession" (Francisco

2006). In this sense, the radio station was viewed as a way to reach out to prostitutes and to improve dominant society's views of prostitution. However, the station was also intended to discuss issues that affect other marginalized communities in the Centro Histórico.[10]

Aprosba paid university professors and found volunteers to help set up the radio station and planned to train prostitutes to serve as on-air hosts. The Ministry of Culture promised R$180,000 to cover the hiring of personnel and the purchase of technical equipment and other materials (*Globo* 2006). Fabiana explained why prostitutes need this means of communication: "Since we always do workshops for students, we discussed the possibility of propagating our actions via a radio station. Today, in Brazil, there are radio stations for politicians, businessmen, salespeople, and doctors, for example. Why can't prostitutes have a channel at their disposal?"

The Without Shame Project

In May 2007, Aprosba hosted the Projeto sem Vergonha (Without Shame Project), a weeklong training that brought together fifteen activists who represented sex workers' associations from various cities in Brazil's Northeast. The workshop was sponsored by the Rede Brasileira de Prostitutas in conjunction with the Brazilian Ministry of Health. Of all the sex workers' associations in the Northeast, Aprosba was selected to host the workshop and train the regional representatives. The project's motto was "Without shame to fight for our rights, without shame to use a condom, without shame to be a prostitute." The image on the cover of the pamphlet distributed at the workshop features a light-skinned, red-haired woman leaning on a windowsill. She has large, round eyes, bright red lips, and exposed cleavage. Given Brazil's racial demographics, the choice of a very pale-skinned woman to represent sex workers reveals the persistent dominance of whiteness in the country's visual culture.

In addition to receiving training in skills that would enhance the sex workers' leadership skills and activism in their home cities, the workshop provided a space for sex workers to come together as a community and share experiences. One of the women noticed that of the fifteen participants, only three were married, while the rest were divorced; nearly all had children.

The Without Shame Project featured a booklet produced by the Ministry of Health that covered topics such as HIV/AIDS, STIs, breast self-exams, sexual violence, and advice on beauty, the home, love horoscopes, and financial management, as well as issues of labor and citizenship. The booklet told readers, "Being a prostitute is not a crime. It is your job, and you don't need to explain to anyone what you do." There were also "Dicas para a Batalha" (Tips for the Battle), and a section on rights: "In your profession, you will be exposed to various types of violence, from clients to police. Often, the aggressor depends on your silence to go unpunished. If you suffer any type of violence, make your rights count. Denounce it, seek help, but don't stay silent." This theme of violence at the hands of police also appeared in *Women Are Equal in Whatever Profession*, a pamphlet created by Apros-PB, a sex workers' association from the state of Paraíba that participated in the workshop: "If you are arrested, police cannot beat you or demand sex. If this happens, it is a crime. Report it!"

At the workshop, Fabiana again described the autonomy, freedom, and mobility that she found in sex work. She emphasized that prostitutes sell not their bodies but fantasies and sexual services: "If we are the owners of our bodies, then we have to do what we want with them." The colloquial expression used to describe a woman who engages in sex work, "fazer vida" (to make/do life), she said, originates from the idea that prostitutes were the only women free to leave the sanctuary of the home in a context where heteropatriarchal gender norms confined women to the domestic sphere. Fabiana told the audience that at one time, she was living in a brothel where clients could stay for a maximum of only three minutes before a security guard would come knock at the door to make them leave. At this brothel, she normally did twenty-eight *programas* a day, charging ten reais per *programa*. Despite these extreme and unfortunate labor conditions, Fabiana never saw herself as a victim. She told me, "I hate it when journalists think that we're 'poor things' [*coitada*] who come from horrible families. My whole family is . . . very religious, educated, and they're not poor." She situated herself boldly as a woman who is confident with her life choices, and she actively resists people's attempts to position her as a subjugated victim.

The discussions at the workshop ranged from serious human rights violations to candid and jovial conversations about sex. The participants swapped stories about clients' strange fetishes. One man wanted the woman to defecate in his mouth; another wanted to bite the sex worker's armpits; another requested that the woman walk rather than take the bus to their rendezvous point in the hot sun so that she would arrive sweaty. In the middle of the group luncheon on the first day of the workshop, Bárbara, an Aprosba member, received a call from a new client who had seen her advertisement in the newspaper. Everyone at the table listened as she told the man that she charged sixty reais for a massage, which included the options of oral, vaginal, and anal sex. Another issue that became a major point of discussion at the workshop was a report featured on national and local network television news shows about sex tourism at the Aeroclube Plaza Show.

The Aeroclube was a major shopping center and tourist attraction in a coastline neighborhood, Boca do Rio. In an ominous tone, the reporter revealed with dismay that despite the Aeroclube's previous popularity among foreign tourists and middle- and upper-middle-class Bahians, the shopping center was now almost completely abandoned as a consequence of the prevalence of sex tourism. The major perpetrators of this economic and social fall from grace were racialized as Italian male sex tourists and black female sex workers. Workshop participants were concerned that the reporters' use of hidden cameras to capture images of the women would not only increase the persecution and criminalization of sex workers but also increase threats to the safety, integrity, and privacy of the women whose faces were broadcast. Bárbara in particular accused two local news anchors of endangering these women by plastering their faces all over local and national television without their consent. Participants discussed appropriate reactions such as emailing or calling to complain or going to the Aeroclube to talk to the women.

The Aeroclube situation reveals how local media constructs sex tourism in ways that criminalize and pathologize Italian men and black Bahian women. Why should the security guards be chided for failing to impede adult prostitution if it is legal? This story also highlights sex workers' anxieties regarding the risks of being caught on camera and thus being outed to their communities as sex workers. The tension between expressing pride and openness in one's profession, as Fabiana advocated, and succumbing to the stigma attached to sex work pervades some of my interviews with Aprosba members, particularly those of African descent.[11]

The Without Shame Project highlights the important role that Aprosba plays in regional and national networks of sex workers' associations. However, such associations' involvement in the Rede was not without controversy. Some sex workers from the northeastern region complained that they felt out of the loop with the Rede. They felt that the Rede was dominated by Leite, with members of small associations from poor, peripheral parts of the country not adequately included in plans and events. Representatives from the Paraíba sex workers' association could not stay abreast of information from the Rede because their office lacked internet access. Fabiana, however, pointed out that she had traveled to Rio de Janeiro three times to be involved in the development of the Without Shame project and that she regularly called Leite to learn the latest news. Aprosba clearly had more resources and infrastructure than associations in other parts of the region.

HIV/AIDS Prevention Education

On one occasion, Pérola, a black lesbian sex worker, invited me to accompany her to distribute condoms to sex workers in nearby brothels, bars, and plazas in Cidade Baixa (Lower City). As we went to various *bregas* (brothels), we traversed long alleys with steep steps, twists and turns, various levels, and peeling pastel-colored paint. When Pérola knocked on the door of one brothel, we could hear a woman in the shower. A few moments later, she came to the door; there were three other *garotas*, as Pérola called them, in the house on that late afternoon weekday. One came out of her room wearing a denim miniskirt and a towel draped over her bare chest. She was what Bahians would call *fofinha* (soft/fluffy/chubby), and she had dark wavy hair cascading down her back. She immediately began asking whether Aprosba was distributing vaginal cream. Pérola said no but told the woman about a clinic where she could get free medical exams as well as vaginal cream. I later learned that Aprosba buys vaginal gel and sells it to women for fifty cents.

Pérola gave each sex worker she encountered three condoms and an Aprosba brochure. At one *brega*, a woman exclaimed, "Only three? I could use that right now!" After visiting the brothels, we moved on to a few bars, which were crowded with people drinking at 4:00 in the afternoon on a weekday. Nearly every woman there seemed not only to be a prostitute but also to know Pérola. Other women asked, "Only three?"; some men also asked to receive condoms, though Pérola refused such requests. Pérola expressed disappointment that even though she was doing the women a favor by bringing them condoms despite their failure to attend the Aprosba meeting, they complained about the small number they received.

Aprosba has played an active role as a peer health educator among prostitutes in Bahia. As such, the group has a history of close collaboration with municipal, state, and federal government agencies despite its status as an NGO. To raise awareness about HIV/AIDS prevention, Aprosba has worked closely with the Ministry of Health, often sending leaders to rural areas of Bahia to help improve the living and working conditions of prostitutes in those areas. Fabiana and Zulema traveled to a small, factory town in southern Bahia full of single men who had migrated there in search of work. The town had a high incidence of rape and was not considered a safe place for women, and its brothels closed at 9:00 P.M., before the factory workers ended their shifts.

Fabiana and Zulema did safer sex workshops for the factory men, brothel owners, and prostitutes. Fabiana was amused by the fact that the factory workers assumed that she and Zulema were doctors or social workers, presumably because they were articulate and white. Fabiana relished the exclamations and looks of surprise she received when she proclaimed, "I'm a prostitute—not because anyone forced me to be. I'm a prostitute because I wanted to be one, because I like to have sex. I like to come, and why not earn money by doing this?" Fabiana anticipated the assumption that she had been "forced into" prostitution by clearly pointing out that the pleasures of sex had led her to engage in sexual labor.

In the process of conducting safer sex workshops in the rural town, Fabiana and Zulema discovered that several of the sex workers there did not know the proper way to put on condoms. Even more disturbing, clients sometimes offered to pay women extra to have sex without a condom. Fabiana and Zulema embraced their leadership roles as peer health educators who could share information that could very well save the lives of the men and women in this factory town. After sharing this experience with the Aprosba members, Zulema quipped, "My only regret about the trip was that I didn't get to try out those men!" Zulema, too, emphasized her agency and pleasure in *programas* with clients. Fabiana quickly reminded her that their purpose in that town was to do a different kind of work—sexual health education, not *programas*.

Aprosba has found creative and engaging ways to spread the message of HIV/AIDS prevention to the sex worker community of Salvador and the state of Bahia as a whole. In one brochure, Aprosba strategically transforms a popular element of Afro-Brazilian culture into an advertisement for safer sex. Placing a condom on a *berimbau*, the musical instrument used in capoeira, was a creative and culturally specific way to raise awareness about the prevention of HIV and STIs. Another Aprosba pamphlet features the slogan "Camisinha não esqueça. Na batalha, este ainda é o melhor programa" (Don't forget the condom. In the battle, this is still the best program). In addition to using the colloquialism of *battle*, the slogan plays on the double entendre of *programa*—both as commercial sexual transaction and program in general.

This pamphlet also informs readers about the appropriate use of both male *and* female condoms. Attendees at Aprosba meetings commonly discussed female condoms as a way for women to exercise agency over the *programa*. By discreetly inserting female condoms before *programas*, sex workers could both satisfy clients who did not want to use male condoms and protect themselves from unwanted pregnancies and HIV/AIDS and other STIs. Despite the high demand, however, female condoms were not as readily available from the Ministry of Health.[12]

In addition to local health education efforts, Aprosba has also taken on national and regional legislation that affects sex workers. The organization protested a law in the southern state of Rio Grande do Sul that called for mandatory testing of prostitutes for HIV/AIDS and other STIs (Nogueira 2007). Fabiana called mandatory testing "a violation of human rights" because it is based on the premise that prostitutes are "vectors of disease." In reality, Fabiana argued, anyone is susceptible to get any STI; therefore, prostitutes should not be singled out. Fabiana was not alone in her condemnation of this law. Activists in Brazil's HIV/AIDS and women's movements also considered mandatory testing a crime and a discriminatory practice that results in a form of "social apartheid" (Nogueira 2007).

While Aprosba's leadership in the arena of sexual health and the prevention of sexually transmitted infections and unwanted pregnancies is laudable, another reading may see their collaboration with state agencies as limiting or restricting the type of work they can do. Scholars have described the "NGO-ization" of women's movements in Brazil, a process that involves the recruitment of activists to serve as experts and implementers of government and international donors' programs (Alvarez 1999, 182; Thayer 2010, 47–48). Similarly, Aprosba leaders have been recruited to implement programs of the Ministry of Health. Fabiana was well aware that the best way to secure funding from government agencies and donors was to configure Aprosba's actions in terms of HIV/AIDS prevention. On the one hand, this approach is good because Aprosba leaders see peer health education as a central and important aspect of their work. On the other hand, this tactic can limit Aprosba's work. Restricting Aprosba to sexual health work may also reassert the problematic assumption of sex workers as vectors of disease and reinforce the idea that the state is interested in collaborating with sex workers only with regard to protecting public health (from sex workers). Sex workers commonly contend with this stigma even though they may actually be more rigorous about condom use than women who are not engaged in sex work.

Racial Politics of Sex Work in Salvador

Aprosba's logo features a voluptuous, fair-skinned, though slightly tanned woman with long blond hair, large round eyes, and bright red lips wearing a short, tight, green dress and swinging a small red purse. This image certainly does not reflect the actual demographics of Bahia, a state where roughly 80 percent of the population is of African descent and where blondness is extremely rare. Bahians have a term, *branco da Bahia* (white from Bahia), that usually refers to a white person with brown hair and eyes. The idea is that even phenotypically white Bahians may be racially mixed somewhere in the course of their family history. Given the black majority in Bahia, the prevalence of black sex workers, and the racialized erotics of sex tourism, I was surprised to discover that white Brazilian women were overrepresented among Aprosba's leaders. This issue often came up in conversations, especially at meetings where the majority of the members were women of African descent, while their leaders—and the association's public face—were (bleached) blond white women.

The overrepresentation of white women in Aprosba was also unusual considering the "controlling images" of black and brown women as hypersexual and available—as always already sex workers. According to Patricia Hill Collins, "controlling images" are dominant stereotypes of black femininity, such as the mammy, matriarch, Jezebel, or Sapphire, that seek to "make racism, sexism, and poverty appear natural, normal and an inevitable part of everyday life" (1990, 69). Collins's theory was formulated with the U.S. context in mind, and these particular images of black womanhood cannot necessarily be applied to the Brazilian context. Nonetheless, the conceptualization of "controlling images" resonates in Brazil. Black Brazilian feminist scholars have situated the *mulata*, *mucama* (colonial-era domestic worker), and *mãe preta* (black mother) as Brazil-specific controlling images of black womanhood (Williams 2014; Caldwell 2007; Carneiro and Santos 1985; Gonzalez 1980, 1982).

My conversations with Aprosba members demonstrated that black prostitutes had to confront things that their white counterparts did not. Fabiana, a forty-year-old blond white woman from Paraíba, was aware of the racial disparities that affected sex workers in Bahia: "I've seen that black prostitutes suffer more. They were arrested and detained while I was able to leave the police station." Since women of African descent are more likely to be read as sex workers, they are arrested, while white sex workers often pass under the radar. With Fabiana's advancing age and an increasingly vigilant police force, she had fewer foreign clients than had previously been the case: "Now I don't do *programas* with tourists anymore because it was prohibited to go to the ships. Well, it was never really allowed—we went hidden—but now the police are watching. I don't know how to search for tourists in the street. I'm forty years old. They prefer younger women, black and *mestiça* women. But sometimes [tourists] call me in the street. When we used to go to the ships, there were around twenty *mestiças* and five white women. But dialogue is also valuable. I'm educated, I like to converse, and I'm extroverted." Despite the European standard of beauty that privileges whiteness, the standard of sensuality is dominated by black and mixed-race women, even among the women who did *programas* with foreign seamen (Williams 2010). However, Fabiana was by no means completely excluded from the tourist sexual economy. She had done *programas* with several European men as well as a

Trinidadian man staying at some of Salvador's most luxurious hotels. In fact, her experience as a white Brazilian with a black Trinidadian man suggests that the cross-racial liaisons that are typically thought to characterize sex tourism operate in reverse as well. She claimed that what she lacked in age and color, she made up for with her gregarious personality and intelligence.

Discourses of racial democracy have shaped commonsense understandings of Afro-Brazilian women's proper social location: it is "socially expected and accepted that Afro-Brazilian women will be servants, sexual objects, and social subordinates" (Caldwell 2007, 57). These assumptions of black women's place created a situation in which foreign clients regularly asked black women to combine their sexual labor with domestic labor, though white women (to the best of my knowledge) were never asked to do so. Valquíria, an Afro-Brazilian sex worker and ballroom dancer from Fortaleza, Ceará, and an active Aprosba member, had several experiences with Italian tourists who invited her to their rented apartments not only to have sex but also to work as an *empregada doméstica* (housekeeper or domestic worker).

The gendered racism that affects black women ultimately relegates them to a place in which domestic work and sex work are seen as two sides of the same coin. However, low-income black Bahian women often saw sex work as a more lucrative and autonomous alternative to domestic work, echoing M. Jacqui Alexander's concept of "erotic autonomy" as posing a danger to respectability (2005, 23). Domestic work was seen as the ultimate form of exploitation, with black women poorly paid, subject to harsh working conditions, and often vulnerable to sexual assault by their employers. Thus, the ambiguities implicit in the sexual economies of tourism in Salvador refer not only refer to the spectrum between *programas* and *namoros* but also to the overlapping realms of domestic and sex work.

What role do these black Brazilian sex/domestic workers play in constituting the subjectivities of white foreign male tourists? Peter Stallybrass and Allon White's notion of the "low Other" offers a theoretical framework for understanding this situation. In their analysis, the "topography of desire . . . is traced out on the body of a paid servant"—in this case, one who provides both sexual and domestic service (1986, 153). For Stallybrass and White, class constitutes the primary difference between the "high" man and the "low" servant. But in the racially charged touristscape of Salvador, the distinction between "high" and "low" relies on differences of race, gender, and nationality as well. Stallybrass and White point out that "the low was internalized under the sign of negation and disgust. But disgust always bears the imprint of desire" (191). This relationship of elite white masculinity to the low Other black Brazilian sexual and/or domestic worker is not merely the domain of foreign tourists who come to Salvador seeking sex. Rather, such relationships are deeply entrenched in Brazil's cultural and social fabric, preceding the advent of mass tourism. Brazil's historically constructed dynamics of race and sex create the conditions of possibility for the *mulata* as sex object and erotic icon. While sensationalist media and governmental campaigns often construct sex tourism as a foreign invasion bringing particular kinds of immoral, racist, and sexist behaviors and practices, many of these practices and behaviors existed in Brazil long before globalized tourism became a common phenomenon. Thus, the racial and sexual dynamics of both the national and transnational context are connected in more ways than might at first seem apparent.

Prostituta or *Garota de Programa*: The Politics of Category Making

In *Global Sex Worker: Rights, Resistance, Redefinition*, Kamala Kempadoo and Jo Doezema (1998) contend that reconceptualizing prostitution as sex work enabled sex workers to mobilize for basic human rights and struggle against injustice and stigma. Whereas prostitution was seen as an identity, sex work was seen as an income-generating activity or form of labor that could either be short-lived or occur alongside other forms of work (3). Several pro–sex worker rights feminists rejected the term *prostitute* because of its connotations of "shame, unworthiness, or wrongdoing" (Bernstein 2007b, 11; see also Kempadoo and Doezema 1998). Conversely, the term *sex worker* suggested that "the sale of sex was not necessarily any better or worse than other forms of service work or embodied labor" (Bernstein 2007b, 11). Amalia Cabezas highlights how Modemu, a Dominican sex workers' organization, strategically deployed the term *sex worker* and human rights discourses to reposition "its members from fallen women to legal-juridical subjects worthy of protection" (2009, 159).

All too often, those who voluntarily engage in sex work are not seen as entitled to make claims on the state. Cabezas criticizes the "violence against women" discourse in international human rights regimes for being "couched in narrow terms of female victimhood" (2009, 153).[13] This notion of female victimhood creates a situation in which "women who sell sexual services to complement low wages, raise funds in a financial crisis, migrate, leave violent husbands, or achieve economic mobility do not fit the model of woman-as-victim, worthy of protection and deserving of salvation" (153). Something seems to be terribly wrong when constructing oneself as a victim is a prerequisite for state protection. Furthermore, the fact that the global movement to end violence against women has largely ignored violence directed against prostitutes suggests that "prostitution seemingly renders women deserving of abuse" (164). The focus on domestic violence under the rubric of violence against women also reveals a heteronormative bias that overlooks sex workers not only because they are "outside the bounds of patriarchal protection, religious mores and legality" but also because they violate norms of respectable and submissive femininity (153).

Despite the fact that adult prostitution is legal in Brazil, it remains stigmatized. Recent ethnographies about violence against women in Brazil such as those by Sarah J. Hautzinger (2007) and Cecilia McDowell Santos (2005) offer little or no discussion of violence against sex workers. The same can be argued for the Lei Maria da Penha (Brazil's Federal Law 11340), which was implemented in 2006 to reduce domestic violence. The fact that efforts to eradicate violence against women overlook sex workers suggests that they are viewed as disposable bodies with no rights worth protecting. In this sense, Brazilian sex workers of all races have something in common with black women, who have long dealt with the history of sexualization, Othering, and the lack of bodily autonomy and integrity.[14] A contemporary parallel exists in the case of the Slut Walks, which crisscrossed the globe in 2011.[15] Salvador's Slut Walk united Afro-Brazilian Candomblé priestesses, educators, feminists, lesbians, and activists with sex workers and other sex radicals to protest the notion that women could be justifiably raped if they dressed "like sluts" (Williams 2011b).

As Julia O'Connell Davidson points out in *Prostitution, Power, and Freedom*, sex workers are constructed as "moral and sexual outsiders" because they "trade in something which cannot honourably be traded" (1998, 129). The moral condemnation of prostitution divides women into those who are good and innocent and thus deserve protection (nonprostitutes) and those who are bad and guilty (prostitutes) and thus can be abused with impunity (Wijers and Doorninck 2002, 2). A harmful consequence of characterizing prostitution as immoral is that it further marginalizes women in the sex trade and results in their invisibility as workers with rights (Kempadoo 1999; Mellon 1998). Furthermore, making sex work illegal forces it underground and "removes it from public view, making it more dangerous for sex workers and society by raising the risk of violence, abuse, disease, and involvement by criminal elements" (Dewey and Kelly 2011, 6). In the Caribbean context, Kempadoo observes that sex workers experience and define oppression not as an inherent part of the sex act itself but rather as a result of the conditions that they must endure (2001b, 44). I found a similar sentiment among Aprosba members: they viewed the sources of oppression in their lives as mistreatment, discrimination, stigma, and police violence rather than the act of selling sexual services. As Susan Dewey and Patty Kelly point out in *Policing Pleasure: Sex Work, Policy, and the State in Global Perspective*, "Criminalizing sex work criminalizes sex workers, making them more vulnerable to social stigmatization, abuse, rape, and even murder" (2011, 7). Similarly, Alexander's (1991) analysis of how the state utilizes morality to regulate sex and manage sexuality suggests that only certain women (that is, wives) have the privilege of making claims on the state; others (nonwives, prostitutes, lesbians) do not enjoy that privilege.

Despite Aprosba's political activism regarding rights and recognition, which is common among sex workers' movements, the group's leaders advocate the use of the term *prostituta* as opposed to *sex worker* (*trabalhadora do sexo* or *profissional do sexo*). They do so as an effort to reclaim the term and to remove the associated stigma with it as well as to refer explicitly to women who do sex work. *Trabalhador do sexo* and *professional do sexo* are gender-neutral and thus also include men and *travestis*. Despite feelings of solidarity with male and *travesti* sex workers, the leaders of Aprosba felt the need to have their own space as women. At one Aprosba meeting, Marisa called for more unity among prostitutes by pointing out that "*putas* often have closer relationships to gays and lesbians than with other *putas*." Marisa's statement reveals that the organization's decision to focus exclusively on women did not result from homophobia or a lack of solidarity with *travesti* and male sex workers. Rather, Aprosba leaders felt that their particular gendered experiences as cis-gender female sex workers were worth exploring and supporting. Similarly, Gregory Mitchell's work points out that *michês* in Brazil's tourist zones are uncomfortable with the sex workers' rights movement because it hinges "on the pride of professionalization" and identification as a prostitute (2011a, 171). *Michês* do not want to identify themselves because of machismo, stigmatization, and fear of being wrongly categorized as gay.

People in Salvador often used two interchangeable terms to refer to the women who became sexually and/or romantically involved with *gringos*: *garota de programa* and *prostituta*. Antonio Jonas Dias Filho describes *garotas de programa* as those who have agents and a structure to enter into contact with tourists in hotels, bars, restaurants, and so forth (1998, 9). Filho introduces the term *gringólogas* (gringologists) to refer to women of African descent who migrate daily from the periphery to the Centro to meet foreign tourists in hopes of finding an opportunity to escape poverty. While I initially thought that the distinction that João made between the *boca do lixo* (trash heap) and the *boca do luxo* (lap of luxury) in Salvador's touristscape on his Web site for high-end *garotas de programa* was his creation, I later learned that these phrases referenced an important moment in the history of the Brazilian sex workers' movement. The movement originated in an area of prostitution in the center of São Paulo known as the Boca do Lixo. In 1979, Wilson Richetti, a police officer who presided over this district, began harassing prostitutes indiscriminately with arrests and physical assaults. The violence resulted in the deaths of three sex workers—two *travestis* and one pregnant woman. The public response to these atrocious abuses of police power did not reach full voice until four months later, when a large march drew not only sex workers but also people from other ranks of society. Richetti ultimately was removed from his position (Ministério da Saúde 2002).

João maintained that foreign tourists seeking sex would rather do *programas* with high-end *garotas de programa* (such as those featured on his Web site) than the poor prostitutes of the Centro Histórico (who comprise most of the members of Aprosba). Maurício, a middle-aged Afro-Brazilian man who was very familiar with Salvador's commercial sex industry, also upheld this distinction between *prostitutas* and *garotas de programa*. He claimed that *prostitutas* could be found in the Terreiro de Jesus plaza in Pelourinho or other parts of the Centro. They displayed themselves openly in the streets and charged between ten and fifteen reais for a *programa*. *Garotas de programa*, conversely, were often married or had stable families, were in college, and were careful not to sully their reputations. Maurício apparently was not aware that many of the women in Aprosba also have families and are married or in long-term relationships. Maurício insisted that tourists seek out *garotas de programa*, not *prostitutas*. However, my conversations and interactions with Aprosba members seemed to contradict this belief.

The question of self-identifying as a *prostituta* was irrevocably tied up with the class politics of category making and struggles over inclusion. For the leaders of Aprosba, the term *garota de programa* was laden with class pretensions. The term enabled university students, many of whom worked in the more elite clubs and agencies, to distance themselves from sex workers, who often worked on the streets, in bars, and in brothels. Bárbara, an Aprosba member who worked both on the coastline and in the Centro, said that *garotas de programa* see themselves as pretty, middle-class *moças simpáticas* (nice girls) who pretend that they are not prostitutes even though they earn money from *programas*. In Salvador, Bárbara said, it is very common to find *garotas de programa* on college campuses and hanging out in the food courts of major shopping malls. In the Shopping Iguatemi food court in particular, Fabiana said, "between 12:00 and 3:00 P.M. or 7:00 P.M.

to close, what you'll see the most is *patricinha de programa*." *Patricinha* is a colloquial word that translates to "princess" or "spoiled brat." Fabiana saw no difference between a *prostituta* and a *garota de programa*: "Both take off their clothes and have sex, and both are stigmatized by society." Fabiana continued, "High-end prostitutes don't come to Aprosba. They don't [even] identify as *garotas de programa*, they identify as students. It's difficult to reach them to do our work—they have pimps and madams. They say that Aprosba is low end. But it's at the low-end that the movement begins. The girls who come [to Aprosba] are those who earn less money and suffer more violence. [The high-end girls] don't want to mix with us. I say, 'People, it's all the same whore.'" Fabiana believed that whether they worked on the streets, in agencies, or in bars and however they procured their clients, all women who engaged in sexual labor would be perceived by society in similar ways. Therefore, all the women should come together as a group, regardless of class differences or whether they occupied the *boca do luxo* or the *boca do lixo*.

As identity categories, terms like *prostituta*, *puta*, and *garota de programa* are all built on exclusions. As Judith Butler claims, "Identity categories are never merely descriptive, but always normative, and as such, exclusionary" (1992, 15). Fabiana self-identified as a *puta*, a usually derogatory term meaning "whore" or "slut." However, several sex workers affiliated with Aprosba embraced this term as a positive and powerful label of identification. The appropriation of this term seemed to provide protection from the potential injury of the words of others. As Fabiana put it, "The worst gossip is when one neighbor tells another neighbor that you're a prostitute. They don't have anything else to say if I'm saying it myself." The plethora of terms and labels for women who engage in sexual and romantic liaisons with foreign tourists and the controversy over the meanings of these terms as well as over who is included and excluded elucidate the politics of category making.

David Valentine's (2007) theorization of the ways in which the transgender category has been constructed in the United States since the 1990s offers useful insights for understanding the complexities of identifying as a prostitute in Salvador. Valentine points out that "people everywhere categorize themselves and others" and that how "these categorizations are made, and which categories come to have effects in the world, are never neutral" (2007, 5). The term *transgender* has been institutionalized to include all gender variance. Despite its limitations, the term was "potentially transformative and powerful" in its ability to draw "attention to a group which was subject to violence, danger, and discrimination" (22). Simply put, what people call themselves is at least as significant as what others call them. The term *transgender* enabled people to see themselves as being a part of this category, which resulted in efforts toward social change.

Like the transgender category, the *prostituta* category possessed powerful and transformative potential to draw attention to the violence, danger, and discrimination that prostitutes in Salvador faced. While rallying support for members who were victimized, abused, or murdered was an integral component of Aprosba's work, these efforts were often hindered by the politics of category making and its attendant exclusions. When Fabiana says, "People, it's all the same whore," she is attempting to position *whore* and *prostitute* as umbrella terms that can bring together all women who sell sexual services, whether on the coastline or in city center, on the beach, in brothels, in shopping malls, or online. While Fabiana views the movement as coming from the low end—or from working-class prostitutes—she emphasizes the fact that the movement must encompass all women who engage in sexual labor. The perennial problem, of course, is that some of those women do not consider themselves to be in the same category as the women of Aprosba.

Several Aprosba members often publicly "disidentified" (Esteban-Muñoz 1999) as *prostitutas*. In reference to queer of color performance art, Jose Esteban-Muñoz describes disidentification as a survival strategy for minority subjects that "works on and against dominant ideology" and "resists a conception of power as being a fixed discourse" (1999, 11, 19). While identification is constantly in motion, disidentification expands and problematizes identity and identification rather than "abandoning any socially prescribed identity component" (29). However, this approach did not always serve its purpose in cases where women refused to identify publicly as *prostitutas*. According to Fabiana, when a rash of police violence against prostitutes occurred in Praça da Sé, a few Aprosba members who worked there reported the situation to the organization, which called Zé Bin, a popular journalist. Fabiana had hoped that when Zé Bin and his cameras descended on the Praça, all the women who worked there would gather to protest the violence. Instead, most of the women disappeared to avoid being caught on camera.

For black women sex workers, self-identifying publicly as a *prostituta* often took on different meanings. Valquíria combined a range of informal activities to make a living. She engaged in sex work in Praça da Sé, modeled for local pornographic magazines, and performed as a ballroom dancer. She regularly participated in Aprosba's activities and was vocal about her occupation in that safe space. However, she did not want her ballroom dance colleagues to know that she was a sex worker and consequently was unwilling to out herself. Since Afro-Brazilian women are presumed to be prostitutes, perhaps they may be less likely to claim the identity of *prostituta* as a badge of pride than their white counterparts.

For Fabiana and the other (largely white) leaders of Aprosba, identifying (publicly) as a *prostituta* was a bold statement in the face of societal disdain. It was also a crucial expression of solidarity necessary for fighting for their rights and improving their living and working conditions. Identifying as a *prostituta* had power—it was a tactical maneuver that enabled them to mobilize more effectively for rights and representation. Assuming *prostituta* as an identity seems to challenge the argument made by some scholars who advocate considering sex work as practice rather than an identity. Steven Gregory (2007) understands "sex work" as one of many formal and informal activities in which people engage to earn a living and consequently avoids constructing "sex worker" as an identity. Similarly, Mark Padilla's (2007b) work on male sex work and HIV/AIDS in the Dominican Republic rejects essentialized notions of "sex workers" that are removed from social and familiar ties. Valquíria's story reflects Gregory's argument about women who do sex work engaging in a range of informal activities to make a living as well as Padilla's point that they should not be seen as removed from their social ties. Gloria Wekker's (2006) compelling ethnography of black women's sexuality in Suriname makes a crucial intervention into the identity-versus-practice debate. Rather than discussing fixed sexual identities (lesbians), Wekker highlights how Afro-Surinamese women discuss their sexuality in terms of an activity (doing the *mati* work) rather than as an identity (I am a *mati*).

However, if assuming *prostituta* as identity is considered a tactic strategically deployed by women for particular purposes, the dichotomy between identity and practice might seem to be false. Before I began my fieldwork, I agreed with the idea of seeing sex work as a practice rather than an identity. Given the complexity and multiplicity of identities, I hesitated to "reduce" someone to any one identity. Altman encourages thinking of prostitution "not as a fixed state or identity, but rather, as a continuum of activities ranging from organized prostitution . . . to unpremeditated transactions resulting from chance encounters" (2001, 103). However, Fabiana's perspective forces me to wonder if this scholarly position inadvertently further stigmatizes sex workers? Does it perpetuate the underlying assumption that sex work is not a "worthy," "appropriate" occupation and thus "sex worker" not a morally redeemable identity? Does conceiving of sex work as a practice instead of an identity take away some of the power that can be gained by organizing for social change as a group or category with a shared identity?

Conclusion: Citizenship, Informal Labor, and Human Rights

Aprosba straddles boundaries by representing the kind of labor that the state would like to deny but that is deeply entrenched and plays a leading role in state HIV/AIDS education outreach programs. Aprosba challenges dominant standards of female respectability and codes of sexual and moral conduct by boldly proclaiming sexual labor as a valid occupational category that should be respected and recognized.

While Merry (2006) points out that human rights advocacy initially was primarily an activity of national and transnational elites with ideas that had little resonance on the grassroots level, Aprosba highlights women on the ground articulating demands for rights, recognition, respect, and the removal of stigma. We could read this as an example of how Brazilian social movements in the aftermath of the dictatorship emphasized a robust concept of citizenship that meshes well with the concept of human rights. In *Making Transnational Feminism: Rural Women, NGO Activists, and Northern Donors in Brazil*, Millie Thayer describes citizenship as the "rallying cry" in the struggle against Brazil's military dictatorship (2010, 58). Brazilian social movements conceived of citizenship as encompassing "heretofore suppressed aspirations for social rights—from employment and land, to racial pride and culture, to health and sexual pleasure" (78). SOS Corpo, a feminist NGO in Recife, Pernambuco, had a vision of citizenship as intricately tied to the dissemination of knowledge (75). Moreover, the organization understood citizenship as "not only guaranteeing the right of women and other disempowered groups to make decisions affecting their lives, but also ensuring the social conditions to allow them to take advantage of this right" (77).

Similarly, Aprosba's broad range of activities—participation in the Rede Brasileira de Prostitutas, the radio station, HIV/AIDS education work—reveals the important role that the organization has played in the struggle for prostitutes' rights, recognition, and the full benefits of citizenship in Bahia and Brazil as a whole. By participating in international (South American/ Latin American) meetings and conferences, Aprosba's leaders articulate a vision of transnational connections even while the focus of their work is explicitly local. In other words, although they may not explicitly identify as feminists, Aprosba members have forged what Manisha Desai refers to as "transnational feminist solidarities" through networks, regional meetings, and world conferences. In so doing, they have ensured that "the flow of ideas and activism is no longer unidirectional, from the North to the South, but multidirectional" (2002, 15). Furthermore, Aprosba is a compelling example of an organization that blends "transnational, national, and local elements" to more effectively "negotiate the spaces between transnational ideas and local concerns" (Merry 2006, 134). Thus, Aprosba's political activism to improve the lives and working conditions of sex workers in Bahia disrupts hegemonic Western feminisms' depiction of the Third World Other as a woman who was always already a poor, subservient victim with no agency (Mohanty 1991).

Nevertheless, transnational solidarities among women often reproduce existing inequalities: women in the North and educated women from the South tend to dominate the international networks and NGOs, marginalizing or excluding "grassroots women" (Desai 2002, 31). Desai claims that transnational activism creates divisions at the national level between elites who belong to these networks and the vast majority of grassroots women who do not (31). To whom does this ascription of "grassroots women" apply? Is it code for poor, uneducated, marginalized women of color? In the context of Aprosba, where all of the women, both leaders and members, are sex workers with varying levels of education, all the participants might be considered "grassroots." However, the differing experiences of white and black sex workers demonstrate that race is a major factor that distinguishes the leadership from the membership. At times, white Brazilians seemed more willing to assume leadership roles and be visible in Aprosba than did women of African descent. It was not clear whether this phenomenon resulted from black women wanting to avoid being outed as sex workers or whether other factors were involved. Consequently, these racial divisions have significant implications regarding who can access the regional and transnational networks that facilitate travel opportunities both within Brazil and overseas.

Scholars have argued that the framing of social, political, and economic issues in terms of human rights is a key dimension of neoliberalism (Naples 2002). Cabezas highlights the irony of sex workers' using human rights discourse for mobilization and consciousness-raising, even when the human rights agenda has had a contentious and problematic relationship to sex workers (2009, 156). She points out that although the 1993 United Nations World Conference on Human Rights in Vienna was the first time that violence against women was included on the international agenda, the move to include gender issues in human rights addressed sex workers only as monolithic and "clearly defined victims" of patriarchy, trafficking or "forced" prostitution (152–53). As Merry notes, human rights ideas are powerful in the realm of violence against women because they break from the idea that violence is a natural and inevitable issue between men and women. Instead, "gender violence becomes a crime against the state that the state must punish" (2006, 180). Merry also argues that "rights offer a new vision of the self as entitled to protection by the state, but this promise must be made good" (217). Aprosba members clearly see themselves as workers entitled to rights and protection from the state.

In analyzing Aprosba with a transnational feminist lens, I have argued that the organization serves a very powerful role in the politicization and health education of prostitutes in Salvador while embodying racial politics that are characteristic of Brazilian racial hegemonies. It is important not to see Aprosba members as a monolithic group, even though they do come together on common issues. The stigma, limitations, and risks of doing sex work are often exacerbated for Brazilian women of African descent. Thus, race and class have a significant impact on the politics of identification, subject formation, and category making among Salvador's sex workers.

CHAPTER SIX

Se Valorizando (Valuing Oneself)

Ambiguity, Exploitation, and Cosmopolitanism

A 2005 Brazilian film set in Salvador, *Cidade Baixa* (Lower City), presents a scenario of the interactions between Brazilian sex workers and foreign ship workers in this touristscape. The two male protagonists, Deco (played by Wagner Moura) and Naldinha (Lázaro Ramos), offered Karinna (Alice Braga), a young sex worker, a ride to Salvador. While the expectation of sex is not explicitly discussed, Karinna ends up having sex with both Deco and Naldinha while en route to Salvador. Once they arrive, Deco and Naldinha agree to use their boat to take a group of sex workers to a large ship that is docked in the port. The ship workers speak Spanish, though their country of origin is unclear. The women negotiate with the ship workers and set the price for *programas*. There is one dark-skinned black woman, one *morena*, and Karinna, who may be considered *morena clara* (light brown) and has bleached-blond hair. The *gringo* who is doing the talking reaches first for the black woman. Karinna enters a small room and begins to snort cocaine with the *gringo*. Deco and Naldinha stand on the deck and watch through the peephole. Soon, they hear screams, and everyone goes running. Karinna is lying on the floor, convulsing with foam coming out of her mouth. It appears to be a drug overdose. Deco and Naldinha tell the *gringos* to call the police, but the workers are scared of getting into trouble with the Brazilian authorities. The ship workers give the women all the money that they have. In the next scene, the sex workers, Deco, and Naldinha all enter a club, laughing. It seems that the whole scenario was actually a scam to extort money from the *gringos*.

While this film scene is certainly dramatic in its portrayal of sex workers deceiving ship workers, it nonetheless speaks to the ambiguous entanglements present in sex tourism. It raises questions regarding the ambiguities of exploitation in the touristscape of Salvador: who is exploiting whom? Furthermore, it reveals some understudied dimensions of the sexual economies of tourism. Fabiana described how the process of *batalhando* (battling) on the ships consistently exploited prostitutes: "We would wait for the ships at the shore. We'd spend between three days and a week on the ships. It cost twenty reais to get to the ship, and sometimes our clothes would tear because of the stairs. There was an illiterate woman who sold clothes at double the cost. She had a house here in Salvador, one for her mother in Ilhéus, and a car, all because she exploited prostitutes." The presence of this additional category of foreign travelers in search of sex—foreign ship workers—challenges the notion of sex tourism as the domain of white middle- and upper-class leisure tourists from Europe and North America who are empowered to fulfill their fantasies of adventure while vacationing in the Global South. While sensationalist media accounts often depict sex tourism as the dark side of tourism, where sexual exploitation runs rampant, my ethnographic research taught me that it is important to consider what sex tourism means in the lives of Brazilian sex workers. I met many women who spoke of the advantages of doing *programas* with *gringos*—of feeling needed and valued and of enjoying the anonymity, security, and gifts that come with foreign clients.

Although some of the encounters between local women and foreign ship workers were strictly *programas* in which money was exchanged directly for sexual services, other encounters resembled *namoros*, where the lines between commercial sex and romantic relationship were blurred. The concept of *se valorizando* (valuing oneself) expressed by women of Aprosba reveals the importance of exchanging money for sexual services. This concept challenges feminist literature on prostitution by moving beyond the long-standing dichotomy between victims and agents, a distinction that hinges on totalizing notions of agency. Researchers must take seriously participants' stories and experiences, even when they challenge our assumptions and everything we thought we knew or understood about a given topic.

Sex tourism is a complex subject because it requires interrogating notions of desire, intimacy, love, affect, and reciprocity as well as race, class, and gender. Drawing inspiration from scholars such as Amalia Cabezas (2009) and Adriana Piscitelli (2001, 2006, 2007), I privilege ambiguity as an analytical tool because it is a defining factor of sex tourism in Salvador. In the context of Cuba and the Dominican Republic, Cabezas argues that rather than being an unambiguous commercial endeavor, the exchange of goods and money for sexual services is actually a "discursive construction that is contested and in motion, changing across time and space" (2009, 4).[1] How do ambiguous entanglements in Salvador complicate understandings of how power, agency, and affect circulate transnationally? Furthermore, how do intimate and emotional labors come into play in ambiguous entanglements between foreign tourists and local sex workers? This chapter critically interrogates the concept of exploitation as it pertains to sex workers in their ambiguous entanglements with foreign men. Exploring these issues in depth first requires understanding how some Aprosba members conceptualize their sexual and romantic encounters and exchanges with foreigners.

Bel's Story

I met Bel, a twenty-four-year-old woman who had migrated to Salvador from the northeastern city of Recife at a bar in the Centro Histórico where sex workers gathered to meet foreign *marinheiros* (seamen/ship workers). Aprosba's cofounder and leader, Fabiana, took me to the bar, where unlicensed tour guides brought *marinheiros* directly from the docks. Fabiana introduced me to Dona Zinha, the white Brazilian woman who owned and operated the establishment, and asked her if I could talk to any of the women present. Looking quite bored with the whole matter, Dona Zinha told us to ask *as meninas* (the girls) directly. Fabiana introduced me as a researcher and volunteer English teacher for Aprosba, but all of the sex workers refused to speak with me. Finally, a *morena clara* with bleached-blond hair agreed to sit for an interview.

The other women watched and listened attentively as Bel began to speak. She referred to sex tourism as "the best source of income for pretty women" and said that the worst thing about sex tourism was that "we fall in love and then the ships leave." Bel had worked almost exclusively with Asian seamen and spoke some Tagalog and English. She preferred Asian *marinheiros* because "they pay well and treat me well." "I already entered into depression three times because of Filipinos. The ships leave and I cry. They are very caring." She also preferred Asian men because, she said, they had smaller penises and climaxed quickly. The more Bel talked about her life, the more it seemed that she did not particularly like sex. She then described the intricate workings of the sexual economies involving foreign seamen: "This bar is specifically for *marinheiros*. Sometimes we accompany them to Rio. It's an exchange. I know [sex workers] from Natal, Recife, and Maceió. They all go to different ports. November to March is the summer season, when the tourism ships come in, and we work during the day. During the other months, we only work at night. In the summer we gain more money than in the rest of the year. In the summer, we check online to see what time the ships will dock. We call each other. We go down to wait in the bar at 9:00 or 10:00. Down at the dock, there are women who used to do *programas* but are now too old. They speak English, Filipino, and Greek very well. They bring the men. We give them a tip of five reais. They all come here—even Egyptians have been here!" Bel's statement offers insight into how the system operates and how sex workers' lives and livelihoods are affected by the influx of tourist ships. With a combination of technology, word of mouth, and the collaboration of retired prostitutes, women such as Bel procure foreign clients.

Bel recounted a "love story" about Pierre, a seamen/client from Madagascar whom she referred to as "the beautiful African." When she met this man, she was four months pregnant by a Filipino ship worker. Throughout the course of their relationship, Pierre bought things for her baby and gave her money. When his ship left the port of Salvador, he called and sent money regularly. After two years without seeing each other, he returned in 2006, and when she saw him again, "everything was beautiful. I went to Rio to be with him." Before his second departure, Frâncio told her that she should get a passport because he wanted her to travel with him back to France:

> I got my passport and identity cards, but I didn't believe he was really going to take me. It was US$1,700 just for the fare on the ship, and he only earned US$1,500 a month. I went to Rio, bringing my suitcase and all, but I didn't believe it. I embarked that same day. . . . The room was the most luxurious house in my life. Everything was luxurious. I got off the ship in France, met his family. I spent seventeen days with him, and then I returned to Brazil. I ended up falling in love with him because I didn't have to have sex with him several times a day. I thought that if we were going to be together in the same place, I would have to have sex with him all the time, several times a day. Now he is in Africa and isn't able to send money to me. He says that he's going to stop working on the ships. He's worked on the ships for ten years. He says that he's coming here in April to marry me. I want to marry him. What he did for me, no man has ever done.

Bel's story reflects the ambiguities implicit in sexual/romantic encounters between foreign clients and local sex workers. *Marinheiros* from the Philippines, Greece, Egypt, Madagascar, India, Norway, and several other countries constitute an overlooked group in the transnational sexual economies of the port city of Salvador.[2] The fact that Bel fell in love with the *marinheiro* from Madagascar as well as a few men from the Philippines suggests that there is more to the sexual economies of tourism in Salvador than sex, money, and illicit activity. Rather, socially acceptable behaviors and values, such as travel, romance, leisure, consumption, and sometimes marriage are also a part of the package (Cabezas 2004).[3]

In my interviews with sex workers, I intentionally refrained from asking why they had chosen that line of work. I felt that this question contained underlying moral assumptions that stem from the premise that sex work was something wrong and immoral, a last resort chosen only under extreme circumstances. I felt that my ability to build rapport with sex workers depended on their understanding that I was not making moral judgments about them or their occupation. For this reason, I chose to begin conversations by asking about their experiences as sex workers. However, Bel volunteered to tell me the story of her entry into sex work: "Why did I end up in this life? It was destiny. . . . I was always a good girl from a good family. My mother only let me go to school and mass," she began. Bel migrated to Salvador along with two friends because the port was *mas movimentado* (busier) than Recife, which meant more ships and thus more potential clients. At the time of the interview, Bel had lived in Salvador for five years.

Bel crafted her narrative to highlight her moral upbringing, relationships with men, and decision to begin doing sex work: "I had my first boyfriend when I was fifteen years old. It was only for a week. I was so antisocial. . . . I only had three boyfriends before starting to *piriguetar* [whore]. . . . I found my second boyfriend on the internet. I am an *interesseira assumida* [admitted gold-digger]. . . . I was seventeen years old, and he was twenty-two. He had a car. I started dating him for *interesse* [ulterior motives]. He was awkward, he wasn't cute, and he only talked about work. We dated for six months. I passed the *vestibular* [college entrance exam] at that time. I went to school for the first six months without paying."[4] Bel's narrative shifts from the imposed moral turpitude of her upbringing to her proclaimed *interesseira* attitudes in selecting her boyfriends. By calling herself an *interesseira assumida*, Bel is saying that she proudly proclaims and admits that she is an *interesseira*. She dated a man she did not find attractive or particularly interesting because of the benefits of mobility and money. The fact that he paid for her monthly college fees during their relationship was an added benefit. She continued, "I chose geography because it was the cheapest program of study that I liked. My friends bought books for school, and I would photocopy them. My debt from the Xerox went up to R$600 the first year, and I didn't pay the monthly payment for school. . . . My stepfather became unemployed, so I had to get a job. I earned $R180. That was barely enough to contribute to the household."

The precariousness of her family's financial situation meant that she could no longer be a carefree college student. She quickly realized that her employment options were limited and that the meager salary she earned for her hard work was far from desirable. "I had ulterior motives [in dating the second boyfriend]. I wanted to lose my virginity to a nice guy so that I could begin to *piriguetar*. The first time [I had sex] I was drunk. I didn't feel anything. Afterwards, I felt blood drip down my leg. . . . I cried. Now I was no longer a *moçinha* [respectable young lady]. I only did it two more times with that boyfriend, and I wanted to *entrar na brega* [begin to do sex work]. . . . I met another guy in college. I wanted to marry him because he fulfilled one of my dreams: he took me to the Chapada Diamantina [a region of Bahia known for its ecotourism]. He worked for the *Receita Federal* [federal government treasury] in Recife, and we dated for six months. I really liked the third boyfriend, so much so that I broke up with him when I decided to *entrar na brega*." Bel voluntarily entered the *brega* at age nineteen when she responded to a newspaper advertisement seeking eighteen-year-old girls to work in a restaurant/bar. She was well aware that the jobs involved more than waitressing and bartending. At this establishment, she was asked to do a striptease in front of a table full of men: "I had never done a striptease. I took off my clothes and took off running."

After that first (failed) attempt at sexual labor, she decided to try another approach: "I met a girl who worked at the port [as a prostitute], and she said she would take me there. She worked with foreigners from the ships. I was studying in the university, so I only went to the port Saturday and Sunday. . . . I was studying geography, but I didn't want to. I wanted to be a psychologist. . . . I did a year and a half of college. I even taught classes for first- and fourth-graders. I worked for a year in an office. I worked as an administrative assistant in another office. My boss wanted to have sex with me." Abolitionist scholarship tends to situate sex workers as women who have limited educational and occupational experience and opportunities and who have no option other than "selling their bodies" as a survival strategy. While this narrative may be true in some cases, in other instances, women exercise autonomy in choosing sexual labor over other forms of exploitative labor.

Bel described her first *programa* as an experience in which her naïveté was almost her downfall. Only because a more experienced sex worker showed her the ropes was Bel able to take full advantage of the situation that presented itself: "My first *programa*, I was a bit crazy. A tall and handsome blond man asked how much I charged and I said R$70–100, but the girl who brought me there told me that I could charge R$200 to *gringos*. I told him this. He said, "No, 150"; I said, "180." He paid for the taxi, hotel, and gave me US$180. I said, 'I don't want this. This money is useless. The girl told me that money was worth a lot: 'Take the money!' I went to the *câmbio* and exchanged the dollars for *reais*. I had never seen so much money in my life!" Disappointed at her lack of financial savvy and the difficulties of managing her money, she reflected, "I was young and stupid. I spent money on lots of frivolous things—clothes, shoes, and cell phones—all nonsense. It wasn't until I got pregnant that I realized that this money wouldn't last forever. . . . I've been with men, ship captains, who gave me R$3,000, but I don't know where that money is now."

Bel's narrative illustrates some of the factors and conditions that shape women's lives in the socioeconomic and cultural landscape of northeastern Brazilian port cities. Her story also reveals a cosmopolitan scene in which an exchange occurs among sex workers from different cities as they travel to different ports to engage in sexual labor. Other research participants also expressed the notion of cosmopolitanism and mobility among sex workers. Fabiana claimed that "all prostitutes are tourists" because of their tendency to travel to different places. She explained that in her experience as a prostitute who was "viciada em carona" (addicted to hitchhiking), she was able to "explore Brazil in trucks, and even earn money with the truck drivers." Similarly, Gilmara, a young black sex worker, told the attendees at an Aprosba meeting, "Prostitution has brought me many things. I had the opportunity to travel to other places. For me, it's been marvelous." These stories illustrate themes of self-value, cosmopolitanism, and mobility. Several of the women that I interviewed saw sex work as a tool to access forms of mobility—both in the literal sense and in terms of possibilities to move up the social ladder—that are often foreclosed for poor women. They expressed their dreams of mobility and cosmopolitanism through their sexual and intimate labor with foreigners.

Se Valorizando (Valuing Oneself): Feeling Needed and the Possibilities of Love

Quite a few sex workers with whom I spoke expressed sentiments of "valuing oneself" tied to the act of charging for sexual services. In fact, se valorizando came specifically from charging for sexual services. Fabiana once told a journalist that she became a prostitute "because I wanted to. . . . I like to have sex—orgasms—and earn my money, so why not do it all at the same time?" When the journalist, unsatisfied, again asked why she became a prostitute, Fabiana's responded, "Because I am valuing my body. Before, I was having a lot of sex and I didn't have money to buy bread. Now I'm valuing my body [by charging]." Thus, Fabiana felt exploited not when she sold sexual services but when she had sex for free, a viewpoint that resonates with Anne McClintock's observation that "society demonizes sex workers because they demand more money than women should, for services men expect for free" (1993, 2).

Even after she became a prostitute, Fabiana had negative experiences with men who had made the transition from clients to boyfriends. She had found that men often wanted to take from her financially and emotionally. While she was living in the city of Natal, in the northeastern state of Rio Grande do Norte, "A guy said, 'Do you want to get out of this life and marry me?' I stayed with him, having sex, and after one week he left a note saying, 'I don't want this anymore. You can go.' I left him a note that said 'Okay, but I'm going to take your stereo for the time that I stayed with you.' I told him that the stereo would be at my mother's house and that he could go pick it up if he brought the money to pay me for the week." Such experiences influenced Fabiana's preference for working with *marinheiros* because they "come and go" and consequently were less likely to become regular customers who would eventually seek to evade payment for sexual services.

Foreign tourists often seek much more than sex on their vacations. In addition to *programas*, men often wanted women to stay in their hotels or on their ships for several days, go out to dinner, go shopping, and, particularly for black women, act as domestic servants. Fabiana had nearly twenty years of experience "battling" on the ships and doing *programas* exclusively with foreign clients. She began working as a prostitute at age twenty-three after a bitter divorce. When ships would arrive, Fabiana "would take a ferry out to them. Sometimes I would stay a week on the ship. I charged R$50 for short time, and R$150 to stay the night. There were foreigners who paid more." On one occasion, an American captain gave her US$300 in one night and took her shopping. She loved receiving gifts from clients. These experiences reflect the tensions between money and gifts, as well as *programas* and relationships.

Two women's articulations of their ambiguous entanglements with foreigners were rooted in the idea that they felt "needed" and "valued" by foreign tourists. Josefa, a thirty-nine-year-old sex worker who had spent seventeen years "battling on the ships," bragged about having clients from Croatia, India, Romania, the United States, Greece, the Philippines, and several other countries. Like Bel and Fabiana, Josefa described how the "girls," often accompanied by a tour guide, would meet foreign ship workers at the dock. The existence of tour guides who facilitate sexual-tourist exchanges indicates the broad range of people who profit from the sex tourism industry. When asked if doing *programas* with *gringos* brought any benefits, she responded, "Yes, it gives you more value. They need us more, for tourism, to go sightseeing." For this reason, she felt more of a stigma about being a sex worker from Brazilians than from *gringos*.

Josefa had two relationships with foreign clients that extended beyond *programas*. She had fallen in love with a *marinheiro* from Greece, and she smiled and gazed wistfully out at the horizon as she told me she hoped to "find him again one day." She also had become pregnant by an Indian man she met on the ships, but she never saw him again after his ship left the port. Josefa's experience doing *programas* with ship workers from all over the world gave her access to a kind of cosmopolitanism that would ordinarily have been beyond her reach. Scholars of globalization and transnational processes often describe the "cosmopolitan subject" as a privileged person, a citizen of the world who is open to global influences (Ong 1999; Robbins 1998; Saraswati 2010; Vertovec and Cohen 2002). Cosmopolitanism has come to be associated with transcending the nation-state, with the ability to "to mediate actions and ideals oriented both to the universal and the particular, the global and the local" and to manage "cultural and political multiplicities" (Vertovec and Cohen 2002, 4). The term also "evokes the image of a privileged person" with "independent means, expensive tastes, and a globe-trotting lifestyle" (Robbins 1998, 248). However, my ethnographic research with sex workers, non–sex workers, and foreign tourists engaged in ambiguous entanglements in the touristscape of Salvador reveals alternative, grassroots ways in which people with limited financial means nonetheless find ways to express their desires for cosmopolitanism. While Josefa never traveled to Greece, India, the Philippines, or other countries, she learned about these countries through her clients. Like the *caçadores* who sought out transnational connections with foreign tourists who could allow them to experience their city in ways that were usually reserved for foreigners and Brazilian elites, Josefa can also be seen as someone who "realizes her cosmopolitan identity through her intimate encounters with men" from all over the world (Maia 2012, 169).

The idea of gaining self-value by feeling needed was also expressed by Patrícia, a twenty-five-year-old black woman who enthusiastically told me that she spoke some Spanish and English: "I prefer all *gringos*, they're more caring, and pay well. They need *carinho* [care, affection]. I like it. I'm very caring." Her clients regularly paid her fifty reais and often gave her presents as well. The ways in which sex workers provided both sexual services and other forms of intimate and emotional labor to their foreign clients at times led to opportunities to travel abroad. Piscitelli (2001) found that lower-class women tended to idealize foreigners and harbor dreams of living abroad, a phenomenon that also held true in Salvador. The desire to travel abroad and be a tourist, if not to live abroad, was pervasive.

Advantages of Gringo Clients

One of the major advantages of doing *programas* with *gringos*, Fabiana pointed out, is that "you can ask for one hundred reais from a Brazilian and one hundred dollars from a *gringo*." Originally from the northeastern state of Paraíba, Fabiana chose Bahia as her home for nearly twenty years because of her sexual preference for black men. However, she had a financial preference for the "raça loira" (blond race)—European clients—because "they paid better." She also had many Asian clients, particularly Filipinos, despite her observation that they often preferred young women. Katrina, a twenty-one-year-old Afro-Brazilian woman whom I met while she was working in Praça da Sé, also preferred to do *programas* with foreign men because they paid more: "*Baianos* cry over twenty reais!," she proclaimed.

However, the financial rewards of sex with foreigners are only part of the story. The prospect of gifts, intimacy, affection, and cosmopolitanism are also integral to the advantages some sex workers see in doing *programas* with non-Brazilians. When asked if *gringos* were usually seeking *programas* or *namoros*, Katrina said they generally wanted *programas* but preferred to spend more time than Brazilian clients—up to three or four hours. In addition to the money she earned from *gringos*, Katrina appreciated their presents, which included necklaces, earrings, a television, a DVD player, a bed, and perfume. Katrina seemed to value this nonmonetary compensation as much if not more than the cash payments. Katrina had spent time in Argentina at the invitation of Mario, a seventy-two-year-old doctor whom she met when she was sixteen. When I met her in the Praça, she was waiting for four foreign "amigos" (friends). Most of her clients were *coroas* from Argentina, France, and Italy. The *coroa*, an elderly man who helps a younger woman financially in exchange for sex, company, and even domestic care, is a common figure in the Brazilian context (Goldstein 2003, 108–10; Piscitelli 2011, 553). The first two times that Mario invited Katrina to his rented apartment, he asked her to do domestic work and sex work, and she robbed him. A few years later, Mario paid for her to visit Argentina for three months, her first trip outside Brazil. "I enjoyed it so much," she said; "I did a lot of sightseeing and ate good food." As Piscitelli (2011) notes, *coroas* are gradually being replaced by foreign tourists, many of whom are younger and more appealing than their Brazilian counterparts because they offer the possibility of marriage and migration.

Sex workers in Salvador often highlighted the nationalities of the various men with whom they had done *programas*. Fabiana, for example, proudly mentioned that she had done *programas* with Hawaiian men as well as Argentines, Greeks, and Japanese, joking that the only nationality with whom she had not done *programas* was "Eskimos." Martin Manalansan makes the related point that "mobile queers" expand our understandings of mobility and highlight "the ways in which cosmopolitanism is not always privileged" (2003, 9). Doing *programas* with foreign clients also offered an impermanence and anonymity that many sex workers desired. For years, local people did not know what Fabiana did for a living.

Aproveitando (Taking Advantage): Money, Gifts, and Exploitation

The Humanitarian Center for the Support of Women (CHAME) is a Salvador-based nongovernmental organization that strives to raise awareness about sex tourism and the trafficking of women. Founder Jacqueline Leite defines sex tourism exclusively as "transactions in which the local women are NOT paid in currency." While this definition may seem counterintuitive, Leite believes that exploitation is a prerequisite for sex tourism. In this perspective, exploitation occurs when women who are dating or involved in ambiguous entanglements with foreign tourists have sex with them and play a variety of other roles for free. Conversely, as long as sex workers are paid (adequately) for sex with tourists, then the women are not exploited; such transactions therefore should not be placed under the rubric of sex tourism. Leite claims that to save money, sex tourists do not enlist the services of professional sex workers. Instead, "they want a girlfriend because it comes out cheaper. They look for romantic involvement to take advantage, realize erotic fantasies, and save money" (Carla Ferreira 2004).[5] Leite sees this gray area of the girlfriend as the true site of exploitation that warrants being called "sex tourism."

Perhaps unsurprisingly, the majority of these "girlfriends" are low-income women of African descent who feel an elevated status by their ambiguous entanglements with (white) foreigners. These women, Leite argues, are exploited on multiple levels as they are often asked to serve as impromptu tour guides, security people, translators, cultural brokers, and more for their tourist *namorados*. Moreover, Leite contends, sex tourists see "all Brazilian women" as "disposable," which explains "why [the foreign man] doesn't want a prostitute." In other words, notions of black hypersexuality that circulate in the transnational tourist imaginary lead foreign tourists to see any Brazilian woman of African descent as a potential object of desire. In 2008, Leite told me,

> The sex industry is a legitimate industry. If you are enjoying this service, it is not exploitation. There is a verbal agreement—she charges a certain amount, and he pays. When [the sex tourist] dates [*namora*], he doesn't want a sex professional; he wants whoever will do it for free. He doesn't want a prostitute because he doesn't want to pay for her service. She'll take him to tourist places and he won't have to pay a tour guide. She'll take him to safe places and be his

security guard and make sure he's not being ripped off. And once again, he's not paying for this. She's doing all this, and he's exploiting the country he came to visit. This is exploitation, not sex tourism—payment or not. Brazil wants tourists who come here and pay. It's not sex that defines it, it's the intention. I can have sex when I travel—why not? But they use the structure of the city without paying for it. When he comes and hooks up with a woman, it is deception. *Exploitation* and *deception* are the key words.

CHAME wanted to replace the term *sex tourism* with *exploitation in tourism development in Brazil* (*exploração no desenvolvimento do turismo no Brasil*) to call attention to the fact that "this tourism isn't only sexual, there are other modalities as well," Leite said. In other words, CHAME is "trying to take the sex out of sex tourism because it carries with it a moralistic baggage and hides many other things. Sex tourism is exploiting various professionals in the Third World. If we don't make this distinction, we will always look at sex work as something different." This semantic move resembles progressive critiques of trafficking discourse that emphasize sexual labor and exploitation over other forms of labor exploitation in the global economy.

I interviewed one sex worker whose perspectives seemed to correspond with Leite's notions of exploitation. In August 2007, Fabiana asked me to assist Aprosba with a survey research project on violence against sex workers in the Centro Histórico. Through this project, I met María, a woman in her early forties. She told me that she had done *programas* mostly with Italians and Germans. The *ponto* where she waited for and solicited clients was in Praça da Se, and she charged between twenty and fifty reais for a *programa*, depending on whether the men were locals or foreigners. Maria felt strongly that it was a "disgrace" for sex workers to do *programas* with tourists for free. When asked if tourists generally wanted a *programa* or something more, she responded, "That's why I don't like [tourists]. They don't want to pay for the *programa*. They want company. I'm not going with them. I'm a *puta*. There are *garotas* who kiss and walk hand in hand [with *gringos*] for nothing. They feel good hooking up with the *gringo* for free. I feel ashamed." Thus, while some sex workers did not charge *gringos* because these women perceived their attachments to foreigners as providing elevated social status, Maria preferred to restrict her interactions with foreigners to the realm of strictly commercial sexual transactions. She liked it when the *gringos* gave her presents—as long as they also paid her. Maria bore an obvious disdain for foreign tourists who assumed that their class, racial, and economic privilege would enable them easily to transform a commercial sexual transaction into an ambiguous open-ended liaison.

Leite's point about the role of monetary exchange in defining sex tourism raises important questions about the distinction between gifts and money. Her understanding of the relationship between sex tourism and exploitation presumes a distinction between gifts and money that privileges hard currency rather than considering the varied social and economic significance of gifts. Martin Opperman points out that exchange in sex work can often take the form of "soft-selling techniques" in which gifts rather than cash are the predominant currency (1998, 14). Furthermore, Linda Anne Rebhun (2007) contends that in northeastern Brazil, gifts are often seen as an expression of love despite the common presumption that "true love" requires a complete separation between sentiment and economics. Furthermore, in *Intimate Labors: Culture, Technologies, and the Politics of Care*, Eileen Boris and Rhacel Salazar Parreñas point out that "relations of intimacy already involve the exchange of money" (2010, 8). Feminist scholars such as Adrienne Davis (2009), Viviana Zelizer (2005, 2009), Amalia Cabezas (2009), Kamala Kempadoo (2004), and Adriana Piscitelli (2007), among others, have also delineated the intersections between intimacy and money.

Gabriela Leite, a well-known Brazilian sex workers' rights activist, complicates the idea of sex tourism as inherently exploitative by pointing out that "in Rio, everybody earns money from tourism, so why can't women [prostitutes] earn money from tourism?" In Salvador, many people earn their livings from the tourism industry—taxi drivers, hair braiders, capoeiristas performing in public plazas and charging tourists to pose for pictures, unlicensed tour guides who hawk their services on the street. Gabriela Leite raises an important question: if so many people make a living off of tourism, why is there public outcry when prostitutes also attempt to take advantage of the tourism industry? Who has the power to determine what is exploitative and who is being exploited? How can researchers or activists with nongovernmental organizations far removed from sex workers' lives evaluate whether receiving thirty reais or three hundred dollars for the sale of sexual services is "less exploitative" than gifts such as new clothes, a month's rent, airfare, or dinner at a fancy restaurant?

Furthermore, how do we reconcile Jacqueline Leite's articulations of sex tourism as defined by the existence of exploitation and a lack of monetary exchange with sex workers' experiences that revealed the importance of valuing oneself, feeling needed, and the benefits of doing *programas* and having ambiguous entanglements with foreign tourists?[6] Thus, Leite might see Josefa as exploited because tourists demand more from her than paid sexual encounters. However, this feeling of being needed in nonsexual ways gave Josefa a sense of importance and cosmopolitanism. Furthermore, many of the ways that sex workers are exploited have little to do with the act of selling sex: Aprosba members' perceptions of exploitation often had more to do with the ramifications of criminalization, stigma, and police violence than the mere fact of having ambiguous entanglements or doing *programas* with foreign tourists.

Conclusion

The women's stories featured in this chapter highlight the complexity of transactions, liaisons, and relationships between foreign men and Bahian women. More than a mere exchange of money is often at stake. These encounters are ripe with notions of intimacy, hope, desire, and cosmopolitan dreams and aspirations. Furthermore, these stories present another side of how people commonly discuss sex tourism. Instead of focusing on victims and oppressors, exploitation and objectification, these stories reveal that complex emotions and desires are also involved. Even in the context of transnational encounters based on global hierarchies and inequalities, women can feel valued and cared for, can care for others, can date, and can experience the possibilities of love and cosmopolitanism. As Kempadoo asks, can we explore these dimensions of the lives of women of color in the sex industry without "dismissing them as unconscious, unfeminist, or unliberated" (2001b, 41)?

Taking seriously the lives and experiences of these women will require scholars to move beyond dichotomies that situate sex workers as either victims or agents. Feminist scholars have helped us understand that people do not exercise agency in isolation from institutions of power. Dorinne Kondo (1990) urges us to recognize the contradictions and creative tensions inherent in people's lives, while Paulla Ebron (1997) reminds us that agency does not necessarily erase oppression. Similarly, McClintock understands agency in terms of the "difficult ways in which people's actions and desires are mediated through institutions of power" such as the family, the media, the law, armies, and nationalist movements (1995, 15). In Salvador, sex workers must negotiate their agency within a society that stigmatizes their trade and a police system that often abuses and criminalizes them rather than offering protection and security.

Recent feminist scholarship on intimate labor can also help us make sense of this concept of valuing oneself. Boris and Parreñas define *intimate labor* as a range of activities that entail touch, bodily or emotional closeness, and personal familiarity. Found in both the formal and informal labor market, *intimate labor* joins together sex work, domestic work, and care work under one rubric, an important development because all three realms are stigmatized as a result of "the presence of dirt, bodies, and intimacy" (2010, 2). Intimate labor can involve both "fleeting encounters and durable ties" and consists of "tending to the intimate needs of individuals" (3–5). Boris and Parreñas's formulation of intimate labor builds on feminist literature on reproductive and emotional labor. Arlie Russell Hochschild's concept of emotional labor is "the management of feeling to create a publicly observable facial and bodily display" (1983, 7). Emotional labor is sold for a wage, has an exchange value, and behaves like a commodity in the marketplace. Hochschild points out that women have more frequently used emotion management in exchange for economic support, that they "make a resource out of feeling and offer it to men as a gift in return for the more material resources they lack" (20, 163). However, Boris and Parreñas claim that emotional labor is not necessarily a prerequisite for intimate labor (2010, 7).

In the sexual economies of tourism in Salvador, sex must also be understood alongside intimacy, affect, and care. Boris and Parreñas's concept of intimate labor is a useful tool for making sense of the ambiguous entanglements between the city's sex workers and foreign visitors. Foreign ship workers and leisure sex tourists do not land in Salvador in search of sex alone—they are often seeking temporary companions, tour guides, domestic servants, and conversation partners. Salvador's sex workers have diverse ways of understanding the significance of their sexual and intimate labors and how those labors intersect with the exchange of money, gifts, and other resources. As Kempadoo points out, although it is "tricky" for transnational or postcolonial feminists to emphasize the "sexual agency, needs, and desires" of women of color who engage in sex work because of the history of sexualization and the risk of reinforcing that sexualization, doing so is nonetheless crucial (2001b, 42).

CHAPTER SEVEN

Moral Panics

Sex Tourism, Trafficking, and the Limits of Transnational Mobility

Pérola, a black sex worker whom I met at Aprosba, once told me a story that made me think about the possibilities of transnational mobility for Brazilian women who sell sex. Pérola showed me a picture of Ivete, a brown-skinned sex worker in her late thirties or early forties who had just come back from a month in Germany.[1] Ivete had gone to visit a *gringo* whom she met in Salvador, returning to share news, pictures, and stories about her positive experiences abroad. Experiences such as Ivete's story offer a significant contrast to sensationalist news media accounts that depict any scenario where a foreign tourist facilitates a Brazilian woman's trip to his country as a case of "trafficking," with the underlying connotation that the woman will be "forced" into prostitution.

Conversely, Fabiana, cofounder and lead organizer of Aprosba, shared with me a completely different perspective on the risks and possibilities of transnational mobility and migration for sex workers. She had had a foreign boyfriend who had started out as a client. For her, the defining factor that marked the man's transition from client to boyfriend was that he no longer paid her for sex. He wanted to marry her and take her to Europe. However, Fabiana did not see this as an once-in-a-lifetime opportunity. She had significant reservations about traveling abroad with a client turned boyfriend: "I'm afraid to leave Brazil. I'm afraid of the cold, of language difficulties, of not having money to return." Another sex worker, Lydia, shared a story of how a *cafetina* (madam) invited her to go to Spain. She was excited at the opportunity and got a passport. However, at the last minute, she refused to go, because she believed that Spanish men only liked to have sex without condoms, and she was not willing to subject herself to that kind of risk overseas. In other words, traveling abroad involved heightened vulnerability, a potential inability to negotiate, and less autonomy than remaining in one's home country. Lydia did point out, however, that a lot of *travestis* go to Spain, implying perhaps that they are more willing to accept those circumstances.

In these women's stories, the specter of trafficking threatens what is often seen as the ultimate fantasy of women who engage in sex work with foreign tourists—transnational migration (Brennan 2004, 13–14). Instead of eagerly taking advantage of the opportunity to travel abroad, Fabiana was much more cautious about putting herself in a situation in which she might lose autonomy. A friend of hers had gone to Germany and been miserable because of the cold weather and because she was forced to drink a lot. Stories from acquaintances as well as information from the Humanitarian Center for the Support of Women (CHAME) about the specter of trafficking informed Fabiana's opinions about what might happen if she were to travel abroad with a client/boyfriend. Fabiana said, "The work of CHAME is very important for us, sex workers, because through CHAME we can inform ourselves about things that we previously didn't know. Knowing how the traffic in women happens, we can prevent it and pass the information along to other women in our group." Fabiana fearlessly defended sex workers' right to migrate or travel abroad if they chose to do so: "If you want to go [abroad], go, but don't go with money from an agent"—that is, someone who advances the travel money with the expectation that he or she will be repaid and receive exorbitant interest.

These scenarios raise interesting questions about the possibilities of transnational mobility for socioeconomically disadvantaged Brazilian women. Intimate encounters with foreigners often provide the context and opportunity for travel or migration. As Suzane Maia points out in *Transnational Desires: Brazilian Erotic Dancers in New York*, "transnational mobility does not take place in a vacuum"; rather, it is "constrained by state and cultural institutions that both delineate and are delineated by everyday practices of particular individuals" (2012, 169). My point in juxtaposing Fabiana's and Lydia's fears with Ivete's positive experiences is not necessarily to ask to what extent the sensationalized horror stories of trafficking are true. Serious cases of trafficking happen all over the world. Rather, my critique is that campaigns against sex tourism and trafficking often fall into the trap of problematically constructing any and all situations in which "vulnerable" women travel abroad with the help of foreigners as potential cases of trafficking.

Ideas of agency, subjectivity, power, and oppression inform the ways in which people talk and think about trafficking, especially considering the fact that "victims of trafficking" are almost always seen as women (never men)—more particularly, as women who engage in sex work (never other forms of labor). This chapter analyzes public debates regarding sex tourism as well as the effects and limitations of state and civil society campaigns against sex tourism in Salvador. Although sex tourism and trafficking are two separate issues, they are often conflated in official policies established by national and international agencies. What are the divergent ways in which governmental and nongovernmental agents understand sex tourism and trafficking, and how do these understandings shape their efforts? How do campaigns against sex tourism and trafficking run the risk of reaffirming patriarchal values and placing further restrictions on (particular) women's mobility, especially women of African descent? In this way, we can see how anti-trafficking discourse in Brazil is informed by fears and beliefs about race. Despite good intentions, CHAME's campaigns often reproduce stock images and sensationalized stories that contribute to a "moral panic" (Carby 1992; Stanley Cohen 1972; Herdt 2009) about interracial sex and transnational border crossings.

The chapter begins with a historical overview of the concept of trafficking and of global antitrafficking movements as well as the ways in which "trafficking" has been confused and conflated with "sex tourism." This background information will enable an understanding of the ways in which trafficking and sex tourism have been constituted as objects of knowledge. Second, I analyze CHAME's campaign activities through an in-depth visual analysis of the images presented in the group's educational materials that illustrates the complexity of campaigns against sex tourism and trafficking. The collection of CHAME educational campaign materials constitutes an "archive of racialized sexuality" (Reddy 2005, 114–15) that reflects society's perspectives about black Brazilian women, foreign (European) men, and the possibilities of sex, intimacy, migration, love, marriage, and exploitation.

CHAME and Aprosba: Coming Together to Combat Violence against Women

On November 28, 2006, I participated in an exposition in downtown Salvador organized by CHAME to commemorate the International Day to End Violence against Women.[2] Two women from Aprosba and I stood at one entrance of the plaza, handing out CHAME pamphlets. Fabiana was very gregarious and charismatic, calling out to attractive male passersby by calling them "saradão" (sexy), "machadão" (macho), or "gostoso" (tasty). She boldly asked men if they beat their wives or girlfriends and asked women if they "já apanhou" (had ever been beaten). Participating in this event helped me appreciate how CHAME brought together a diverse group of people in an effort to educate the public and foster social change. By collaborating with Aprosba, CHAME revealed its support for sex workers' rights. A poster that CHAME produced for the event announced, "Before opening your heart, open your eyes. There are Brazilian women being enslaved abroad. A good marriage. A job. Foreign currency. The Brazilian woman doesn't have to stop having these dreams. But she needs to pay attention. Because along with them, there is a sad reality. A slavery without color. Sexist, silent, and cowardly. Before you open your heart, open your eyes. To be happy or earn a living in another country, you don't need to lose your freedom." This statement intimately links the risk of trafficking with romantic sentiments as well as aspirations of socioeconomic mobility and cosmopolitanism. Here, cosmopolitanism refers to the appeal of experiencing the world outside Brazil's borders, the chance to live and work abroad, which may put some women at risk for being "enslaved." However, these dreams of cosmopolitanism must be understood in the context of the lack of educational and employment opportunities available to many Afro-Brazilian women. Though CHAME contends that this slavery is "without color," the ways in which racialized sexualities are implicated in the transnational circulation of notions of black hypersexuality suggests that this slavery is indeed racialized. In other words, women of African descent are specifically targeted as the potential victims of trafficking.

CHAME is the only NGO engaged in campaigns to raise public awareness about sex tourism and trafficking in Brazil. Founded in 1994 by Jacqueline Leite, CHAME became an independent NGO in 2001. It's mission is to "alert society to the risks of exploitation of young and adult women in the different forms of migration and recruitment for forced labor (sexual, domestic, and other modalities of slavery, usually linked to physical or psychological violence), respecting her freedom of choice. Though such terms as *slavery, forced labor,* and *exploitation* parallel language of abolitionist organizations, the use of the phrase *freedom of choice* indicates that Leite positions herself within a sex worker's rights' framework that respects women's choice to do sex work.

Leite created CHAME after working for the Center for Information for Women from Asia, Africa, and Latin America (FIZ), a Swiss organization that combats the exploitation of foreign migrant women. At FIZ, Leite noticed that many Latin American women and especially Brazilians found themselves in precarious situations abroad. They arrived with little information about how to live in another country, let alone about their rights and restrictions as foreign migrants. The FIZ team recognized the need for a project that would provide information to women before they traveled abroad so that they would not see Europe as a paradise.

CHAME focuses on three primary areas of activity: preventing trafficking through documentation and raising awareness; political work on local, regional, national, and international levels; and international research. CHAME organizes events, workshops, seminars, and courses in schools, neighborhood associations, unions, and other groups. The organization has also developed a packet of course materials (*módulo*) for training a cadre of people (*multiplicadores*) who can go back to their home communities and educate their peers. Leite sees working with grassroots communities as one of CHAME's major strengths, and she hopes that this work will prevent trafficking, so that women "may know that when they travel there could be dangers." "What motivates this project," Leite says, "is the fight for a better condition of women": "Our objective is to give more power to women by disseminating information so that they can decide their own futures. This requires awakening the consciousness, understanding their social condition and the role that they play in this society. From this base, women will certainly have greater opportunities to choose whether to migrate" (CHAME n.d.[b], n.p.). Thus, CHAME works to empower women with knowledge so that they can make informed decisions about traveling abroad.

Coming to Terms with Sex Tourism and Trafficking

While sex tourism is complex and ambiguous, trafficking is often seen as a clear-cut, black-and-white issue, always unequivocally negative. Moreover, trafficking is presented in a simplistic way that erases the complexities of race, class, place, and citizenship that mark it. However, for some, sex tourism and trafficking are virtually indistinguishable. Reginaldo Serra, an officer with the Delegation for the Protection of Tourists, the specialized police force that deals with tourist issues, conflates sex tourists with "mafiosos" and traffickers and assumes that sex tourists are hunting for women to bring back to their home countries: "It's a very serious problem. . . . [Foreign men] take women [to Europe to live, but] it's nothing like they thought it would be. They're held hostage by elements of the mafia and can't return home again. Sex tourism is really ambiguous, but it's criminal. The tourist comes seeking people to take back with him." In reality, according to Fabiana, the foreign men who were largely responsible for trafficking Brazilian women were not leisure tourists on their first few trips to Bahia. Rather, mafia-connected migrants from other countries already living in Salvador were involved in these transnational circuits of deception and exploitation. Furthermore, his assertion that sex tourism is "ambiguous" yet "criminal" highlights the entanglements implicit in such practices. Police officers find sex tourism ambiguous because it is often difficult to distinguish an encounter between a foreign tourist and a paid sex worker from a budding relationship between a foreign tourist and a Bahian who may or may not be a sex worker. Furthermore, the statement that sex tourism is criminal is debatable—while it is certainly criminal with adolescents, it is not a crime when consenting adults are involved.

The term *trafficking* was first used in the early twentieth century to refer to the "white slave trade" in European women, brought across the Atlantic to serve as concubines and prostitutes in U.S. brothels (Altink 1995, 1). Two opposing factions emerged in the fight against white slavery: the "regulationists," who distinguished between the "willing prostitute" and the "victimized white slave," and the "purity campaigners" (abolitionists), who saw all prostitutes as "victims in need of rescue" (O'Connell Davidson 1998, 16; Doezema 2002, 22–23).[3] Abolitionists embraced a "moralistic, middle-class urge to protect the virtue of young, working class, and immigrant women" (Doezema 2002, 23). Sex worker rights activist Jo Doezema asserts that this urge was rooted in notions of the (usually black, working-class, colonial, or Other) "suffering body" posed in opposition to the (usually white and middle-class) "Western saving body" (2001, 22).

In the mid-1990s, "trafficking" resurfaced as a "modern form of slavery" (Agustín 2007, 36). Trafficking has been defined as a "transnational, transcontinental movement of the new human cash crop" in which "bodies of Third World women are purveyed as affordable specialty items in the international sex industry" (Hugh Johnston and Khan 1998, 136). Although most antitrafficking literature tends to focus on "sex slavery," or trafficking for prostitution, people are also trafficked for other purposes, among them marriage (mail-order brides), sweatshop labor, adoption, and domestic work. However, the outcry from international human rights NGOs, feminists, and journalists is loudest about trafficking for sex work as a consequence of the assumption that sexual labor is more pernicious and devastating than other forms of labor because commercial sex is morally reprehensible. Grace Chang (2004) suggests that the exclusive focus on trafficking for sex work perpetuates governmental antitrafficking discourses, which focus specifically on sex trafficking because prostitution is an easy target that most people agree should be abolished and because the state has a vested interest in maintaining other forms of exploitative labor.

Global trafficking in persons has become one of the most lucrative illicit businesses in the world today, trailing only drugs and guns as sources of

profits for organized crime (Miko and Park 2002; Commonwealth Secretariat 2002, 6).[4] While the U.S. government estimates that between six
hundred thousand and nine hundred thousand people are trafficked each
year around the world (Wyler and Siskin 2010), it is very difficult to acquire
reliable statistics on this underground activity. The general description of
trafficking in news and documentaries suggests that women are forced,
deceived, or coerced into traveling abroad and that once they arrive at their
destinations, they face debt bondage, forced servitude, and slavery-like conditions (Global Alliance against Trafficking in Women 2000). Some scholars
indicate that trafficking occurs less than the police, politicians, and some
feminist organizations and media assume (Thorbek and Pattanaik 2002, 4).
Susanne Thorbek and Bandana Pattanaik point out the ambiguity regarding
the victims of trafficking: "It is very difficult to distinguish between who
is trafficked and who is not. A woman may decide to go abroad, knowing
she will work as a prostitute, and then find the conditions under which
she has to work unacceptable; in this sense she may be considered a victim
of trafficking. Another woman may be lured or cheated into the trade but
decide that, in the circumstances, her best option is to go on. Has she been
trafficked if she does not want to be liberated?" (Thorbek and Pattanaik
2002, 5). Consent and coercion thus figure prominently in determining who
qualifies as a victim of trafficking. Furthermore, categories such as gender,
race, age, and sexuality inform who is seen as in need (read: worthy) of
intervention, protection, and rescue by the state and civil society (Agustín
2007, 8; Alexander 1991, 142).

Like the twentieth-century campaign against white slavery, the contemporary global antitrafficking movement is divided into two camps. In the
summer of 2000 when the United Nations Commission on Crime Prevention
and Criminal Justice convened in Vienna to draft the "Protocol to Prevent,
Suppress, and Punish Trafficking in Persons, Especially Women and Children" (the UN Trafficking Protocol),[5] two blocs of feminist antitrafficking
groups lobbied with very different perspectives and goals. Because this protocol represented the first attempt to define *trafficking* in the international
legal arena, the opposing feminist factions were embroiled in a brutal dispute
over whose viewpoint would be enshrined in this important document. The
Human Rights Caucus, which consisted of twelve NGOs from all over the
world, embraced a sex workers' rights perspective that saw prostitution as
a legitimate form of labor and sought guarantees that the UN Trafficking
Protocol would not harm sex workers' human rights. This perspective rejects
the assumption that sex work is something morally reprehensible from which
women must be rescued. An example of this perspective can be seen in the

Global Alliance against Trafficking in Women (GAATW), a Thailand-based organization that strives to ensure that the human rights of trafficked persons are protected by authorities and that women are empowered rather than treated as victims.[6]

Conversely, the abolitionist group, led by the Coalition against Trafficking in Women (CATW), views prostitution itself as a violation of women's human rights. Founded by Kathleen Barry, the New England–based CATW is actively involved in the United Nations and has antitrafficking and antiprostitution coalitions in more than fifteen countries. CATW maintains that "all prostitution exploits women, regardless of women's consent" (Barry 1984, 6). Jo Doezema (2001) accuses CATW's antitrafficking discourses of portraying Third World sex workers as backward, innocent, helpless, and in need of rescue. Furthermore, she contends that CATW perpetuates Orientalist ideas by blaming trafficking on traditional, religious, and social structures.[7] By engaging in an insidious Othering of people from the Global South, CATW's antitrafficking discourses participate in what Chandra Talpade Mohanty (1991) refers to as Western feminism's indulgence in notions of Third World difference that effectively homogenize Third World women and cast them as "ourselves undressed" (Rosaldo 1980, 392).[8] What began as a concern for white slavery has become racialized so that women of color from the Global South are seen as the primary victims of trafficking and sexual exploitation.

The Vienna negotiations ultimately illustrate how the contentious debate between abolitionists and sex worker rights advocates has revolved around the politics of naming. Thus, an issue central to Aprosba also plays out in the international arena. Supporters from the two sides have disagreed about whether to refer to those for whom they advocate as "trafficked prostitutes," "kidnapped innocents," or "migrant sex workers." The narrow representation of the "average third world woman" (Mohanty 1991, 56) elucidates what Agustín identifies as a problem within the violence against women framework: "perpetrator" and "victim" are treated as identities rather than temporary conditions (2007, 39). Subsequently, Agustín asserts, "victims become passive receptacles and mute sufferers who must be saved" (39). Fabiana and other sex workers understood exploitation in a much different way than Barry and other abolitionists. Rather than seeing exploitation as an inherent part of sex work, they saw it as a result of the conditions of illegality, criminalization, and stigma of sex work. How do these discourses about trafficking in the international human rights regime play out in the context of Brazilian campaigns to raise awareness regarding sex tourism and trafficking?

CHAME's Perspectives on Sex Tourism and Trafficking

CHAME understands trafficking not only as a problem of morality, migration, and organized crime but also as a fundamental violation of human rights and "one of the most perverse forms of violence against women." CHAME identifies eight factors as contributors to trafficking: (1) social and economic inequality, (2) unemployment, (3) social exclusion, (4) sex tourism, (5) gender discrimination, (6) laws and politics about migration and migrant work, (7) corruption of authorities, and (8) organized crime. CHAME conflates sex tourism and trafficking by referring to sex tourism as the gateway to trafficking or the tip of the trafficking iceberg.

CHAME's educational materials reflect the limits of mobility of people deemed vulnerable—particularly low-income Brazilian women of African descent. One pamphlet features a European man, superimposed on a landmass marked *Europa* and standing in a doorway and reaching out to someone whom we cannot see. The inside of the pamphlet has an image of a white man's hand holding a postcard or photograph of a curvaceous brown-skinned Bahian woman in a miniscule bikini. The back of the pamphlet shows a black Bahian woman superimposed on a landmass marked *Brasil*. In heels, short-shorts, and a midriff-baring tank top, she stands with her knees slightly bent as if ready to leap, with her arms outstretched to the European man on the front. Her lips are puckered and her eyes are wide and bright; three hearts circle around her head, suggesting that she is smitten. This final image evokes hopefulness, eagerness, and desire. However, its location in a brochure warning about the dangers of trafficking leaves an unsettling feeling that things may not turn out the way the Bahian woman hopes.

These campaign materials cast European men as evil and sinister perpetrators who always have ulterior motives in their interactions with black Brazilian women. The front cover of another brochure, *Travel Is a Dream? Sometimes a Nightmare!*, drawn by Mario Brito, features a black woman and a blond, blue-eyed, European man who are embracing. The woman's eyes are closed, and a circle of hearts flutters above her head. She imagines this man as a smiling prince with a crown, an angelic halo, and a big heart. However, she cannot see that his face is contorted into a sinister snarl. He imagines her holding a broom while dressed in sexy lingerie with a ball and chain tied to her ankle. The comic strip tells the tragic (love) story of this couple, who met during Carnaval. As the woman puts the finishing touches on her makeup, she says to herself with a conniving grin, "Who knows, maybe I'll hook up with a *gringo* in the streets." Next, we see two blond tourists enjoying Carnaval and having a conversation about how "easy" [*oferecidas*] Bahian women are and how different they are from the "civilized white women" of Europe. One of the men says, "We're going to get the most out of these [women]. They fall easily for our game and even think we're rich." At that moment, they spot the black woman dancing seductively by herself. After their encounter in the street, she and the man sit at a table full of empty beer bottles and cans before she accompanies him back to his hotel; the next scene shows them in bed, with crumpled sheets. The man asks if she would like to go to his country with him and she responds, "That's all I've ever wanted. It's like a dream!" The narrative's seamlessness is striking, although it is obviously oversimplified for the sake of brevity and clarity.

After the Brazilian woman travels to his (unidentified European) country, however, she is alone in an empty, run-down room with four locks on the door. Pregnant and crying, she laments about how she feels used and vulnerable in a foreign country far from her family. She continues, "He keeps me in prison and doesn't let me leave. . . . I thought I was smart . . . that I would marry him. I want to go back, but the jerk hid my travel documents. I don't have any money." Thus, the man she thought was her Prince Charming turned out not to be so charming after all. Finally, the last frame zooms in on the woman's face and pregnant belly as she screams: "THE DREAM TURNED INTO A NIGHTMARE!!! I WANT TO GO HOME!!!" She regrets her naïveté, her eagerness to trust this foreigner and put her fate into his hands in hopes of a better future.

The idea that the Prince Charming turns into a frog once the Brazilian woman is safely ensconced in his home on the other side of the world is one that emerges repeatedly in CHAME publications. The CHAME *Sumário* (n.d.) contains brief quotations from anonymous women that reflect this unfortunate transformation:

> He was no longer that polite, caring man who I met in Brazil. He turned into a perverse person.
> My husband did horrible things to me. He took my children away from me and even put me in a psychiatric clinic for two months.
> I met a person in Brazil who invited me to do folkloric dance shows in Switzerland. When I arrived there, I realized that it was an erotic show. In the club, they made me drink with the clients. In the club, if you don't drink, you're worthless.

CHAME represents the dangers of sex tourism and trafficking as being deeply tied to the naïveté and unrealistic expectations of Brazilian women of African descent. While the first two testimonies might represent any relationship or marital situation in which one spouse reveals his or her true colors over time, the involvement of transnational migration and its consequent vulnerability makes these situations dramatic and worthy of attention in the CHAME brochures. Can the situation of these women be seen as an example of trafficking, or simply as a case of a transnational romance and migration gone awry? If trafficking generally occurs for the exploitation of some kind of labor, what kind of labor are the women expected or forced to perform?

Would these campaigns see a situation involving a Brazilian man who traveled abroad at the invitation of an American woman lover as a victim of trafficking if things went horribly wrong? One of my informants, Washington, a thirty-year-old supermarket employee, dreamed of migrating to the United States and marrying an American woman. Much like the Brazilian women I interviewed who preferred to date *gringos* because they thought Bahian men were rude, domineering, and unfaithful, Washington had had negative experiences with Brazilian women and felt that they were not seeking commitment. In December 2006, he met an American woman online, and they quickly fell in love—or so he thought. She visited Bahia so they could meet in person, and he subsequently visited her in Kansas for three weeks. They were together for nine months before she told him she was married. Despite this bad experience, he still wanted to pursue a relationship with an American woman. As a man of African descent from a working-class background, Washington can be seen as a part of the vulnerable population that is not privileged enough to migrate legally. Because of the difficulty of securing a visa, he recognized transnational marriage as the only viable strategy to achieve his dream of living abroad. If we think of mobility as corporeal travel associated with privilege, knowledge, and the promise of liberation (Frohlick 2007), how do we define privilege when the traveler is marginalized?

Pablo, a twenty-six-year-old indigenous man and undocumented immigrant from Paraguay who worked in a Barra *pousada*/internet café, was deceived by a fifty-one-year-old Portuguese woman who said she would take him to Portugal to play professional soccer. Pablo quit his job and moved out of his apartment in preparation for the trip. One day, he went to speak to his boss, and when he returned to the apartment where he was living with the woman, she was gone and his clothes were strewn all over the floor. Pablo was bitter about her false promises, particularly since he had never asked her for anything. Humiliated, he had to beg for his job back. If he had been in the country legally, he said, he would have denounced her for sex tourism. However, given the gendered bias that defines sex tourism as a problem to be eradicated to protect Brazilian women and children from unscrupulous foreign men, Brazilian state authorities would have been unlikely to have taken an interest in Pablo's case.

Another CHAME brochure, *Travel Abroad: Dream or Nightmare?*, shows a Brazilian woman and European man on their wedding day. The groom is imagining his Brazilian bride wearing lingerie and handcuffed to a bed while he stands in front of her holding a whip. This brochure warns women who marry foreigners to register their marriages at the consulate of the groom's country in Brazil as well as at the Brazilian consulate in the groom's country. Another image in this brochure depicts the Brazilian woman boarding a plane with the European man. He holds a leash wrapped around her neck, and the drawing is captioned, "Travel: A freedom of choice . . . but don't believe in all of the stories." Such an approach might make people afraid to travel, even though doing so is their choice and their right. The text warns, "Your passport belongs to you. Don't give or even loan your passport to anyone. Always keep it with you. Your return airfare is your guarantee, don't give it to anyone." Recurrent themes in these campaign materials are the notions of dreams and nightmares, controlling men, racial differences, and the idea that the dream is not all that it is cracked up to be.

A CHAME poster that addresses trafficking in a more straightforward way features a close-up of the face of a young brown-skinned woman peeking through the crack in a door. Only one of her eyes and a small part of her nose and mouth are visible. The caption reads, "In this market, promises of jobs become acts of violence," and a large circular stamp on the image reads, "Stop. The Traffic of Women: A Cruel Industry." In many ways, this poster resembles one produced by the Brazilian federal government that Thaddeus G. Blanchette and Ana Paula da Silva analyzed. This poster shows the back of a slim, naked woman with her head buried between her knees and bears the ominous caption, "First they take your passport; next, your freedom," and "If someone offers you a house, food, and clean clothes abroad, don't trust them." Both posters are subtitled, "Don't be the next victim. Don't trust fantastic proposals of a better life abroad" (Blanchette and Silva 2008, 15).

While CHAME respects women's choice to travel, some of the organization's educational materials employ scare tactics that run the risk of limiting the possibilities of mobility for "vulnerable" women. In raising awareness about the dangers of sex tourism and trafficking, CHAME both supports women's right to have transnational aspirations and highlights the risks involved in the means through which many women have access to transnational mobility—that is, through people they meet in the touristscape of Salvador. Bahians' access to transnational connections and mobility is profoundly affected by disparities of race and class. A working-class black Bahian woman, regardless of her level of education, is unlikely to have opportunities to travel abroad unless she obtains them through romantic, friendly, or familial connections with foreigners. Jafari Sinclaire Allen (2007), Denise Brennan (2004), and others have also discussed this phenomenon in the context of Cuba and the Dominican Republic. Young black Brazilian students, activists, hip-hop artists, and dancers were stuck, unable to travel abroad as a consequence of financial constraints, the inability to secure tourist visas, and other reasons. However, they routinely encountered young North American and European students, researchers, and volunteers visiting Bahia.

Moral Panics

CHAME's campaign materials construct an image of Brazilian women of color as naive, vulnerable, innocent victims of unscrupulous foreign men. The images as well as the unparalleled attention that sex tourism and trafficking have garnered are indicative of a moral panic that has emerged regarding questions of interracial sex and sexuality, national image, and transnational tourism and mobility in Brazil (Herdt 2009; Carby 1992; Stanley Cohen 1972). Although the travels and travails of European men are the source of the moral panic, its implications are shifted onto the bodies of women of African descent. In other words, the mobility of Brazilian women of African descent is curtailed in an effort to protect them. As vulnerable subjects and the target of the moral panic, black women and sex workers (neither synonymous nor mutually exclusive) are constructed in a way that calls into question their right to transnational mobility. Thus, the specter of sex tourism has created a situation in which Brazilian women of African descent who desire to move beyond their borders are not only discouraged because of the "risks and dangers" of trafficking but are also automatically suspected of being victims of trafficking, migrant sex workers, or unsuspecting women traveling for some combination of love and self-interest. Again, the discourses of sex tourism profoundly affect how foreign tourists and locals interact with each other as well as what they think about each other's motivations and intentions regarding sex and intimacy. Agustín asserts that discourse "develops . . . a series of conventions, and becomes institutionalised through use. The discourse defines the socially accepted, mainstream or apparently official version, the version that seems obvious or natural" (2007, 8–9). Discourses leave out experiences that do not fit into their hegemonic narratives, thus effectively silencing differences.

According to Stanley Cohen, moral panics occur when "a condition, episode, person or group of persons emerges to become defined as a threat to societal values and interests" (1972, 9). Moral panics create a flurry of mass media activity in which the object of the panic is presented in "stylized and stereotypical fashion" and experts propose solutions and develop coping strategies for the issue (9). Moral panics provoke new techniques for governing the self and others and "produce state and non-state stigma, ostracism, and social exclusion" (Herdt 2009, 3). Hazel Carby's work on black women's migration to northern cities in the early twentieth-century United States helps our understanding of the racialized and gendered dimensions of moral panics as they relate to black women. Carby argues that this migration generated a series of moral panics in which black female migrants were characterized as "sexually degenerate and socially dangerous" (1992, 739). These women were constructed as needing protection and being "at risk" or "vulnerable" to falling into prostitution (741).

This idea resonates with the discourse of Brazilian campaigns against sex tourism and trafficking. Brazilian women of African descent are depicted not only as naive but also as eager to utilize their transnational ties to foreigners in get-rich-quick schemes. The underlying implication might be that without the necessary skills to reach a higher standard of living in Brazil, these women seek risky opportunities abroad. They see transnational romance and marriage or job opportunities as the most efficient strategy for upward mobility. But these dreams of transnational mobility violate the moral and social order in which they are always already depicted as poor, marginalized, and unable to move. Like M. Jacqui Alexander's concept of the "queer fetishized native" (2005, 70) Afro-Brazilian women are discursively stuck in place, never allowed to move or travel. As Allen points out, "Black subjects remain the primordial, fixed object while other groups are traveling, changing their minds and sex partners, and exchanging goods and ideas on the global market" (2009, 91). Ironically, while Afro-Brazilian women have long been situated at the bottom of the country's racial/gender hierarchy, they are overwhelmingly sought out by foreign tourists seeking erotic adventures with exotic Others. Thus, Afro-Brazilian women who travel abroad and have success represent a major disruption of this racial social order.

According to Carby (1992), black women in the early twentieth-century United States who migrated from the South to the North evoked a plethora of fears about uncontrolled black female sexuality and desire as well as miscegenation. These fears resulted in an increase in supervision and policing of black women's sexuality. Similarly, in contemporary Bahia, black women's mobility and sexuality evoke innumerable fears and raise questions about the gendered aspects of travel. In her work on Northern European female sex tourists in Gambia, Paulla Ebron highlights how women travelers are generally portrayed as morally distasteful and sexually promiscuous, while men's travels are seen as "stories of masculine agency" (1997, 225). As Agustín has pointed out, why should the travels of people from less wealthy countries be understood as fundamentally different from those of Europeans? (2007, 11). While many observers seem to think that the term *cosmopolitan* should be reserved for "elite, urbane globetrotters," Agustín contends that there is no reason poorer travelers should be disqualified from cosmopolitanism (44).

CHAME's educational materials utilize stock images that depict black Brazilian women as naive, ignorant, and willing to do anything to migrate to Europe. Conversely, European men are cast as evil and sinister perpetrators who always have ulterior motives in their interactions with Brazilian women. CHAME's cartoons seem to use a representational strategy that unwittingly reproduces stereotypes of both Brazilian women of African descent and European men. Furthermore, CHAME's materials reflect the limits of mobility of people deemed vulnerable, particularly low-income Brazilian women of African descent. In this sense, then, the repertoire of images contained in the CHAME educational materials can be read as an "archive of racialized sexuality" (Reddy 2005, 114–15) that reflects society's perspectives about black Brazilian women, foreign (European) men, and the possibilities of sex, intimacy, migration, love, marriage, and exploitation. Rather than being understood as a passive domain, the archive is actually an "active technique by which sexual, racial, gendered, and national differences . . . are suppressed, frozen, and redirected as the occasion for universal knowledge" (115).

Why did CHAME consistently use the comic strip or cartoon as a representational strategy to create images that would resonate with the public? According to Jacqueline Leite, the organization's leaders did not want to use photos that "could link anyone directly to crime or criminal connotation." Moreover, she and other CHAME officials thought that cartoons would appeal to youth, who understand things in a more thematic way, and would avoid making a direct connection to any one community in Salvador, unlike photographs, which make a direct link to a person. In her view, "the cartoon is more impersonal."[9]

The sensationalist images used in CHAME's educational materials contradict Leite's critique of government campaigns against sex tourism not only as being xenophobic but also as creating a hysteria regarding sex tourism. Leite views the government's campaigns as focusing "a lot on the foreign tourist and very little on the question of patriarchy and machismo. It's a young person's choice whether they want to have a foreign boyfriend or not." Furthermore, she asserts that sexual tourism is "very sensationalized. Any foreigner in Salvador is seen as if he were a sex tourist. The line between who is a sex tourist and who is not is very tenuous." Through the services of skilled cartoonists, CHAME controls the form of the story that is told. In a sense then, the organization is molding the "ideal" narrative of the dangers of sex tourism and trafficking in Brazil. The comic strips and testimonies in CHAME's educational materials rely almost exclusively on the use of terrifying life narratives of trafficked persons. As Donna Hughes points out, "Victims of trafficking remain one-dimensional figures whose terrifying stories are condensed and simplified for media reporting" (2002, 33).

Moralizing Discourses

The limitations of the CHAME campaign materials reveal the importance of distinguishing between sex tourism and trafficking. Fabiana differentiated the two concepts when she said, "Sex tourism is valid. There are many foreigners who come here to work, so why can't the prostitute also travel to work? Sex tourism will never end. I'm against the trafficking of women—it's completely different." Adriana Piscitelli's (2008) work on sex tourism in Fortaleza and the sex and marriage industry involving Brazilian women in Italy and Spain highlights the problems of confusing these concepts. She found that because the Brazilian migrant sex workers are terrified of the Spanish police, their illegal status can encourage migrant sex workers to say they were trafficked to avoid prosecution. Similarly, Brazilian sex worker activist Gabriela Leite (2005) claimed that women who travel with their own money are seen as "victims of trafficking": "If a prostitute is caught in Europe, of course they're going to say they were trafficked!" Strategically claiming to be a victim of trafficking may have become a tool that migrant sex workers use to escape punishment.

The fact that the CHAME materials depict Brazilian women as naive and as falling in love (or feeling self-interested lust) rather than as sex workers reproduces the notion prevalent in global antitrafficking discourses that the appropriate victims of trafficking must be "innocent." Women must have been tricked or lured—they cannot have consented to travel with the knowledge of the kind of labor in which they would engage or the conditions they would face. The juxtaposition between deceived subjects and those who knowingly consent is central to these moralizing discourses. Women who are deceived into engaging in sex work can be pardoned, forgiven, excused, and even rescued despite their involvement in "deviant" sexual practices; women who knowingly consent are beyond forgiveness for their transgressions. As Barbara Limanowska and Ann Rosga point out in their analysis of antitrafficking strategies in the Balkans, "The 'ideal type' of trafficking victim" is one who has been kidnapped or deceived. Any suggestion that she 'suspected her fate' might lead law enforcement officers to believe that she was partly culpable (2004, 166).

Consent figures into antitrafficking discourses in very complicated and problematic ways. In the UN Trafficking Protocol, consent emerged as a central element in the definition of trafficking (Doezema 2002).[10] In many countries, admitting consent effectively excludes one from protections under the law as a victim of trafficking. However, as Agustín notes, knowing the type of labor in which one will engage abroad is a poor measure of exploitation and unhappiness, since no one can anticipate their future working conditions (2007, 30). As an analytical point of departure, a focus on moralizing discourses can illuminate how notions of agency, consent, coercion, and morality are marshaled to demarcate what kinds of subjects can be considered victims of trafficking. International human rights regimes require a clearly defined victim to rescue (Altink 1995, 2). The idea that some women are worthy of support, assistance, rescue, and human rights while others are not indicates the need for an analysis of moralizing discourses that attends to the ways in which international human rights regimes and their affiliated NGOs have created an idealized victim of human trafficking.

The figure of the innocent trafficking victim that is central to the moralizing discourses of international human rights regimes can be analyzed in light of Gayatri Chakravorty Spivak's notion of the "new subaltern," the "monolithic woman-as-victim who is the constituted subject of justice under (the now-unrestricted) international capitalism" (2000, 306). Following Spivak's analysis, the subaltern trafficking victim is not portrayed in terms of her agency, strategies, or actions, but rather, she is essentialized as the suffering object of the cruel actions of others. Trafficking victims as subjects of state intervention are constituted by excluding immoral Others who knowingly consent to migrate for sex work. Alexander points out that certain types of consent are more legitimate and authoritative than others and that adulthood sometimes serves as a "proxy for consent" (1991, 141). The crucial factor in regulating consent, Alexander argues, is morality, which can either "dispense or revoke" consent (142).

The (presumably) unintended consequences of repressive antitrafficking strategies include restricting or preventing the migration of women and increasing the surveillance and deportation of migrant sex workers (Agustín 2007; Doezema 2002). These restrictions include tightened visa policies, increased border control, closer supervision of mixed marriages, and the criminalization of migrants and third parties who facilitate illegal entry or stay. Once again, when the twin concepts of consent and morality cannot guarantee their status as innocent, unknowing victims, sex workers do not qualify as subjects of rights under international human rights regimes. These unintended consequences of campaigns against sex tourism and trafficking reflect Agustín's argument that in positioning themselves as "benevolent help-ers," NGO advocates, journalists, government officials, and others involved in the "rescue industry" "consistently deny the agency of large numbers of working-class migrants" (2007, 8).

Conclusion

The specter of vulnerability creates a moral panic in which already margin-alized people are stigmatized even further. In their analysis of the Brazilian government's efforts to combat trafficking, Blanchette and da Silva contend that the government focuses almost exclusively on preventing international travel by people deemed vulnerable to trafficking. Vulnerability in this context is clearly linked to poor, marginalized people of color (2008, 14).[11]

Campaigns carried out by the Brazilian state and NGOs construct sex tourism as a problem to be eradicated by conflating sex tourism with traffick-ing and the sexual exploitation of children and adolescents. The moralizing discourses of antitrafficking NGOs have produced trafficking as an object of knowledge. With Agustín's insightful critique in mind, perhaps CHAME can be seen as an organization of "social helpers" and an integral part of the Brazilian "rescue industry." Even while espousing the rights of women to travel, the CHAME campaign materials unwittingly perpetuate the moral panic that situates the potential risk of trafficking as the ultimate represen-tation of the fantasy of transnational mobility for working-class Brazilian women of African descent.

Conclusion

The Specter of Sex Tourism in a Globalized World

I met Sueli, a nineteen-year-old *morena*, in the summer of 2005 through Nathan, her fifty-year-old American expatriate boyfriend.[1] At the time of our interview, she had been dating Nathan for six months. Born and raised in a poor neighborhood on the outskirts of Salvador, Sueli had recently moved into Nathan's apartment in the beachfront neighborhood of Barra. She met Nathan while working there at a pizzeria, where she had also met men from France, Norway, Germany, and other countries. Sueli bragged about her exposure to and experiences with people of different cultures, saying that she preferred foreigners because "they treat you better, respect you more, and give you more attention and affection." Sueli noticed that people often seemed bothered when they saw her and Nathan walking in the streets: "It messes with them. They say, 'Oh, what a pretty girl.' They don't respect [our relationship]. Brazilians and Italians especially feel jealous."

Despite her youth, Sueli said that she had "already suffered too much" in relationships with Brazilian men. In fact, she had a two-year-old by a Brazilian man whom she described as extremely jealous and controlling. While she said she did not "see disadvantages to dating foreigners," she quickly added that she "wouldn't leave the country with another person." Her caution suggests that the efforts of the Humanitarian Center for the Support of Women (CHAME) to spread awareness about the risks of trafficking may be reaching the group's intended audience. Sueli differentiated not only between Brazilian and foreign men but also between younger and older men: "I've already dated younger men. I sought an older man because they know how to converse with you, they won't say things that hurt your feelings, and they want you to always make progress. Younger men, they're jealous, they fight. I've already been through this." The often large age disparities between foreign tourists and local women can be understood within the local cultural practice of dating older men, known colloquially as *coroas* (Piscitelli 2001). Suelí also preferred to date foreigners because she felt that Brazilian men were "only interested in sex," a viewpoint that complicates the assumption that foreign men come to Brazil in search of sex. Thus, she saw older foreign men as more trustworthy, more generous, and better potential partners for a serious romantic relationship, whereas local men were controlling, unfaithful, and only interested in sex.

Suelí's cynicism about Brazilian men is a common feature of the sexual economies of tourism, where foreign men are privileged over local men. The major quality that attracted Simone, a twenty-nine-year-old Afro-Brazilian woman, to European men was *a gentileza* (niceness), which she found lacking in Brazilian men: "The European man is such a gentleman!" Though she had had two six-year relationships with Brazilian men prior to meeting her German boyfriend Günther, Simone said that neither had been as kind, romantic, and attentive: "If we spend a week together, it's like we've spent years together," she exclaimed. Günther sent her money to take German classes and called every day to speak with her. The work of Adriana Piscitelli (2006) and Jessica Gregg (2006) in other northeastern Brazilian cities finds similar preferences for European men. In Fortaleza, Ceará, Brazilian women who preferred to date foreigners as well as the European men themselves associated Brazilian masculinity with explosive tempers, alcoholism, stupidity, infidelity, aggression, possessiveness, lack of respect, and exacerbated sexuality. Conversely, European masculinity was interpreted as romantic, delicate, open, and invested in equality (Piscitelli 2006).[2] Similarly, women residents of a favela in Recife saw local men as aggressive, irresponsible, lazy, and malicious (Gregg 2006). These women did not believe in romantic love. Rather, they felt all men were *safado* (shameless) and would inevitably mistreat any woman who was good to them. Moreover, Gregg's informants were convinced that men took pleasure in ruining women's lives. The "bleak state of gender relations and . . . the economic system" made marriage an undesirable option for many women in impoverished northeastern Brazil (158). Conversely, pursuing *liberdade* (freedom) was seen as a way to be independent and to protest the gender system. Those who sought out ambiguous entanglements in the touristscape of Salvador may be seen as attempting to pursue independence, *liberdade*, upward mobility, and cosmopolitanism. Thus, Suelí and the sex workers of Aprosba can be seen as pursuing *liberdade*.

The sex workers' stories in this book attest to the fact that the process of globalization is woefully uneven. Although it has in some ways worked to women's advantage, globalization can also "unleash forces of inequality that will further disadvantage women" (Ferree and Tripp 2006, 22). This game has both winners and losers: some people have access to travel, mobility, communication, and commodities from all over the world, while others have little or no access to these things. As Manisha Desai points out, even the progressive field of transnational feminisms has mostly drawn on "the expertise of educated, privileged women from the global North and the South" who can raise money for travel (2007, 800). However, these categories of winners and losers are not fixed or static, in part as a consequence of the agency of people who imagine different possibilities for their lives as they navigate the impact of globalizing processes (Appadurai 2001).

One of the key features of the sexual and cultural economies of tourism in Salvador is that marginalized, low-income Bahian women and men are taking matters into their own hands to ensure that the trickle-down promises of the transnational tourism industry are fulfilled. As Malik, an African American expatriate in Salvador, stated, "Most Brazilian women know that foreign men want to have sex with them. Most Bahians don't have a lot of opportunities for upward mobility. They use the resources that they have. This is the reality of the imbalance of this country." This book contributes to the anthropology of globalization by considering how people on the ground are negotiating global inequalities in their sexual practices and intimate lives. As Tom Boellstorff (2007) points out, questions of globalization have moved to the forefront of anthropological research on sexuality. While top-down globalization in the form of the tourism industry still promises to spread the wealth to reach more Brazilian citizens, Bahian sex workers, tour guides, tourism industry workers, and cultural producers are enacting what Boaventura de Sousa Santos calls "insurgent cosmopolitanism" in the form of "counter-hegemonic solidarity, bottom-up globalization" (2006, 398).

Desires for cosmopolitanism weave throughout the various stories and experiences of Bahian women and men in this book. For sex workers who did *programas* with foreigners but were open to *namoros*, cosmopolitanism meant access to spaces within the touristscape from which they were usually excluded. Similarly, for the *caçadores* who used their Afro-Brazilian cultural expertise to initiate transnational connections with foreigners, cosmopolitanism meant the opportunity to expand transnational networks of friends and acquaintances and to increase the likelihood of traveling abroad. Thus, while cosmopolitanism is often used to describe "elite, urbane globetrotters" (Agustín 2007, 44), the notion of insurgent cosmopolitanism helps us to think about different forms of organized resistance between various social movements and organizations. According to Santos, insurgent cosmopolitanism "refers to the aspiration by oppressed groups to organize their resistance on the same scale and through the same type of coalitions used by the oppressors to victimize them, that is, the global scale and local/global coalitions" (2006, 398). Aprosba can be seen as an example of insurgent cosmopolitanism, particularly because it is deeply embedded in regional, national, and international sex workers' rights organizations.

Perhaps the idea, put forth in campaigns by the government and by nongovernmental organizations (NGOs), journalists, and abolitionist feminists, that sex tourism is a "problem" is ill conceived. While many of these sources focus on sex tourism as the problem of white Western elite men exploiting poor, marginalized, Third World women, sex workers in Salvador saw opportunities for cosmopolitanism, advancement, romance, intimacy, and potential transnational mobility through their ambiguous entanglements with foreigners. From the perspective of these women, their most significant problems were violence from (usually local) clients and police officers and the stigma that being a sex worker carries in the local communities. Some women feel valued and cared for, care for others, and experience the possibilities of intimacy and cosmopolitanism even in the context of transnational encounters rooted in global hierarchies and inequalities. Many of the sex workers I interviewed saw their work as a tool for accessing forms of mobility that are often foreclosed to low-income women. They used this tool to attempt to bring their dreams of mobility and cosmopolitanism to life.

How can feminist scholars make our work matter, especially when the stories of our research participants often contradict the victimizing narratives on which feminist activists rely to inspire their activism and rescue efforts (Agustín 2007)? When I teach my undergraduate Sexual Economies course, students invariably fall into victimizing, rescue narratives despite my efforts to assign work that emphasizes agency, autonomy, and sex workers' rights. In a sense, then, they are embracing a variant of global feminism that, as Inderpal Grewal and Caren Kaplan point out, has "elided the diversity of women's agency in favor of a universalized Western model of women's liberation that celebrates individuality and modernity" (1994, 17). What about the black Bahian sex workers I interviewed who preferred sex work over domestic work? What of the sex workers who saw their ambiguous entanglements with foreign tourists as an advantage over *programas* with local clients who often sexually or physically assaulted them or failed to pay?

I have learned that it is necessary to take seriously the voices and perspectives of sex workers rather than assuming that we speak for them and know what is best for them. This book presents a different viewpoint from how sex tourism is usually discussed—that is, in terms of victims and oppressors—by illuminating the complex emotions and desires involved in people's choices of who to have sex with, date, and love in the sexual economies of tourism in Salvador. As scholars such as Paulla Ebron, Jafari Sinclaire Allen, Amalia Cabezas, and Kamala Kempadoo have shown, it is useful to think of agency in an expansive way, especially when it concerns the daily negotiations that black Bahian women and men are making in the touristscape of Salvador. Allen distinguishes between two interrelated modes of agency, "improvised quotidian action to make one's life easier to manage" and "organized and intentional resistance" (2011, 84). Jorginho, the Afro-Brazilian dance teacher, was also clear about his agency in dating foreign women: "If I want to date or have a relationship with a *gringa*, I'm going to because I'm attracted to her, because I have feelings for her, not because I want to get something from her." He had had some "good experiences" with foreigners who did not see him "in the stereotypical way as a *negão*."

Racialized Sexualities and Transnational Feminisms

As Brazilian feminist scholar Sonia Correia stated at the 2012 Latin American Studies Association meetings in San Francisco, "It is impossible to talk about inequality connected to sexuality without being very clear about intersectionality." Drawing inspiration from M. Jacqui Alexander and Chandra Talpade Mohanty's definition of the transnational as "a way of thinking about women in similar contexts across the world, in different geographical spaces, rather than as all women across the world" (2010, 24), this book highlights the local particularities of a transnational phenomenon. More specifically, the local particularities of this touristscape involve the connections between sex tourism and cultural tourism. In Brazil's Black Mecca, the eroticization and marketing of blackness and black cultural production as a tourist commodity are inextricably linked.

The racialized and gendered effects of tourism in Salvador can also be seen in a video advertisement for a hotel near Praia do Flamengo. The video, found in the Bahiatursa archives, opens with the sound of loud, powerful drums and the image of a black man cleaning the windows. We see a beautiful, idyllic resort with a pristine pool and a *baiana* putting on a necklace and serving a drink to a group of blond tourists. Scenes flash of souvenir shops and well-appointed rooms. All of the tourists are white; all of the workers are black. Young white couples walk and sun themselves on the beach, drink coconut water, surf, and eat *moqueca de peixe*. A black waiter serves drinks; three black musicians play at the hotel. As Natasha Pravaz points out, the discourse of *mestiçagem* that was so central to the Brazilian nation's story about itself relied on "Afro-Brazilian traditions as its icons" (2008b, 98). Salvador's municipal government passed an ordinance that required *baianas de acarajé* to wear typical outfits so that they would uphold the "tradition" and "authenticity" of being a *baiana*. Thus, even "tradition" is strategically produced, performed, and maintained by the state in the interests of tourism. Rather than being natural, "authenticity" is produced, performed, legislated, and disciplined.

Centering a critical analysis of racialized sexualities in the study of the sexual economies of tourism in Salvador allows us to see how notions of blackness, eroticism, and Negrophilia converge with desires for the social mobility and privileges of whiteness and cosmopolitanism in a globalized world. But how does one study racialized sexualities in the context of glo-balization (Allen 2009)? Grewal and Kaplan emphasize the importance of bringing "questions of transnationalism into conversation with the feminist study of sexuality" (2001, 666). I embrace this perspective, exploring the desires, motivations, and practices of Bahians and foreign tourists as they enact their ambiguous entanglements with one another in Salvador's tourist-scape. My work also contributes to articulating comparative racial histories of sexuality in the United States and Brazil by pointing out the similar ways in which black women in both areas of the African diaspora historically have struggled to have their bodies belong to them (Gilmore 2010).

As Beverly Guy-Sheftall notes, "Being black and female is characterized by the private being made public. . . . [T]here is nothing sacred about black women's bodies. [They are] not off-limits, untouchable, or unseeable" (2002, 18). African American women have historically responded to negative im-ages of black sexuality with the "politics of respectability" and "culture of dissemblance" (Hine 1989), distancing themselves from all discussions and expressions of sexuality to prove that they were indeed "respectable" and could assimilate into dominant Euro-American sexual and familial norms (Hammonds 1997; Miller-Young 2008). In the context of white supremacy, this strategy sought to defend black womanhood from all manner of assaults, including portrayal as whores and prostitutes. Bodily integrity was central to the project of black women recuperating their dignity.

However, Mireille Miller-Young raises an important question: "What can we learn from black sex workers' utilization of hypersexuality and self-com-modification as they live and labor within advanced capitalism?" (2010, 221). Within the framework of the politics of respectability, no sexual subjectivity exists outside of domestic, heteronormative, and bourgeois family relations. Furthermore, the culture of dissemblance is a way of disavowing sexuality in black women's lives in an effort to protect them from sexual injury. Miller-

Young ultimately argues that although black women in the pornography industry are "victimized by multiple axes of discrimination and harm," they also "employ an outlaw sexuality to achieve mobility, erotic autonomy, and self-care" (231). This observation is useful for my analysis of black Bahian sex workers, who use the racialized stereotype of them as more *quente* (hot) than European women to their advantage in pursuing ambiguous entanglements with foreign men. Furthermore, as Kempadoo notes, "a transnational feminism that relinquishes colonizing narratives about prostitution and the global sex trade, draws from women of color's experiences and perspectives in sex work, and builds global alliances, could be a useful theory and practice for many women around the world" (2001b, 46).

The Role of the State and the Global Economy

This book demonstrates the Brazilian state's contradictory roles in the sexual economies of tourism. It both produces postcards with the eroticized bodies of Afro-Brazilian women and mounts campaigns to combat (child) sex tourism and human trafficking. How do we make anthropological sense of the Brazilian state's involvement in the tourism industry and sex tourism more specifically? Sex work is not only central to the tourism industry but also materially benefits the Brazilian state. Anthropological approaches focus on how people's understandings of the state "are shaped by their particular locations and intimate and embodied counters with state processes and officials, and how the state manifests itself in their lives" (Sharma and Gupta 2010, 11). In the words of Vrushali Patil, a transnational feminist perspective understands that the state "engages in the (re)production of multiple centers and peripheries . . . each of which invokes particular logics of racialization and sexualization" (2011, 204).

As Kempadoo notes, the global panic about human trafficking incites governments to "clamp down on the sex trade and to intensify border controls, while deepening racialised sexualized divides" (2007, 80). In the United States, this moral panic has led the Christian Right and radical feminists to join forces with the U.S. State Department to combat global trafficking (82). In Brazil, the state has long taken a position of what Correia (2012) calls "ambivalent state neutrality" with respect to prostitution. While the Brazilian state was never fully persuaded by the abolitionist perspective, it also has never adopted a state model of regularization as is the case in the Netherlands and New Zealand (Goodyear and Weitzer 2011). Correia emphasizes that this "ambivalent neutrality" left space open for conflicts, which often took the form of localized battles on the ground in the states that make up the vast nation of Brazil. In 2005, Brazil was one of the few countries that refused to conform to the Bush administration's "prostitution oath" in exchange for U.S. Agency for International Development money (Mitchell 2011a).[3] Furthermore, the Brazilian Ministry of Health and Culture has been a consistent partner with and funder of Aprosba's peer health education efforts.

James Clifford and George Marcus remind us that all ethnographies are merely "partial truths" (1986, 7). This volume merely captures a cross-section of what I witnessed and what people told me at a particular time and place. This time has passed, and the place is always shifting, with tourists coming and going, sex workers migrating from the *interior* (countryside) or other states in the northeastern region, and NGO and governmental campaigns. The implications of the specter of sex tourism in Salvador will remain far-reaching for years to come, particularly as Brazil crystallizes its role as a global economic power.

It remains to be seen how the ever-changing global economic situation will affect the sexual economies of tourism in Salvador and Brazil as a whole. Such changes are particularly important in light of Brazil's prominence, not only in terms of its increasing power on the global stage but also as the host of the 2014 Soccer World Cup and the 2016 Summer Olympics. The global economic crisis has shifted the balance of power: a March 2011 article from the *Guardian* ran under the headline, "Brazil Considers Helping Portugal Ease Debt Crisis" (Wearden 2011). The irony of a former colony offering its erstwhile overlords a financial lifeline is glaring. According to the International Monetary Fund, "The Brazilian economy is now almost 10 times larger than that of Portugal" (Wearden 2011). The phenomena that I have documented may not persist into the future. For example, working-class Italians and other European tourists may have more difficulty "living like kings" while on vacation in Bahia.

The global economic situation has also influenced Brazil's tourism industry. The number of domestic tourists has recently grown to unprecedented levels. According to Vincent Bevins (2012), Brazil's tourism sector is becoming one "of the world's least international," with 95 percent of tourism revenue coming from domestic tourists by 2011. David Scowscill, chief executive officer of the World Travel and Tourism Council, explains this shift by pointing out that Brazil and other emerging countries have a higher rate of domestic tourists because members of the new middle classes are starting to travel within their own countries (Bevins 2012). Similarly, Brazil's *2007–2010 National Tourism Plan* states that while foreign tourist arrivals are important for bringing in foreign exchange, domestic tourism is crucial for providing "the dynamism needed to put Brazilian tourism on the international market" (Brazil 2007, 22).[4]

Implications and Future Research

Nothing is clear-cut or simple in the sexual economies of tourism. There are no quick fixes or easy solutions, no clearly defined victims or villains. Rather, there are ambiguous entanglements that push and pull people with various desires, motivations, hopes, and dreams. Moving forward, researchers of sex tourism in various parts of the world might productively consider recommendations for public policy and transnational feminist activism. As Susan Dewey and Patty Kelly state, "Ethnography's greatest potential contribution to public policy lies in its ability to represent the everyday realities of life for individuals who often constitute a population invisible to policy makers" (2011, 13).

While ambiguity is an important analytical tool for understanding what is taking place in this context, it has a downside. The distinction between the *programa* and the *namoro* is not just a matter of semantics but has significant public health implications. The possibility of developing intimacy in ambiguous encounters with tourists was seen as dangerous—even deadly—because it could lead women to be taken advantage of and to have unprotected sex. As activist Gabriela Leite pointed out, "Amor é a fatalidade de mulher" (Love is the death of women). Even sex workers who are highly politicized about safer sex practices and who consistently use condoms with their clients may overlook those rules when love, intimacy, and emotions come into play (Kempadoo 2001a; Chacham et al. 2007).

Similarly, Jacobo Schifter-Sikora's work on sex tourism and HIV risk in Costa Rica highlights the fact that "if sex tourism would only be about sex, and would not have the love component, there would be fewer dangers to contracting HIV" (2007, 163). As Fabiana pointed out, when foreign tourists seek out an ambiguous encounter rather than a straightforward commercial transaction with a Brazilian woman, they may "seek out a student and think that she's not a prostitute. This is bad because these girls from the working-class neighborhoods don't know anything about prevention. And it's bad for prostitutes because they lose money."

Future researchers could focus more on heterosexual female (Frohlick 2009; Jacobs 2010) and gay and lesbian sex tourism (Mitchell 2011a, b). The question of the impact of social media on these transnational sexual-affective exchanges will also bear investigation, as will the transformations experienced by the sexual economies of tourism in the aftermath of the World Cup and Summer Olympics in Brazil. While an adolescent, Arturo, a gay black Bahian man, met a Dutch tourist at the headquarters of a prominent LGBT organization in Salvador. What started out as flirtation quickly progressed to *amizade* (friendship). When the tourist took him out for a fancy dinner,

Arturo "felt like this was a way to buy me, so I let him think that he was manipulating me. At the restaurant table I asked him for money." Arturo's family had kicked him out because of his sexual orientation, and although he owned a parcel of land in a working-class neighborhood in Cidade Baixa, he lacked the money to purchase construction materials and build a house. Arturo decided to have sex with the Dutch tourist and subsequently asked for money. "At that moment," he reflected, "I was a sex worker." Sex work can be a onetime opportunity, a sporadic or chance encounter, just as much as a full-time occupation or an identity category. Furthermore, Arturo exercised his agency to help improve his difficult living situation. So many stories need to be explored and voices must be heard before we can understand the impact that globalization and transnational processes are having on the lives of people all over the world, as well as how people are responding to these changes.

Notes

Introduction

1. All informants' names and names of businesses are pseudonyms.

2. As of March 2013, one U.S. dollar was equal to about two Brazilian reais.

3. Adriana Piscitelli describes the term *programa* as the explicit exchange of sexual services for money, usually involving specific practices and periods of time (2011, 547).

4. See the Web site of former member of the Brazilian Congress Fernando Gabeira, author of a 2003 bill to legalize prostitution (www.gabeira.com.br) and the Web site of the Brazilian Network of Prostitutes (www.redeprostitutas.org.br).

5. National Penal Code, articles 227–30.

6. Aprosba meeting, December 5, 2006. Marisa identified herself as an "ex-prostitute," a classification that was controversial among some of the other women in Aprosba, who thought it signified that she thought she was better than those who still were prostitutes. Fabiana quipped, "No one says they're an ex-lawyer" (interview, May 15, 2007).

7. Pérola, for example, dropped out of sight and was rumored to have murdered a Bahian police officer who regularly physically and sexually abused prostitutes.

8. I learned that a woman's bikini bottom was enough to identify her as Brazilian or a *gringa*.

Chapter 1. Geographies of Blackness

1. Similarly, Gregory Mitchell (2011b) describes Beto, a Bahian *michê* (a man who has commercial sex with men but who usually does not identify as gay) who sold souvenirs on the beach as a pretense for making contact with the gay foreign tourists who would become his clients.

2. Keith also contrasted male "hustling" with female "prostitution": "It's more ambiguous with Brazilian men, but with the women it's pretty obvious. I can spot a prostitute by how she walks, dresses, how she looks at me. Prostitution is no big deal here—it's a way of life."

3. Although prices vary in brothels, it is customary for sex workers to charge clients fifty reais, of which fifteen reais goes to the house. The owner of the brothel charges a departure fee of forty-five reais if a client wants to take a woman outside the brothel.

4. The Steve Biko Cultural Institute is a nongovernmental organization founded by black movement activists in 1992 to increase college enrollment among underprivileged Afro-Brazilians and to promote public policies to reduce racial inequality.

5. It is beyond the scope of this work to delve into the intricacies of black Brazilian feminist scholarship, though I have done so in a forthcoming essay that will be published in "Transatlantic Feminisms: Women and Gender in Africa and the African Diaspora," edited by Akosua Adomako Ampofo, Cheryl R. Rodriguez, and Dzodzi Tsikata. For more information on black Brazilian feminisms, see Caldwell 2000, 2010; Carneiro 2003; Carneiro and Santos 1985; Gonzalez 1980, 1982, 1988; Perry 2009; Sonia Beatriz dos Santos 2007; Viana 2010; Werneck 2010.

6. They would charge R$50 for "short-time" and R$150 to spend the night, though they could often demand more money from foreign men.

7. Furthermore, Salvador's municipal government passed a tax to support tourism efforts in 1951, a council of tourism was created in 1953, and tourism was a part of Governor Juracy Magalhães's economic development plan in the 1960s (Romo 2010, 152).

8. In July 1992, Embratur launched the National Plan for Tourism (Plantur), which sought to promote regional development by focusing on destinations outside of the South and Southeast. The Prodetur project budget was US$1,670,000, of which approximately US$800,000 came from the Inter-American Development Bank (Tamar Diana Wilson 2008).

9. Prodetur II is the second phase. It had US$400 million earmarked for investments, of which US$240 million came from Inter-American Development Bank loans and US$160 million came from federal matching funds, complemented by state funds (Brazil 2007, 30).

10. The *2007–2010 National Tourism Plan* set a goal of "217 million trips to domestic destinations," which would generate 1.7 million jobs and bring in US$7.7 billion in foreign exchange. The *National Tourism Plan* focuses on inclusion "to reduce regional inequalities." The plan generally seeks to "develop high-quality Brazilian tourist products" that consider the country's regional, cultural, and natural diversity; to "promote tourism along with social inclusion, by generating jobs and income and by making it a consumption item for all Brazilians"; and to "foster the competitiveness of Brazilian tourist products on national and international markets, and attract foreign exchange to the country" (Brazil 2007, 16).

11. The number of international arrivals to Brazil grew from 2 million in 1995 to 4.1 million in 2003, 4.8 million in 2004, 5.4 million in 2005, and 5 million in 2006 (Brazil 2007, table 3).

12. These terms also signify the prevalence of enslaved Africans who were Muslim. The term *Black Mecca* was promoted by black militants from other parts of Brazil who saw Bahia as the principal source of African culture in the country (Patricia de Santana Pinho 2004). In the early twentieth century, Bahia was also referred to as the Mulata Velha (Old Mulatta), which Anadelia Romo says reflected a "national conception of Bahia as overwhelmingly nonwhite and . . . as aging and tradition-bound" (2010, 5).

13. Marcelo complained that obtaining a license would cost him R$150/month to take a tour guide course. Not only is that amount exorbitant, but the time spent taking the

course would subtract from his work time. He worked as a taxi driver until he met three African American professors who sparked his interest in working as a tour guide.

14. Afro-Brazilian cultural practices were also suppressed in other parts of Brazil. For example, in 1796, the military commander of Goiânia suppressed *batuques* (African drumming), and Rio de Janeiro banned drumming and arrested enslaved Africans for dancing to drums (Fryer 2000).

15. This division was created by Bahia governor Jacques Wagner (Workers' Party) in 2007 to focus government efforts on this popular aspect of the tourism economy.

16. Even after Vargas was deposed in 1945, the "nationalistic intent of his cultural policies continued under subsequent presidencies," including the military dictatorship from 1964 to 1985 (Pravaz 2008a, 89).

17. Stephen Selka (2007, 74) also points out that this form of commercialization is controversial in the Candomblé community.

18. Furthermore, Cheryl Sterling argues that in Candomblé, "spiritual power becomes tangible, accessible, and concretely located in the body of the *filha de santo* [daughter of the saint]. No longer is she the denigrated object of the society's gaze, or simply the object of sexual desire, but the revered and esteemed subject who bears messages of divine organization" (2010, 83).

19. In a bold move that demonstrated a sense of ownership over the field of Afro-Brazilian studies, Freyre was openly hostile attitude toward the Salvador congress and was condescending in depicting Candomblé and capoeira as picturesque "local color" (Romo 2010, 67).

20. The tour group was organized by Dr. Rachel Harding, a scholar, *filha de santo* of that *terreiro*, and author of *A Refuge in Thunder: Candomblé and Alternative Spaces of Blackness* (2000).

Chapter 2. Racial Hierarchies of Desire and the Specter of Sex Tourism

1. The Bahiatursa archives also contained a brochure with the same title as the video and using the same *mulata* to represent Gabriela.

2. *Scopophilic* means the "love of looking," or deriving erotic pleasure from gazing upon an object of desire.

3. www.liveauctioneers.com/item/586416.

4. For a historical overview of the Globeleza commercials, see "História" 2009.

5. Valenssa said that she derived great pleasure and satisfaction from dancing before large adoring crowds: "When I see people looking at me, the sound of the *bateria*, the music, the fireworks, this really touches me deep inside, no matter how tired you are, it's impossible to stand still, to think about your tiredness, you forget yourself" (Pravaz 2008b, 107). Valenssa converted to Evangelical Christianity in 2004 after she had two children and Globo fired her (Cavallera 2011).

6. See, for example, Morgan 1997, which discusses how African women were seen as beasts and monsters with long breasts. Early European travelers in Africa saw African women simultaneously as subjects of repulsion and desire.

7. Furthermore, Pravaz interviewed young women in Rio de Janeiro who perform samba at Carnaval events and who refer to themselves as *mulatas* in their work environments but identify as black "outside the sphere of staged samba" (2008a, 97).

8. In 2012, Brazilian singer Tiririca lost a lawsuit involving his song "Veja os Cabelos Dela," which describes a black woman's hair as a scouring pad for pots and pans and complains about her "stench" (Julee Wilson 2012).

9. For a comprehensive review of scholarship advocating and contesting racial democracy, see Reiter and Mitchell 2010.

10. Edward Telles (2004) rejects the binary opposition between racial mixing and exclusion or racism.

11. Antonio Sergio Alfredo Guimarães (2005, 119–34) points out that while the expression *racial democracy* has always been attributed to Freyre, it is not found in his most important works and does not appear in the literature until it was used by Arthur Ramos in 1941.

12. Societal acceptance of Candomblé is contentious, however, as a consequence of the widespread discrimination and religious intolerance of the Evangelical movement that is sweeping Brazil and Latin America as a whole.

13. A *travesti* is someone who was born biologically male but whose gender expression and performance are as female. They can be considered under the umbrella term *transgendered*; however, they are usually not transsexuals. They may engage in bodily practices to appear more feminine—breast implants, silicone injections to create feminine curves, wearing women's clothes and makeup. However, this gender performance and expression is often not accompanied by a desire to have surgery to remove the penis. See Kulick 1998.

14. *Cis-gender* is the term used in queer theory and gender studies to describe people whose gender identity matches their bodies and the gender they were assigned at birth (Schilt and Westbrook 2009).

15. The politics of respectability emerged in the United States in the nineteenth century as a way to challenge black women's ubiquitous portrayal as whores and prostitutes.

Chapter 3. Working-Class Kings in Paradise

1. Other popular destinations include Amsterdam, Argentina, Cape Town, the Caribbean, Costa Rica, and Mexico, among others (Howard L. Hughes 2006).

2. The survey was conducted in ten languages and in eighteen countries. The other nine most popular destinations for gay travel were (in order): the United States, France, Spain, England, Italy, Germany, Australia, Canada, and Argentina ("World's Gayest" 2011).

3. GLS, the common Brazilian acronym for queer communities, stands for *gay, lésbica, simpatizante* (ally).

4. Here, I am building on studies of tourism that emphasize the importance of paying attention to local workers in the tourist economies (Gmelch 2003; Ness 2003). For example, Ness (2003) uses the term *tourate* to describe the population of tourism service providers and locals, and Gmelch (2003) focuses on the working lives of tourism industry professionals as a corrective to the ways in which tourism literature fails to sufficiently portray the "local voice" in the Caribbean.

5. Founded in 1947, the Serviço Nacional de Aprendizagem Comercial is a professional education institution that works to prepare people for the job market, particularly in the areas of commerce, services, and tourism.

6. For recent books exploring sex tourism and women's romance tourism in Kenya and Egypt, respectively, see Kibicho 2009; Jacobs 2010.

7. The report also states that "child sex tourists typically arrive from Europe and, to a lesser extent, the United States" and that "the Brazilian Federal Police estimate that 250,000 to 400,000 children are exploited in domestic prostitution, in resort and tourist areas, along highways, and in Amazonian mining brothels" (U.S. Department of State 2009). The 2011 TIP report stated that "sex trafficking of Brazilian women and girls occurs in all 26 Brazilian states and the federal district, and the federal police continued to estimate that upwards of 250,000 children were involved in prostitution" (U.S. Department of State 2011).

8. The International Convention of the Rights of the Child, the Statute of the Child and Adolescent (ECA, Law 8.069/90), and the Brazilian Penal Code are the predominant legal instruments used in cases of sexual exploitation of children and adolescents (*Turismo Sustentável* n.d.). The Code of Conduct for the Protection of Children from Sexual Exploitation in Tourism was created in 1999 by ECPAT, an international organization that works to end prostitution, pornography, and trafficking of children for sexual purposes. When the Code of Conduct is adopted by companies and people who work in the tourism sector, they must make it clear to their customers that they oppose the sexual exploitation of children and adolescents—for example, through signs in hotels (*Turismo Sustentável* n.d.).

9. The panel included eleven women and six men; three of whom were black (two women and one man). The participants (not all of whom were present) included Ruy Pavan, coordinator of the UNICEF office for Bahia, Sergipe, and Espirito Santo; Emilia Maria Salvador, president of Bahiatursa; Leila Paiva, director of the Program of Assistance for Children and Adolescent Victims of Trafficking for Purposes of Sexual Exploitation of the Program Partners of the Americas; Yulo Oiticia, president of the Legislative Assembly's Commission of Human Rights; Valdenor Cardoso, president of the Municipal Camara of Salvador; Valmir Carlos da Assuncao, state secretary of social development and fighting poverty; Joao Henrique Barradas, mayor of Salvador; Jacques Wagner, governor of Bahia; Carlos Ribeiro Soares, municipal secretary of social development; Lidice da Matta, president of the Legislative Assembly's Commission for the Defense of Children and Adolescents; Cristine Albuquerque, coordinator of the Brazilian president's National Program to Combat Sexual Abuse and Exploitation of Children and Adolescents; Maria Lisabete de Souza Povoa of the School Project that Protects; Edna Sena, director of social responsibility of the Brazilian Association of the Hotel Industry; Jucara Santos, coordinator of the social-environmental sector of the Concessionaria North Coast/Invepar Institute; and Waldemar Oliveira of the Committee to Confront Sexual Violence against Children and Adolescents in Bahia.

10. Even though boys and men are trafficked as well, women and girls are the poster children for antitrafficking campaigns.

11. ww.cedeca.org.br.

12. Programa Sentinela is another Salvador-based nongovernmental organization that works on issues of sexual abuse of children and adolescents, in which foreigners do not play a significant role.

13. Here, Caetano used the English word *book* rather than the Portuguese word, *livro*, even though he was speaking in Portuguese.

14. The Bahian *michês*' willingness to participate in a discourse of diasporic brotherhood and solidarity that (supposedly) crossed class and national boundaries resembles

Hartman's account of Ghanaians who capitulated to African American tourists' desire to hear about slavery (2007, 71).

Chapter 4. Tourist Tales and Erotic Adventures

1. See, for example, Schaeffer-Grabiel (2005) on transnational marriage Web sites featuring Latin American women.

2. For Urry, "touristic practices" involve "a limited breaking with established routines and practices of everyday life" and seeing sights and seeking experiences that offer "distinctive contrasts to work and home" (2002, 2).

Chapter 5. Aprosba

1. For more information on the Ministry of Health's condom distribution campaigns in Bahia, see Biehl (2007, 274).

2. www.aprosba.com.br.

3. Child prostitution is a criminal act, as is benefiting from the sexual labor of others (National Penal Code, articles 227–30). In 2002, the Brazilian Ministry of Labor and Employment officially declared prostitution an economic activity. Furthermore, in 2003, government official Fernando Gabeira presented the Project of Law, which recognizes the existence of sexual services and gives rights to those who provide them. See www .gabeira.com.br; www.redeprostitutas.org.br.

4. The government site lists the general conditions of sex work: they "work for themselves, in diverse locales and irregular hours. In the exercising of some of the activities they can be exposed to bad weather and to social discrimination. There are still risks of contracting STIs and mistreatment, street violence, and death" (*Classificação* n.d.).

5. When Bárbara began working in Patamares, she fell in with a crowd of substance abusers and again became addicted.

6. For more on Women's Police Stations in Brazil, see Cecelia McDowell Santos 2005. Brazil is one of the few countries to have Women's Police Stations.

7. Sex worker rights activist Jo Doezema, for example, argues that the voluntary versus forced dichotomy in conceptualizing prostitution is actually a "new justification for denying sex workers their human rights" (1998, 34). This dichotomy is particularly apparent in discussions of trafficking of women for purposes of sexual labor, in which women are automatically depicted as "victims of evil traffickers," while the structures that violate sex workers' human rights are left unchallenged (42).

8. Bandana Pattanaik, program coordinator of the Thailand-based Global Alliance against Trafficking in Women, argues that careful listening and nonjudgmental attitudes toward sex workers will result in "narratives that neither glorify sex work as liberatory nor denigrate it as soul-destroying" (Pattanaik and Thorbek 2002, 222).

9. http://www.redeprostitutas.org.br/.

10. A newspaper article about the radio station asserted that the women of Aprosba as well as "their children and members of other segments that are also considered marginalized such as *travestis* and the homeless will also be the principal focus of the radio station" (*O Globo* 2006).

11. See also Mitchell 2011a, which discusses the intense stigma that male *michês* experience, which prevents them from even organizing as a group to mobilize for their rights and improved working conditions.

12. Aprosba's partnership with the Ministry of Health and Culture supports Gregory Mitchell's (2011a) point that the Brazilian government assists prostitutes through its efforts toward HIV prevention, education, and treatment.

13. Merry notes that when violence against women was first discussed as a human rights violation in the 1980s, it referred specifically to men's violence against women. However, in the 1990s, the definition expanded to include issues such as female genital circumcision; gender-based violence by members of the police and military; trafficking and prostitution; sexual harassment; forced pregnancy, abortion, sterilization, and marriage; female infanticide; honor killings; and widowhood violations (2006, 21). Furthermore, Saskia Sassen (2001) describes the emergence of the international human rights regime as an example of the transformation of sovereignty under globalization. She traces the shift from the individual being granted rights because of nation-based citizenship to the individual being seen as an object of law and rights whether s/he is a citizen or alien.

14. For an excellent example of this phenomenon in the American South, see McGuire 2010.

15. The Slut Walks initially arose in response to a Toronto police chief's comments that college students could avoid being sexually assaulted on campus if they stopped dressing like "sluts" (http://en.wikipedia.org/wiki/SlutWalk; http://www.slutwalktoronto.com).

Chapter 6. Se Valorizando *(Valuing Oneself)*

1. Similarly, Piscitelli (2001) found that in Fortaleza, the capital of the northeastern state of Ceará, women who engaged in sexual encounters with foreign tourists created a climate of confusion by distinguishing themselves from stereotypes of prostitutes. While some of the women demanded money in exchange for sex, others had stable jobs with low salaries and accepted gifts rather than cash. Still others dated foreigners with no expectations of cash or presents but simply to obtain access to the tourist experience—leisure, dining in nice restaurants, shopping, and so forth.

2. For maritime prostitution, see Trotter 2009.

3. One must beware of assuming that marriage is the great equalizer in power relations—an expression of true, pure love (Giddens 1992, 58).

4. *Piriguete* is a colloquial term used in Bahia to refer to promiscuous women. Thus, *piriguetar* is making this colloquial noun into a verb form to refer to whoring, or engaging in sex work. An *interesseira* is a woman who dates someone to seek social mobility or material benefits.

5. In the context of the Dominican Republic, Denise Brennan notes that although the women "try to take advantage (to the extent that they can) of the men . . . who are in Sosúa to take advantage of them," these relationships "inevitably fall short of mutual exploitation" since the tourists are better positioned than the sex workers to "leave Sosúa satisfied with their experiences there" (2004. 24–25).

6. For more of Jacqueline Leite's perspectives on sex tourism and trafficking, see José Antônio Gomes de Pinho et al. 2008.

Chapter 7. Moral Panics

1. A previous version of this chapter was published as Williams 2011.

2. The International Day to End Violence against Women (November 25) was established to honor the Mirabal sisters, who were assassinated under the dictatorship of Rafael Trujillo in the Dominican Republic. The event in Salvador was planned by a group of two men and ten women: two were staff of CHAME, two were trained volunteer peer educators, and the rest were representatives of other organizations.

3. Regulationists believed that prostitution was a necessary evil that should be controlled by stringent state regulations. For example, the state could regulate prostitution by enforcing registration and compulsory medical exams for the women involved. The abolitionist perspective on white slavery was deeply enmeshed in Victorian ideals of femininity that considered women sexually passive and virtuous. By engaging in illicit sexual behavior, women lost their virtue, quickly transforming their sexuality into something nefarious and dangerous (Doezema 2002, 23).

4. Jordan and Burke (2011) have posted an interesting article that questions the validity of the assertion that trafficking is the third-largest industry of organized crime, trailing only drugs and guns.

5. According to the protocol,

    (a) "Trafficking in persons" shall mean the recruitment, transportation, transfer, harbouring or receipt of persons, by means of the threat or use of force or other forms of coercion, of abduction, of fraud, of deception, of the abuse of power or of a position of vulnerability or of the giving or receiving of payments or benefits to achieve the consent of a person having control over another person, for the purpose of exploitation. Exploitation shall include, at a minimum, the exploitation of the prostitution of others or other forms of sexual exploitation, forced labour or services, slavery or practices similar to slavery, servitude or the removal of organs;

    (b) The consent of a victim of trafficking in persons to the intended exploitation set forth in subparagraph (a) of this article shall be irrelevant where any of the means set forth in subparagraph (a) have been used;

    (c) The recruitment, transportation, transfer, harbouring or receipt of a child for the purpose of exploitation shall be considered "trafficking in persons" even if this does not involve any of the means set forth in subparagraph (a) of this article;

    (d) "Child" shall mean any person under eighteen years of age. (United Nations 2000, Article 3)

6. GAATW contends that trafficking violates human rights, including the right to life, liberty, and security; freedom from slavery, equality before the law, freedom of movement and residence; freedom from arbitrary arrest, detention, and exile; freedom from torture and cruel punishment; and freedom of thought, conscience and religion (Global Alliance against Trafficking in Women 2000, 68).

7. For example, CATW's codirectors, Kathleen Barry and Donna Hughes, stated that "in the global South and East, victims of the sex trade are often young women and girls who are desperately poor in cultures where females are expected to sacrifice themselves for the well-being of their families" (Leidholdt 1999, 4).

8. Mohanty writes, "This average third world woman leads an essentially truncated life based on her feminine gender (read: sexually constrained) and her being 'third world'

(read: ignorant, poor, uneducated, tradition-bound, domestic, family-oriented, victimized, etc.) . . . in contrast to the (implicit) self-representation of Western women as educated, as modern, as having control over their own bodies and sexualities, and the freedom to make their own decisions" (1991, 56).

9. Email to author, October 20, 2009.

10. The CATW's proposed definition of trafficking included "all forms of recruitment and transportation for prostitution." This broad conception of trafficking lends itself to the assumption that all migrant sex workers are victims of trafficking and therefore need to be rescued. On the contrary, the Human Rights Caucus asserted the centrality of force and/or deception in defining trafficking, pointing out that "an adult woman is able to consent to engage [in prostitution.] [I]f no one is forcing her . . . then trafficking does not exist" (Doezema 2002, 21).

11. Blanchette and Silva find that most female sex workers who migrate abroad do so voluntarily after forging transnational connections with foreign tourists. The women who migrate abroad to do sex work are usually not indebted to pimps or intermediaries, as much trafficking literature claims (2008, 14). Blanchette and Silva also criticize the Survey on Trafficking of Women, Children, and Adolescents for the Purposes of Sexual Exploitation for considering cases of voluntary migration of prostitutes as cases of trafficking even when there are no human rights violations, a practice that clearly suggests that the survey is operating from an abolitionist perspective that considers all prostitution to be sexual exploitation (13). This perspective seems to be in line with Article 231 of the Brazilian Penal Code, the main legal instrument applicable in cases of human trafficking in Brazil. Article 231 defines trafficking as the "simple circulation of sex workers, especially if this movement crosses the country's borders" and as "promoting, intermediating or facilitating the entry, into national territory, of a person to work as a prostitute or the departure of a person from the country for the same purpose abroad" (Blanchette and Silva 2008, 1, 6).

Conclusion

1. I heard from various people in Barra that he consistently dated young black and *morena* women. I asked him for an interview, but he politely declined, noting that he was not comfortable discussing this topic with me.

2. Conversely, European women were perceived as independent and masculinized, prioritizing careers and money, and "spoiled by feminist ideas," while Brazilian women were seen as embodying a tender, warm, simple, and submissive femininity (Piscitelli 2006, 14).

3. Pedro Chequer, director of Brazil's National HIV/AIDS Commission, condemned the Bush mandate as theological and fundamentalist. He saw prostitutes as the government's "partners" in HIV prevention, education, and treatment efforts (Mitchell 2011a).

4. The Brazilian tourism industry is responding to these shifting demographics by working to stimulate the domestic market—specifically retired people, workers, and students (Brazil 2007, 29).

Bibliography

Agencia de Notícias de AIDS. 2007. *Lei Que Obrigava Profissionais do Sexo a Realizarem Exame de HIV é Criticada por Ativistas.* April 24.

Agier, Michael, and Christian Cravo. 2005. *Salvador de Bahia: Rome Noire, Ville Metisse.* Paris: Autrement.

Agustín, Laura María. 2007. *Sex at the Margins: Migration, Labour Markets, and the Rescue Industry.* London: Zed.

Alexander, M. Jacqui. 1991. "Redrafting Morality: The Postcolonial State and the Sexual Offences Bill of Trinidad and Tobago." In *Third World Women and the Politics of Feminism*, ed. Chandra Talpade Mohanty, Ann Russo, and Lourdes Torres. Bloomington: Indiana University Press.

———. 1997. "Erotic Autonomy as a Politics of Decolonization: An Anatomy of Feminist and State Practice in the Bahamas Tourist Economy." In *Feminist Genealogies, Colonial Legacies, Democratic Futures*, ed. M. Jacqui Alexander and Chandra Talpade Mohanty. New York: Routledge.

———. 2005. *Pedagogies of the Crossing: Meditations on Feminism, Sexual Politics, Memory, and the Sacred.* Durham: Duke University Press.

Alexander, M. Jacqui, and Chandra Talpade Mohanty. 2010. "Cartographies of Knowledge and Power: Transnational Feminism as Radical Praxis." In *Critical Transnational Feminist Praxis*, ed. Amanda Lock Swarr and Richa Nagar. Albany: SUNY Press.

Allen, Jafari Sinclaire. 2007. "Means of Desire's Production: Male Sex Labor in Cuba." *Identities: Global Studies in Culture and Power* 14:183–202.

———. 2009. "Blackness, Sexuality, and Transnational Desire: Initial Notes toward a New Research Agenda." In *Black Sexualities: Probing Powers, Passions, Practices, and Politics*, ed. Juan Battle and Sandra L. Barnes. New Brunswick, N.J.: Rutgers University Press.

———. 2011. *Venceremos! The Erotics of Black Self-Making in Cuba.* Durham: Duke University Press.

Altink, Sietske. 1995. *Stolen Lives: Trading Women into Sex and Slavery.* London: Scarlet.

Altman, Dennis. 2001. *Global Sex.* Chicago: University of Chicago Press.

Alvarez, Sonia. 1990. *Engendering Democracy in Brazil: Women's Movements in Transition Politics*. Princeton: Princeton University Press.

———. 1999. "Advocating Feminism: The Latin American Feminist NGO 'Boom.'" *International Feminist Journal of Politics* 1: 181–209.

Alves, Dirceu. 2002. "O Mestre das Mulatas." *Isto é Gente*. http://www.terra.com.br/istoegente/142/aconteceu/index.htm.

Amado, Jorge. 1962. *Gabriela, Clove and Cinnamon*. New York: Knopf.

Appadurai, Arjun. 1996. *Modernity at Large: Cultural Dimensions of Globalization*. Minneapolis: University of Minnesota Press.

———. 2001. "Grassroots Globalization and the Research Imagination." In *Globalization*, ed. Arjun Appadurai. Durham: Duke University Press.

Araújo, Joel Zito. 2009. *Cinderelas, Lobos, e um Principle Encantado*. Pipa Produções.

Araújo, Luis Edmundo. 1999. "Sargentelli Traz de Volta o Ziriguidum." *Isto é Gente*. www.terra.com.br/istoegente/15/reportagens/rep_sargentelli.htm.

Arons, Nicholas Gabriel. 2004. *Waiting for Rain: The Politics and Poetics of Drought in Northeast Brazil*. Tucson: University of Arizona Press.

Arruda, Marcos. 1999. *External Debt: Brazil and the International Financial Crisis*. London: Pluto.

Azevedo, Aluísio. 2000 (1890). *The Slum*. New York: Oxford University Press.

Babb, Florence. 2007. "Queering Love and Globalization." *GLQ: A Journal of Lesbian and Gay Studies* 13:111–23.

———. 2010. *The Tourism Encounter: Fashioning Latin American Nations and Histories*. Stanford: Stanford University Press.

Bahiatursa. 1998. *Bahiatursa 30 Anos 1968–1998*. Salvador: Bahiatursa.

Bahiatursa and the Ministry of Culture and Tourism. N.d.(a). *Bahia, Brazil*. Salvador: Bahiatursa and the Ministry of Culture and Tourism.

———. N.d.(b). *Brasil Sensacional!* Salvador: Bahiatursa and the Ministry of Culture and Tourism.

Bairros, Luiza. 1991. "Mulher Negra: O Reforço da Subordinação." In *Desigualdade Racial no Brasil Contemporâneo*, ed. Peggy Lovell. Belo Horizonte: MGSP.

———. 2000. "Lembrando Lélia Gonzalez, 1935–1994." *Afro-Ásia* 23 (Universidade Federal da Bahia).

Bandyopadhyay, Ranjan, and Karina Nascimento. 2010. "'Where Fantasy Becomes Reality': How Tourism Forces Made Brazil a Sexual Playground." *Journal of Sustainable Tourism* 18: 933–49.

Barneiro, Sara. 2003. "Guerra Prejudicará o Turismo na Bahia." *A Tarde*, March 23.

Barry, Kathleen. 1984 (1979). *Female Sexual Slavery*. New York: New York University Press.

———. 1995. *The Prostitution of Sexuality: The Global Exploitation of Women*. New York: New York University Press.

Bartholo, Roberto, Mauricio Delamaro, and Ivan Bursztyn. 2008. "Tourism for Whom? Different Paths to Development and Alternative Experiments in Brazil." *Latin American Perspectives* 35:103–19.

Bastide, Roger. 1967. "The Present Status of Afro-American Research in Latin America." *Daedalus* 96:111–23.

Bauer, Thomas, and Bob McKercher. 2003. *Sex and Tourism: Journeys of Romance, Love, and Lust*. New York: Haworth Hospitality Press.

Beleli, Iara, and José Miguel Nieto Olivar. "Mobilidade e Prostituição em Produtos da Mídia Brasileira." In *Gênero, Sexo, Amor, e Dinheiro: Mobilidades Transnacionais Envolvendo o Brasil*, ed. Adriana Piscitelli, Glaucia de Oliveira Assis, and José Miguel Nieto Olivar. Campinas: Pagu/Núcleo de Estudos de Gênero, UNICAMP.

Bennett, Ramos, and Eliana Guerreiro. 1999. "Gabriela Cravo e Canela: Jorge Amado and the Myth of the Sexual Mulata in Brazilian Culture." In *The African Diaspora: African Origins and New World Identities*, ed. Jorge Isidore Okpewho, Carole Boyce Davies, and Ali A. Mazrui. Bloomington: Indiana University Press.

Bernstein, Elizabeth. 2007a. "Buying and Selling the 'Girlfriend Experience': The Social and Subjective Contours of Market Intimacy." In *Love and Globalization: Transformations of Intimacy in the Contemporary World*, ed. M. Padilla, Jennifer Hirsch, Miguel Munoz-Laboy, Robert Sember, and Richard Parker. Nashville: Vanderbilt University Press.

———. 2007b. *Temporarily Yours: Intimacy, Authenticity, and the Commerce of Sex*. Chicago: University of Chicago Press.

Bevins, Vincent. 2012. "Brazil Tourism: Forget the Gringos." *FT.com*, April 5. blogs.ft.com/beyond-brics/2012/04/05/brazil-tourism-forget-the-gringos/#ixzz1sA79E9uh.

Biehl, João. 2007. *Will to Live: AIDS Therapies and the Politics of Survival*. Princeton: Princeton University Press.

Blanchette, Thaddeus G. 2011. "'Fariseus' e 'Gringos Bons': Masculinidade e Turismo Sexual em Copacabana." In *Gênero, Sexo, Amor, e Dinheiro: Mobilidades Transnacionais Envolvendo o Brasil*, ed. Adriana Piscitelli, Glaucia de Oliveira Assis, and José Miguel Nieto Olivar. Campinas: Pagu/Núcleo de Estudos de Gênero, UNICAMP.

Blanchette, Thaddeus G., and Ana Paula da Silva. 2005. "'Nossa Senhora da Help': Sexo, Turismo, e Deslocamento Transnacional em Copacabana." *Cadernos Pagu* 25:249–80.

———. 2008. "Vulnerable Women and Bad Girls: An Anthropological Analysis of Hegemonic Narratives Regarding Human Trafficking in Brazil." Unpublished article, Department of Anthropology, Federal University of Rio de Janeiro.

———. 2011. "Our Lady of Help: Sex, Tourism, and Transnational Movements in Copacabana." *Wagadu: A Journal of Transnational Women's and Gender Studies* 8:144–65.

Boellstorff, Tom. 2007. "Queer Studies in the House of Anthropology." *Annual Review of Anthropology* 36:17–35.

Boris, Eileen, and Rhacel Salazar Parreñas, eds. 2010. *Intimate Labors: Culture, Technologies, and the Politics of Care*. Stanford: Stanford University Press.

Bourdieu, Pierre, and Loïc Wacquant. 1999. "On the Cunning of Imperialist Reason: Theory, Culture, Society." *Theory, Culture, and Society* 16:41–58.

Brazil. 2007. *2007–2010 National Tourism Plan: A Journey towards Inclusion*. http://www.turismo.gov.br/export/sites/default/turismo/o_ministerio/plano_nacional/downloads_plano_nacional/PNT_Ingles.pdf.

"Brazil to Fight Sex Tourism as Carnival Nears." 2004. *China Daily*, February 12. http://www.chinadaily.com.cn/english/home/2004-02/12/content_305401.htm.

"Brazil Urges Visitors to Explore Far and Wide." 2012. *Opodo*, April 13. news.opodo.co.uk/NewsDetails/2012-04-13/Brazil_encourages_visitors_to_explore_far_and_wide.

Brennan, Denise. 2004. *What's Love Got to Do with It? Transnational Desires and Sex Tourism in the Dominican Republic*. Durham: Duke University Press.

Bruner, Edward M. 1991. "The Transformation of Self in Tourism." *Annals of Tourism Research* 18:238–50.

———. 2005. *Culture on Tour: Ethnographies of Travel*. Chicago: University of Chicago Press.

Burdick, John. 1998. *Blessed Anastácia: Women, Race, and Popular Christianity in Brazil*. New York: Routledge.

Butler, Judith. 1992. "Contingent Foundations: Feminism and the Question of 'Postmodernism.'" In *Feminists Theorize the Political*, ed. Judith Butler and Joan Scott. New York: Routledge.

Butler, Kim. 1998. *Freedoms Given, Freedoms Won: Afro-Brazilians in Post-Abolition São Paulo and Salvador*. New Brunswick, N.J.: Rutgers University Press.

Cabezas, Amalia. 2004. "Between Love and Money: Sex, Tourism, and Citizenship in Cuba and the Dominican Republic." *Signs: Journal of Women in Culture and Society* 29:987–1015.

———. 2008. "Tropical Blues: Tourism and Social Exclusion in the Dominican Republic." *Latin American Perspectives* 35 (2008): 21–36.

———. 2009. *Economies of Desire: Sex and Tourism in Cuba and the Dominican Republic*. Philadelphia: Temple University Press.

Caldwell, Kia Lilly. 2000. "Fronteiras da Diferenca: Raça e Mulher no Brasil." *Estudos Feministas* 8:91–108.

———. 2007. *Negras in Brazil: Re-Envisioning Black Women, Citizenship, and the Politics of Identity*. New Brunswick, N.J.: Rutgers University Press.

———. 2009. "Transnational Black Feminism in the 21st Century: Perspectives from Brazil." In *New Social Movements in the African Diaspora*, ed. Leith Mullings. New York: Palgrave Macmillan.

———. 2010. "A Institucionalização de Estudos sobre a Mulher Negra: Perspectivas dos Estados Unidos e do Brasil." *Revista da Associação Brasileira de Pesquisadores Negros* 1:18–27.

Cantalice, Tiago. 2011. "Turismo, Sexo, e Romance: *Caça-Gringas* da Praia da Pipa-RN." In *Gênero, Sexo, Amor, e Dinheiro: Mobilidades Transnacionais Envolvendo o Brasil*, ed. Adriana Piscitelli, Glaucia de Oliveira Assis, and José Miguel Nieto Olivar. Campinas: Pagu/Núcleo de Estudos de Gênero, UNICAMP.

Carby, Hazel. 1992. "Policing the Black Woman's Body in an Urban Context." *Critical Inquiry* 18:738–55.

Cardoso, Fernando Henrique. 1965. "Colour Prejudice in Brazil." *Presence Africaine* 24:120–28. Reprinted in *Race and Ethnicity in Latin America*, ed. Jorge I. Domínguez. New York: Garland.

Carneiro, Sueli. 1999. "Black Women's Identity in Brazil." In *Race in Contemporary Brazil*, ed. Rebecca Reichmann. University Park: Pennsylvania State University Press.

———. 2003. "Mulheres em Movimento." *Estudos Avancados* 17:117–32.

Carneiro, Sueli, and Thereza Santos. 1985. *Mulher Negra*. São Paulo: Nobel/Conselho Estadual da Condição Feminina.

Cavalcante, Rodrigo. 2007. "O Nordeste Portugues." *Exame, Anuário de Turismo 2007–2008*. http://exame.abril.com.br/revista-exame/edicoes/0890/noticias/o-nordeste-portugues-m0125876.

Cavallera, Renato. 2011. "Ex Globeleza Valeria Valenssa Conta o Que Mudou em Sua Vida Depois Que Se Tornou Evangélica." *Gnotícias*, March 9. http://noticias.gospelmais.com.br/globeleza-valeria-valenssa-evangelica-testemunho-17274.html.

Cerqueira, M. 2009. "Bahia é um Destino Pronto, diz Ernesto Camacho da Prime Travel." *Grupo Gay da Bahia.* http://www.ggb.org.br/turismo_gay_bahia_comodestino.html.

Chacham, Alessandra, Simone Diniz, Monica Maia, Ana Galati, and Liz Mirim. 2007. "Sexual and Reproductive Health Needs of Sex Workers: Two Feminist Projects in Brazil." *Reproductive Health Matters* 15:108–18.

CHAME. N.d.(a). *Migração Feminina Internacional: Causas e Consequências.* Salvador: CHAME.

———. N.d.(b). *Sumário.* Salvador: CHAME.

———. 1998. *What's Up in Bahia: The Other Side of Tourism in Salvador.* Salvador: CHAME.

Chang, Grace. 2004. "Con/Vergences: Critical Interventions in the Politics of Race and Gender." Paper Presented in Transnational Political Economies, University of California, Berkeley.

Channel News Asia. 2004. "Brazil Inherits Sex-Tourism Crown from Tsunami-Struck Thailand: Hotelier." March 17. http://www.channelnewsasia.com/stories/afp_world _business/view/137747/1/.html.

Cidade Baixa [Lower City]. 2005. Directed by Sérgio Machada. Palm Pictures.

Classificação Brasileira de Ocupações. N.d. http://www.mtecbo.gov.br/cbosite/pages/ pesquisas/BuscaPorTituloResultado.jsf.

Clifford, James, and George Marcus. 1986. *Writing Culture: The Poetics and Politics of Ethnography.* Berkeley: University of California Press.

Clift, Stephen, and Simon Carter, eds. 2000. *Tourism and Sex: Culture, Commerce, and Coercion.* Leicester: Pinter.

Cobb, Jelani. 2006. "Blame It on Rio." *Essence,* September.

Cohen, Cathy. 2005. "Punks, Bulldaggers, and Welfare Queens: The Radical Potential of Queer Politics?" In *Black Queer Studies: A Critical Anthology,* ed. E. P Johnson and M. G. Henderson. Durham: Duke University Press.

Cohen, Stanley. 1972. *Folk Devils and Moral Panics: The Creation of the Mods and Rockers.* London: Routledge.

Collier, Stephen J., and Aihwa Ong, eds. 2005. *Global Assemblages: Technology, Politics, and Ethics as Anthropological Problems.* Malden, Mass.: Blackwell.

Collins, John. 2008. "But What If I Should Need to Defecate in Your Neighborhood, Madam? Empire, Redemption, and the 'Tradition of the Oppressed' in a Brazilian World Heritage Site." *Cultural Anthropology* 23: 279–328.

Collins, Patricia Hill. 1990. *Black Feminist Thought: Knowledge, Consciousness, and the Politics of Empowerment.* Boston: Unwin Hyman.

———. 2004. *Black Sexual Politics: African Americans, Gender, and the New Racism.* New York: Routledge.

Commonwealth Secretariat. 2002. *Report of the Expert Group on the Strategies for Combating the Trafficking of Women and Children: Best Practice.* London: Commonwealth Secretariat Human Rights Unit. http://www.thecommonwealth.org/Shared_ASP_Files/ UploadedFiles/%7B9DA75C65-FBFE-4F33-8CA1-99D014B52989%7D_Trafficking %20of%20Women.pdf.

Constable, Nicole. 2007. "Love at First Site? Visual Images and Virtual Encounters with Bodies." In *Love and Globalization: Transformations of Intimacy in the Contemporary World,* ed. Mark Padilla, Jennifer Hirsch, Miguel Munoz-Laboy, Robert Sember, and Richard Parker. Nashville: Vanderbilt University Press.

Correia, Sonia. 2012. "Brazilian Sexualities and Norms: A Shifting Landscape." Paper presented at meeting of Latin American Studies Association, San Francisco, May 25.

Costa, Ana Paula. 2001. "Bahia Quer Melhorar Turismo." *Tribuna da Bahia*, June 24.

Craide, Sabrina. 2008. "Trabalhadoras Domésticas Negras São Maioria sem Carteira Assinada, Aponta OIT." http://www.agenciabrasil.gov.br/2008/04/25/materia.2008.

Crepaldi, Iara, and Guilherme Maciel. 2005. *Os Endereços Curiosos de Salvador*. São Paulo: Panda.

Crick, Malcolm. 1989. "Representations of International Tourism in the Social Sciences: Sun, Sex, Sights, Savings, and Servility." *Annual Review of Anthropology* 18:307–44.

Crook, Larry, and Randal Johnson, eds. 2000. *Black Brazil: Culture, Identity, and Social Mobilization*. Los Angeles: UCLA Latin American Center Publications.

Da Silva, Ana Paula. 2011. "'Cosmopolitismo Tropical': Uma Análise Preliminar do Turismo Sexual Internacional em São Paulo." In *Gênero, Sexo, Amor, e Dinheiro: Mobilidades Transnacionais Envolvendo o Brasil*, ed. Adriana Piscitelli, Glaucia de Oliveira Assis, and José Miguel Nieto Olivar. Campinas: Pagu/Núcleo de Estudos de Gênero, UNICAMP.

Dalevi, Alessandra. 2002. "In Praise of *Mulatas*." *Brazzil*. http://www.brazzil.com/pages/po6apro2.htm.

"Daspu Faz Encontro Nacional de Prostitutas no Rio: ONU Participa." 2008. *Folha On-line*, December 2. http://noticias.bol.uol.com.br/brasil/2008/12/02/ult4733u26196.jhtm.

"Daspu Faz Sucesso em Salvador." 2007. *Beijo da Rua*, August 31. http://www.beijodarua.com.br/materia.asp?edicao=28&coluna=6&reportagem=777&num=1.

Davis, Adrienne. 2009. "Don't Let Nobody Bother Your Principle: The Sexual Economy of American Slavery." In *Still Brave: The Evolution of Black Women's Studies*, ed. Stanlie M. James, Frances Smith Foster, and Beverly Guy-Sheftall. New York: Feminist Press.

Davis, Darien. 1999. *Avoiding the Dark: Race and the Forging of National Culture in Modern Brazil*. Brookfield, Vt.: Ashgate.

———. 2009. *White Face, Black Mask: Africaneity and the Early Social History of Popular Music in Brazil*. East Lansing: Michigan State University Press.

D'Eça, Aline. 2007. "Blocos de Carnaval Convocados para Combater Exploração Sexual." Ministério Público do Estado da Bahia, Procuradora Geral da Justiça, Assessoria de Comunicação. http://www.mp.ba.gov.br/noticias/2007/jan_04_blocosCarnaval.asp.

Decena, Carlos. 2011. *Tacit Subjects*. Durham: Duke University Press.

Degler, Carl. 1971. *Neither Black nor White*. New York: Macmillan.

Desai, Manisha. 2002. "Transnational Solidarity: Women's Agency, Structural Adjustment, and Globalization." In *Women's Activism and Globalization: Linking Local Struggles and Transnational Politics*, ed. Nancy A. Naples and Manisha Desai. New York: Routledge.

———. 2007. "The Messy Relationship between Feminisms and Globalizations." *Gender and Society* 21:797–803.

Dewey, Susan, and Patty Kelly, eds. 2011. *Policing Pleasure: Sex Work, Policy, and the State in Global Perspective*. New York: New York University Press.

Diegues, Antonio Carlos. 2001. "Regional and Domestic Mass Tourism in Brazil." In *The Native Tourist: Mass Tourism within Developing Countries*, ed. Krishna B. Ghimire. London: Earthscan.

Doezema, Jo. 1998. "Forced to Choose: Beyond the Voluntary v. Forced Prostitution Dichotomy." In *Global Sex Workers: Rights, Resistance, Redefinition*, ed. Kamala Kempadoo and Jo Doezema. New York: Routledge.

————. 2001. "Ouch! Western Feminists' 'Wounded Attachment' to the 'Third World Prostitute.'" *Feminist Review* 67:16–38.

————. 2002. "Who Gets to Choose? Coercion, Consent, and the UN Trafficking Protocol." In *Gender, Trafficking, and Slavery*, ed. R. Masika. Oxford: Oxfam.

Domínguez, Jorge I., ed. 1994. *Race and Ethnicity in Latin America*. New York: Garland.

Donnan, Hastings, and Fiona Magowan. 2010. *The Anthropology of Sex*. London: Berg.

Dunn, Christopher. 2007. "Black Rome and the Chocolate City: The Race of Place." *Callaloo* 30:847–61.

Dzidienyo, Ayani. 1985. "The African Connection and the Afro-Brazilian Condition." In *Race, Class, and Power in Brazil*, ed. Pierre-Michel Fontaine. Los Angeles: Center for Afro-American Studies, UCLA.

————. 2005. "The Changing World of Brazilian Race Relations?" In *Neither Enemies nor Friends: Latinos, Blacks, Afro-Latinos*, ed. Anani Dzidzienyo and Suzanne Oboler. New York: Palgrave Macmillan.

Ebron, Paulla. 1997. "Traffic in Men." In *Gendered Encounters: Challenging Cultural Boundaries and Social Hierarchies in Africa*, ed. Maria Grosz-Ngate and Omari H. Kokole. New York: Routledge.

Edmonds, Alexander. 2010. *Pretty Modern: Beauty, Sex, and Plastic Surgery in Brazil*. Durham: Duke University Press.

Enloe, Cynthia. 1990. *Bananas, Beaches, and Bases: Making Feminist Sense of International Politics*. Berkeley: University of California Press.

Esteban-Muñoz, José. 1999. *Disidentifications: Queers of Color and the Performance of Politics*. Minneapolis: University of Minnesota Press.

Esteves, Acúrsio Pereira. 2004. *A "Capoeira" da Indústria do Entretenimento: Corpo, Acrobacia, e Espectáculo para "Turista Ver."* Salvador: Esteves.

Exame. 2007. *Anuário de Turismo 2007–2008*. São Paulo: Abril.

Ferguson, Roderick. 2004. *Aberrations in Black: Toward a Queer of Color Critique*. Minneapolis: University of Minnesota Press.

Fernandez, Nadine. 2010. *Interracial Couples in Contemporary Cuba*. New Brunswick, N.J.: Rutgers University Press.

Ferree, Myra Marx, and Aili Mari Tripp, eds. 2006. *Global Feminism: Transnational Women's Activism, Organizing, and Human Rights*. New York: New York University Press.

Ferreira, Carla. 2004. "Sol e Praia Sem Turismo Sexual." *A Tarde*, December 19.

Ferreira, Francisco H. G., Phillippe G. Leite, and Julie A. Litchfield. 2008. "The Rise and Fall of Brazilian Inequality, 1981–2004." *Macroeconomic Dynamics* 12:199–230.

Filho, Antonio Jonas Dias. 1998. "Fulôs, Ritas, Gabrielas, Gringólogas, e Garotas de Programa: Falas, Práticas, Textos, e Imagens em Torno de Negras e Mestiças, a Partir da Sensualidade Atribuída a Mulher Brasileira." Master's thesis, Federal University of Bahia.

Filho, Ubaldo Marques Porto. 2006. *Bahia: Terra da Felicidade*. Salvador: Bahiatursa.

Fontaine, Pierre-Michel. 1985. *Race, Class, and Power in Brazil*. Los Angeles: UCLA Center for Afro-American Studies.

Francisco, Luiz. 2006. "Prostitutas Vão Administrar Radio FM em Salvador (Prostitutes Are Going to Run a Radio Station in Salvador)." *Folha Online—Agencia Folha*. http://www1.folha.uol.com.br/folha/cotidiano/ult95u119147.shtml.

Frank, Katherine. 2007. "Playcouples in Paradise: Touristic Sexuality and Lifestyle Travel." In *Love and Globalization: Transformations of Intimacy in the Contemporary World*, ed.

M. Padilla, Jennifer Hirsch, Miguel Munoz-Laboy, Robert Sember, and Richard Parker. Nashville: Vanderbilt University Press.

Freyre, Gilberto. 1956 (1933). *The Masters and the Slaves: A Study in the Development of Brazilian Civilization*. Trans. Samuel Putnam. 2nd ed. New York: Knopf.

———. 1963. *The Mansions and the Shanties: The Making of Modern Brazil*. Trans. Harriet de Onís. New York: Knopf.

Friedman, Mack. 2006. "The Beaches and Boys of Brazil." *Out Traveler*, Winter. http://www.outtraveler.com/features.asp?did=528.

Frohlick, Susan. 2007. "Fluid Exchanges: The Negotiations of Intimacy between Tourist Women and Local Men in a Transnational Town in Caribbean Costa Rica." *City and Society* 19:139–68.

———. 2008. "Engaging Ethnography in Tourist Research: An Introduction." *Tourist Studies* 8:5–18.

———. 2009. "Pathos of Love in Puerto Viejo, Costa Rica: Emotion, Travel, and Migration." *Mobilities* 4:389–405.

Frohlick, Susan, and Lynda Johnson. 2011. "Naturalizing Bodies and Places: Tourism Media Campaigns and Heterosexualities in Costa Rica and New Zealand." *Annals of Tourism Research* 38:1090–1109.

Fryer, Peter. 2000. *Rhythms of Resistance: African Musical Heritage in Brazil*. Middletown, Conn.: Wesleyan University Press.

Giacomini, Sonia M. 1991. "Aprendendo a Ser Mulata: Um Estudo sobre a Identidade da Mulata Profissional." In *Entre a Virtude e o Pecado*, ed. Albertina de Oliveira Costa and Cristina Brushini. Rio de Janeiro: Rosa dos Tempos.

———. 1994. "Beleza Mulata e Beleza Negra." *Estudos Feministas* 94:217–27.

Giddens, Anthony. 1992. *The Transformation of Intimacy: Sexuality, Love, and Eroticism in Modern Societies*. Cambridge: Polity.

Gille, Zsuzsa, and Seán Ó Riain. 2002. "Global Ethnography." *Annual Review of Sociology* 28:271–95.

Gilliam, Angela. 1994. "The Brazilian Mulata: Images in the Global Economy." *Race and Class* 40:57–69.

———. 2001. "A Black Feminist Perspective on the Sexual Commodification of Women in the New Global Culture." In *Black Feminist Anthropology: Theory, Politics, Praxis and Poetics*, ed. Irma McClaurin. New Brunswick, N.J.: Rutgers University Press.

Gilmore, Danielle. 2010. *At the Dark End of the Street: Black Women, Rape, and Resistance—A New History of the Civil Rights Movement from Rosa Parks to the Rise of Black Power*. New York: Knopf.

Global Alliance against Trafficking in Women. 2000. *Human Rights and Trafficking in Persons: A Handbook*. Bangkok: Global Alliance against Trafficking in Women.

O Globo. 2006. "Prostitutas de Bahia Terao Emissora da FM." March 9. http://www.gabeira.com.br/noticias/noticia.asp?id=1901.

Gmelch, George. 2003. *Behind the Smile: The Working Lives of Caribbean Tourism*. Bloomington: Indiana University Press.

Goffman, Erving. 1959. *The Presentation of Self in Everyday Life*. New York: Anchor.

Goldstein, Donna. 1999. "'Interracial' Sex and Racial Democracy in Brazil: Twin Concepts?" *American Anthropologist* 101:563–78.

———. 2003. *Laughter Out of Place: Race, Class, Violence, and Sexuality in a Rio Shanty-town*. Berkeley: University of California Press.

Gonzalez, Lélia. 1980. "Racismo e Sexismo na Cultura Brasileira." In *IV Encontro Anual da Associação Nacional de Pos Graduação e Pesquisa em Ciencias Sociais*. Rio de Janeiro. ANPOCS.

———. 1982. "A Mulher Negra na Sociedade Brasileira." In *O Lugar da Mulher: Estudos sobre a Condição Feminina*, ed. Madel T. Luz. Rio de Janeiro: Graal.

———. 1988. "For an Afro-Latin American Feminism." In *Confronting the Crisis in Latin America: Women Organizing for Change*. Santiago: Isis International and Development Alternatives.

Goodyear, Michael, and Ronald Weitzer. 2011. "International Trends in the Control of Sexual Services." In *Policing Pleasure: Sex Work, Policy, and the State in Global Perspective*, ed. Susan Dewey and Patty Kelly. New York: New York University Press.

Graburn, Nelson H. H. 1977. "Tourism: The Sacred Journey." In *Hosts and Guests: The Anthropology of Tourism*, ed. Valene Smith. Philadelphia: University of Pennsylvania Press.

———. 1983. "The Anthropology of Tourism." *Annals of Tourism Research* 10:9–33.

Gregg, Jessica. 2006. "He Can Be Sad Like That: Liberdade and the Absence of Romantic Love in a Brazilian Shantytown." In *Modern Loves: The Anthropology of Romantic Courtship and Companionate Marriage*, ed. Jennifer Hirsch and Holly Wardlow. Ann Arbor: University of Michigan Press.

Gregory, Steven. 2003. "Men in Paradise: Sex Tourism and the Political Economy of Masculinity." In *Race, Nature, and the Politics of Difference*, ed. Donald Moore, Jake Kosek, and Anand Pandian. Durham: Duke University Press.

———. 2007. *The Devil behind the Mirror: Globalization and Politics in the Dominican Republic*. Berkeley: University of California Press.

Grewal, Inderpal. 1996. *Home and Harem: Gender, Empire, and the Cultures of Travel*. Durham: Duke University Press.

Grewal, Inderpal, and Caren Kaplan. 1994. "Introduction: Transnational Feminist Practices and Questions of Postmodernity." In *Scattered Hegemonies: Postmodernity and Transnational Feminist Practices*, ed. Inderpal Grewal and Caren Kaplan. Minneapolis: University of Minnesota Press.

———. 2001. "Global Identities: Theorizing Transnational Studies of Sexuality." *GLQ* 7:663–79.

Guillermoprieto, Alma. 1990. *Samba*. London: Cape.

Guimarães, Antonio Sérgio Alfredo. 2001. "The Misadventures of Nonracialism in Brazil." In *Race and Inequality in Brazil, South Africa, and the United States*, ed. Charles Hamilton, Lynn Huntley, Neville Alexander, and Antonio Sérgio Alfredo Guimarães. Boulder, Colo.: Rienner.

———. 2005. "Racial Democracy." In *Imagining Brazil*, ed. Jessé Souza and Valter Sinder. Lanham, Md.: Lexington Books.

———. 2006. "Depois da Democracia Racial." *Tempo Social, Revista de Sociologia da USP* 18: 269–90.

Gutterman, David S. 2001. "Postmodernism and the Interrogation of Masculinity." In *The Masculinities Reader*, ed. Stephen Whitehead and Frank J. Barrett. London: Polity.

Guy-Sheftall, Beverly. 2002. "The Body Politic: Black Female Sexuality and the Nineteenth Century Euro-American Imagination." In *Skin Deep, Spirit Strong: Critical Essays on the Black Female Body in American Culture*, ed. Kimberly Wallace Sanders. Ann Arbor: University of Michigan Press.

Hall, Stuart. 1978. *Policing the Crisis: Mugging, the State, and Law and Order*. New York: Palgrave Macmillan.

Hamilton, Russell G. 2007. "Gabriela Meets Olodum: Paradoxes of Hybridity, Racial Identity, and Black Consciousness in Contemporary Brazil." *Research in African Literatures* 38:181–93.

Hammonds, Evelyn. 1997. "Toward a Genealogy of Black Female Sexuality: The Problematic Silence." In *Feminist Genealogies, Colonial Legacies, Democratic Futures*, ed. M. Jacqui Alexander and Chandra Talpade Mohanty. New York: Routledge.

Hanchard, Michael. 1994. *Orpheus and Power: The Movimento Negro of Rio de Janeiro and São Paulo, Brazil, 1945–1988*. Princeton: Princeton University Press.

———. 1999. *Racial Politics in Contemporary Brazil*. Durham: Duke University Press.

———. 2003. "Acts of Misrecognition: Transnational Black Politics, Anti-Imperialism, and the Ethnocentrisms of Pierre Bourdieu and Loïc Wacquant." *Theory, Culture, and Society* 20:5–29.

Harding, Rachel. 2000. *A Refuge in Thunder: Candomblé and Alternative Spaces of Blackness*. Bloomington: Indiana University Press.

Harrison, Julia. 2003. *Being a Tourist: Finding a Meaning in Pleasure Travel*. Vancouver: University of British Columbia Press.

Hartman, Saidiya. 2007. *Lose Your Mother: A Journey along the Atlantic Slave Route*. New York: Farrar, Straus, and Giroux.

Hasenbalg, Carlos. 1979. *Discriminação e Desigualdades Raciais no Brasil*. Rio de Janeiro: Graal.

Hasenbalg, Carlos, and Suellen Huntington. 1982. "Brazilian Racial Democracy: Reality or Myth?" *Humboldt Journal of Social Relations* 10:129–42.

Hautzinger, Sarah J. 2007. *Violence in the City of Women: Police and Batterers in Bahia, Brazil*. Berkeley: University of California Press.

Hellwig, David, ed. 1992. *African-American Reflections on Brazil's Racial Paradise*. Philadelphia: Temple University Press.

Herdt, Gilbert, ed. 2009. *Moral Panics, Sex Panics: Fear and the Fight over Sexual Rights*. New York: New York University Press.

Hine, Darlene Clark. 1989. "Rape and the Inner Lives of Black Women in the Middle West." *Signs* 14:912–20.

"A História da Globeleza." 2009. *Globo.tv*. http://globotv.globo.com/rede-globo/video-show /v/a-historia-da-globeleza/971921/.

Hita, Maria Gabriela, and John Gledhill. 2009. "Anthropologies of the Urban Periphery: Salvador, Bahia." http://www.bwpi.manchester.ac.uk/resources/Working-Papers/bwpi -wp-9709.pdf.

Hochschild, Arlie Russell. 1983. *The Managed Heart: Commercialization of Human Feeling*. Berkeley: University of California Press.

Hoje em Dia. 2007. Rede Record. February 2.

Howe, Alyssa Cymene. 2001. "Queer Pilgrimage: The San Francisco Homeland and Identity Tourism." *Cultural Anthropology* 16:35–61.

Hughes, Donna. 2002. *Trafficking for Sexual Exploitation: The Case of the Russian Federation*. Geneva: International Organization for Migration.

Hughes, Howard L. 2006. *Pink Tourism: Holidays of Gay Men and Lesbians*. Oxfordshire: CAB.

Ilhéus, a Terra da Gabriela [Ilhéus, the Land of Gabriela]. Ca. 1980. Directed by Carlos Rosalos. Narrated by Luzia Santiago. ECRAN Audiovisual Productions.

Inda, Jonathan Xavier, and Renato Rosaldo, eds. 2002. *The Anthropology of Globalization: A Reader*. Malden, Mass.: Blackwell.

Jacobs, Jessica. 2010. *Sex, Tourism, and the Postcolonial Encounter: Landscapes of Longing in Egypt*. Burlington, Vt.: Ashgate.

Johnson, E. Patrick, and Mae G. Henderson, eds. 2005. *Black Queer Studies: A Critical Anthology*. Durham: Duke University Press.

Johnston, Hugh, and Sona Khan, ed. 1998. *Trafficking in Persons in South Asia*. Calgary: Shastri Indo-Canadian Institute.

Jordan, Ann, and Lynn Burke. 2011. "Is Human Trafficking Really the Third Most Profitable Business for Organized Crime?" *rightswork.org*, March 1. http://rightswork.org/2011/03/is-human-trafficking-really-the-third-most-profitable-business-for-organized-crime-3/.

Kang, Joo-Hyun. 2009. Paper presented at Queer Politics in Transnational Contexts seminar, Cornell University.

Kelsky, Karen. 2001. *Women on the Verge: Japanese Women, Western Dreams*. Durham: Duke University Press.

Kempadoo, Kamala. 1999. *Sun, Sex, and Gold: Tourism and Sex Work in the Caribbean*. Lanham, Md.: Rowman and Littlefield.

———. 2001a. "Freelancers, Temporary Wives, and Beach-Boys: Researching Sex Work in the Caribbean." *Feminist Review* 67:39–62.

———. 2001b. "Women of Color and the Global Sex Trade: Transnational Feminist Perspectives." *Meridians* 1:28–51.

———. 2004. *Sexing the Caribbean: Gender, Race, and Sexual Labor*. New York: Routledge.

———. 2007. "The War on Human Trafficking in the Caribbean." *Race and Class* 49:79–85.

Kempadoo, Kamala, and Jo Doezema, eds. 1998. *Global Sex Workers: Rights, Resistance, Redefinition*. New York: Routledge.

Kibicho, Wanjohi. 2009. *Sex Tourism in Africa: Kenya's Booming Industry*. Burlington, Vt.: Ashgate.

Kincaid, Jamaica. 1988. *A Small Place*. New York: Farrar, Straus, and Giroux.

Kingstone, Steven. 2004. "Brazil Struggles to Curb Sex Tourism." *BBC News*. December 2. http://news.bbc.co.uk/2/hi/americas/4061325.stm.

Kondo, Dorinne. 1990. *Crafting Selves: Power, Gender, and Discourses of Identity in a Japanese Workplace*. Chicago: University of Chicago Press.

Kraay, Hendrik. 1998. *Afro-Brazilian Culture and Politics: Bahia, 1790s to 1990s*. Armonk, N.Y.: Sharpe.

Kulick, Don. 1998. *Travesti: Sex, Gender, and Culture among Brazilian Transgendered Prostitutes*. Chicago: University of Chicago Press.

Landes, Ruth. 1947. *The City of Women*. New York: Macmillan.

Larvie, Patrick. 1997. "Homophobia and the Ethnoscape of Sex Work in Rio de Janeiro." In *Sexual Cultures and Migration in the Era of AIDS: Anthropological and Demographic Perspectives*, ed. Gilbert Herdt. Oxford: Oxford University Press.

———. 1999. "Natural Born Targets: Male Hustlers and AIDS Prevention in Urban Brazil." In *Men Who Sell Sex: International Perspectives on Male Prostitution and AIDS*, ed. Peter Aggleton. London: Taylor and Francis.

Leidholdt, Dorchen. 1999. "Prostitution—A Modern Form of Slavery." In *Making the Harm Visible: Global Sexual Exploitation of Women and Girls, Speaking Out and Providing Services*, ed. Donna Hughes and Claire Roche. Kingston, R.I.: Coalition against Trafficking in Women.

Leite, Gabriela. 2005. Presentation at the Central Única dos Trabalhadores conference on Transforming the Relationship between Labor and Citizenship: Production, Reproduction, and Sexuality, August 11.

Lenz, Flavio. 2008. "Rede Divulga Carta de Principios [Network Publicizes Letter of Principles]." *Beijo da Rua.* http://www.beijodarua.com.br/materia.asp?edicao=28&coluna =6&reportagem=833&num=1.

Lewellen, Ted C. 2002. *The Anthropology of Globalization: Cultural Anthropology Enters the 21st Century.* Westport, Conn.: Bergin and Garvey.

Limanowska, Barbara, and Ann Rosga. 2004. "The Bar Raid as 'Outcome Space' of Anti-Trafficking Initiatives in the Balkans." In *Traveling Facts*, ed. E. Dunn, Daniel Dor, Caroline Baillie, and Yi Zheng. Berlin: Campus.

Lipsitz, George. 2007. "The Racialization of Space and the Spatialization of Race: Theorizing the Hidden Architecture of Landscape." *Landscape Journal* 26: 10–23.

Lofgren, Orvar. 1999. *On Holiday: A History of Vacationing.* Berkeley: University of California Press.

Lucinda, Elisa. 1998. "Mulata Exportação." In *O Semelhante.* 3rd ed. Rio de Janeiro: Record.

Lyrio, Alexandre. 2007. "Americano É Preso Acusado de Exploração Sexual." *Correio da Bahia*, January 25. http://www.correiodabahia.com.br.

MacCannell, Dean. 1992. *Empty Meeting Grounds: The Tourist Papers.* London: Routledge.

———. 1999 (1976). *The Tourist: A New Theory of the Leisure Class.* Berkeley: University of California Press.

MacLachlan, Colin. 2003. *A History of Modern Brazil: The Past against the Future.* Wilmington, Del.: Scholarly Resources.

Maia, Suzana. 2012. *Transnational Desires: Brazilian Erotic Dancers in New York.* Nashville: Vanderbilt University Press.

Malkki, Liisa H. 1995. *Purity and Exile: Violence, Memory, and National Cosmology among Hutu Refugees in Tanzania.* Chicago: University of Chicago Press.

Manalansan, Martin. 2003. *Global Divas: Filipino Gay Men in Diaspora.* Durham: Duke University Press.

Manalansan, Martin, and Arnaldo Cruz-Malave, eds. 2002. *Queer Globalizations: Citizenship and the Afterlife of Colonialism.* New York: New York University Press.

Manderson, Lenore, and Margaret Jolly, eds. 1997. *Sites of Desire, Economies of Pleasure: Sexualities in Asia and the Pacific.* Chicago: University of Chicago Press.

Martínez, Samuel. 1996. "Indifference without Indignation: Anthropology, Human Rights, and the Haitian Bracero." *American Anthropologist* 98:17–25.

Marx, Anthony W. 1998. *Making Race and Nation: A Comparison of the United States, South Africa, and Brazil.* Cambridge: Cambridge University Press.

Massey, Doreen. 1994. *Space, Place, Gender.* Minneapolis: University of Minnesota Press.

Matory, James Lorand. 2005. *Black Atlantic Religion: Tradition, Transnationalism, and Matriarchy in the Afro-Brazilian Candomblé*. Princeton: Princeton University Press.

McCallum, Cecilia. 2007. "Women Out of Place? A Microhistorical Perspective on the Black Feminist Movement in Salvador da Bahia, Brazil." *Journal of Latin American Studies* 39:55–80.

McCann, Bryan. 2008. *The Throes of Democracy: Brazil since 1989*. Halifax, N.S.: Fernwood.

McClintock, Anne. 1993. "Sex Workers and Sex Work: Introduction." *Social Text* 37:1–10.

———. 1995. *Imperial Leather: Race, Gender, and Sexuality in the Colonial Contest*. New York: Routledge.

McGuire, Danielle. 2010. *At the Dark End of the Street: Black Women, Rape, and Resistance—A New History of the Civil Rights Movement from Rosa Parks to the Rise of Black Power*. New York: Knopf.

McKittrick, Katherine. 2006. *Demonic Grounds: Black Women and the Cartographies of Struggle*. Minneapolis: University of Minnesota Press.

Meade, Teresa A. 2003. *A Brief History of Brazil*. New York: Facts on File.

"Measuring Brazil's Economy: Statistics and Lies." 2011. *Economist*, March 10. http://www.economist.com/node/18333018/print.

Mellon, Cynthia. 1998. "A Human Rights Perspective on the Sex Trade in the Caribbean and Beyond." In *Global Sex Workers: Rights, Resistance, Redefinition*, ed. Kamala Kempadoo and Jo Doezema. New York: Routledge.

Mendes, Renato. 2007. "A Difícil Escalada Brasileira." In *Anuário de Turismo 2007–2008*. São Paulo: Abril.

Menezes, Bernardo de. 2002. "O Lado Cruel de Turismo Nacional." *A Tarde*, February 6.

Merry, Sally Engle. 2006. *Human Rights and Gender Violence: Translating International Law into Local Justice*. Chicago: University of Chicago Press.

Miller-Young, Mireille. 2008. Review of *The Politics of Passion: Women's Sexual Culture in the Afro-Surinamese Diaspora*, by Gloria Wekker. *Feminist Theory* 9:119–20.

———. 2010. "Putting Hypersexuality to Work: Black Women and Illicit Eroticism in Pornography. *Sexualities* 13:219–35.

Miko, Francis T. and Grace (Jea-Hyun) Park. 2002. *Trafficking in Women and Children: The U.S. and International Response*. Washington, D.C.: Congressional Research Service. http://fpc.state.gov/documents/organization/9107.pdf.

Ministério da Saúde. 2002. *Profissionais do Sexo: Documento Referencial para Ações de Prevenção das DST e da AIDS*. Ed. Secretaria de Políticas de Saúde Coordenação Nacional de DST e AIDS. Brasilia: Coordenação Nacional de DST e AIDS.

Minority Rights Group. 1995. *No Longer Invisible: Afro-Latin Americans Today*. London: Minority Rights Publications.

Mitchell, Gregory. 2010. "Fare Tales and Fairy Tails: How Gay Sex Tourism Is Shaping the Brazilian Dream." *Wagadu: A Journal of Transnational Women's and Gender Studies* 8:93–114.

———. 2011a. "Organizational Challenges Facing Male Sex Workers in Brazil's Tourist Zones." In *Policing Pleasure: Sex Work, Policy, and the State in Global Perspective*, ed. Susan Dewey and Patty Kelly. New York: New York University Press.

———. 2011b. "Turbo Consumers in Paradise: Tourism, Civil Rights, and Brazil's Gay Sex Industry." *American Ethnologist* 38:666–82.

Mohanty, Chandra Talpade. 1991. "Under Western Eyes: Feminist Scholarship and Colonial Discourses." In *Third World Women and the Politics of Feminism*, ed. Chandra Talpade Mohanty, Ann Russo, and Lourdes Torres. Bloomington: Indiana University Press.

Montgomery, Heather. 2001. *Modern Babylon? Prostituting Children in Thailand*. New York: Berghahn.

Morgan, Jennifer L. 1997. "Some Could Suckle over Their Shoulder: Male Travelers, Female Bodies, and the Gendering of Racial Ideology, 1500–1770." *William and Mary Quarterly*, 3rd. ser., 54:167–92.

Nagel, Joane. 2003. *Race, Ethnicity, and Sexuality: Intimate Intersections, Forbidden Frontiers*. New York: Oxford University Press.

Naples, Nancy A. 2002. "The Challenges and Possibilities of Transnational Feminist Praxis." In *Women's Activism and Globalization: Linking Local Struggles and Transnational Politics*, ed. Nancy Naples and Manisha Desai. New York: Routledge.

Nash, Dennison. 1989. "Tourism as a Form of Imperialism." In *Hosts and Guests: The Anthropology of Tourism*, ed. Valene L. Smith. Philadelphia: University of Pennsylvania Press.

Needell, Jeffrey D. 1995. "Identity, Race, Gender, and Modernity in the Origins of Gilberto Freyre's Oeuvre." *American Historical Review* 100:51–77.

Negreiros, Adriana. 2001. "O Amor Sem Fronteira." *Veja*, August 15. http://veja.abril.com .br/150801/p_088.html.

Nencel, Lorraine. 2001. *Ethnography and Prostitution in Peru*. London: Pluto.

Ness, Sally Ann. 2003. *Where Asia Smiles: An Ethnography of Philippine Tourism*. Philadelphia: University of Pennsylvania.

Nogueira, Leo. 2007. "Lei Que Obrigava Profissionais do Sexo a Realizarem Exame de HIV e Criticada Por Ativistas." Agencia de Noticias da Aids. April 24. http://www .agenciaaids.com.br/noticias/interna.php?id=7398.

O'Connell Davidson, Julia. 1998. *Prostitution, Power, and Freedom*. Ann Arbor: University of Michigan Press.

Oliveira, Beatriz, and Jakzam Kaizer. 2002. *Embratur: O Turismo na Economia Nacional, a Revolução Silenciosa*. Florianopolis: Letras Brasileiras.

Oliveira, Luciano Amaral. 2002. *Turismo para Gays e Lésbicas: Uma Viagem Reflexiva*. São Paulo: Roca.

Oliveira, Mauricio. 2007. "A Maior Indústria do Mundo." *Annuário de Turismo 2007–2008*. São Paulo: Abril. http://exame.abril.com.br/revista-exame/edicoes/0890/noticias/a-maior -industria-do-mundo-m0125844.

O'Neill, Jim. 2001. *Building Better Global Economic BRICs*. http://www.goldmansachs.com/ our-thinking/archive/archive-pdfs/build-better-brics.pdf.

Ong, Aihwa. 1999. *Flexible Citizens: The Cultural Logics of Transnationality*. Durham: Duke University Press.

Opperman, Martin. 1998. *Sex Tourism and Prostitution: Aspects of Leisure, Recreation, and Work*. Elmsford, N.Y.: Cognizant Communication.

Padilla, Mark. 2007a. *Caribbean Pleasure Industry: Tourism, Sexuality, and AIDS in the Dominican Republic*. Chicago: University of Chicago Press.

———. 2007b. "Tourism and Tigueraje: The Structures of Love and Silence among Dominican Male Sex Workers." In *Love and Globalization: Transformations of Intimacy in the Contemporary World*, ed. Mark Padilla, Jennifer Hirsch, Miguel Munoz-Laboy, Robert Sember, and Richard Parker. Nashville: Vanderbilt University Press.

Parker, Richard G. 1991. *Bodies, Pleasures, and Passions: Sexual Culture in Contemporary Brazil.* Boston: Beacon.

———. 1997. "Carnivalization of the World." In *The Gender/Sexuality Reader: Culture, History, Political Economy*, ed. Roger N. Lancaster and Micaela di Leonardo. New York: Routledge.

———. 1999. *Beneath the Equator: Cultures of Desire, Male Homosexuality, and Emerging Gay Communities of Brazil.* New York: Routledge.

Patil, Vrushali. 2011. "Reproducing/Resisting Race and Gender Difference: Examining India's Online Tourism Campaign from a Transnational Feminist Perspective." *Signs* 37:185–206.

Pattanaik, Bandana. 2002. "Conclusion: Where Do We Go from Here?" In *Transnational Prostitution: Changing Patterns in a Global Context*, ed. Susanne Thorbek and Bandana Pattanaik. London: Zed.

Pattanaik, Bandana, and Susana Thorbek, eds. 2002. *Transnational Prostitution: Changing Patterns in a Global Context.* London: Zed.

Perry, Keisha-Khan. 2004. "The Roots of Black Resistance: Race, Gender, and the Struggle for Urban Land Rights in Salvador, Bahia, Brazil." *Social Identities* 10:811–31.

———. 2009. "'The Groundings with My Sisters': Towards a Black Diasporic Feminist Agenda in the Americas." *Scholar and Feminist Online* 7.2. http://sfonline.barnard.edu/ africana/perry_01.htm.

Pesquisa das Nações Unidas para o Desenvolvimento (PNUD). 2006. *Desigualdade é Maior na Grande Salvador Que no Brasil.* December 27. http://www.pnud.org.br/Noticia .aspx?id=1470.

Petenbrink, Troy. 2012. "Brazil: Gay-Murders More Than Double in Five Years." *Examiner. com*, April 9. www.examiner.com/article/brazil-gay-murders-more-than-double-five -years-1.

Pierson, Donald. 1942. *Negroes in Brazil: A Study of Race Contact at Bahia.* Chicago: University of Chicago Press.

Pinho, José Antônio Gomes de, Aniele Marquez, Ivã Coelho, and Mônica Santana. 2008. "Combate à Exploração Sexual de Crianças e Adolescentes no Turismo em Salvador." In *O Setor Turístico Versus a Exploração Sexual na Infancia e Adolescencia*, ed. Fernando G. Tenorio and Luiz Gustavo Medeiros Barbosa. Rio de Janeiro: FGV.

Pinho, Patricia de Santana. 2004. *Reinvenções da Africa na Bahia.* São Paulo: AnneBlume.

———. 2008. "African-American Roots Tourism in Brazil." *Latin American Perspectives* 35:70–86.

Piscitelli, Adriana. 1996. "Sexo Tropical: Comentários sobre Gênero e Raça em Alguns Textos da Mídia Brasileira." *Cadernos Pagu* 6–7:9–34.

———. 2001. "On Gringos and Natives: Gender and Sexuality in the Context of International Sex Tourism in Fortaleza, Brazil." Paper presented at the conference of the Latin American Studies Association, Washington, D.C. http://www.vibrant.org.br/ downloads/a1v1_ogn.pdf.

———. 2006. "Transnational Sex Travels: Negotiating Identities in a Brazilian 'Tropical Paradise.'" In *Translocalities/Translocalidades: Feminist Politics of Translation in*

Latin/a Américas, ed. Sonia Alvarez, Claudia de Lima Costa, Veronica Feliu, Macarena Gomez-Barris, Rebecca Hester, Norma Klahn, and Millie Thayer. Amherst: University of Massachusetts Center for Latin American, Caribbean, and Latino Studies.

———. 2007. "Shifting Boundaries: Sex and Money in the North-East of Brazil." *Sexualities* 10:489–500.

———. 2008. "Looking for New Worlds: Brazilian Women as International Migrants." *Signs* 33784–93.

———. 2011. "Amor, Apego, e Interesse: Trocas Sexuais, Economicas, e Afetivas em Cenarios Transnacionais." In *Gênero, Sexo, Amor, e Dinheiro: Mobilidades Transnacionais Envolvendo o Brasil*, ed. Adriana Piscitelli, Glaucia de Oliveira Assis, and José Miguel Nieto Olivar. Campinas: Pagu/Núcleo de Estudos de Gênero, UNICAMP.

Piscitelli, Adriana, Glaucia de Oliveira Assis, and José Miguel Nieto Olivar, eds. 2011. *Gênero, Sexo, Amor, e Dinheiro: Mobilidades Transnacionais Envolvendo o Brasil*. Campinas: Pagu/Núcleo de Estudos de Gênero, UNICAMP.

Pratt, Mary Louise. 1992. *Imperial Eyes: Travel Writing and Transculturation*. London: Routledge.

Pravaz, Natasha. 2003. "Brazilian *Mulatice*: Performing Race, Gender, and the Nation." *Journal of Latin American Anthropology* 8:116–47.

———. 2008a. "Hybridity Brazilian-Style: Samba, Carnaval, and the Myth of 'Racial Democracy' in Rio de Janeiro." *Identities: Global Studies in Culture and Power* 15:80–102.

———. 2008b. "Where Is the Carnivalesque in Rio's Carnaval? Samba, *Mulatas*, and Modernity." *Visual Anthropology* 21:95–111.

———. 2009. "The Tan from Ipanema: Freyre, *Morenidade*, and the Cult of the Body in Rio de Janeiro." *Canadian Journal of Latin American and Caribbean Studies* 34:79–104.

———. 2012. "Performing Mulata-Ness: The Politics of Cultural Authenticity and Sexuality among Carioca Samba Dancers." *Latin American Perspectives* 39:113–33.

Pritchard, A., and N. Morgan. 2000. "Privileging the Male Gaze: Gendered Tourism Landscapes." *Annals of Tourism Research* 27:884–905.

Programa das Nações Unidas para o Desenvolvimento. 2006. *Desigualdade de Renda é Maior na Região Metropolitana de Salvador-RMS Que no Brasil*. https://docs.google.com/gview?url=http://www.pnud.org.br/publicacoes/atlas_salvador/release_desigualdade.pdf.

Puar, Jasbir K. 2002a. "Introduction." *GLQ* 8:1–6.

———. 2002b. "A Transnational Feminist Critique of Queer Tourism." *Antipode* 34:935–46.

———. 2007. *Terrorist Assemblages: Homonationalism in Queer Times*. Durham: Duke University Press.

Queiroz, Lúcia de. 2002. *Turismo na Bahia: Estratégias para o Desenvolvimento*. Salvador: Secretaria da Cultura e Turismo.

Rajbhandari, Binayak. 1994. *Conceptual Clarity on Trafficking: Proceedings of the Workshop on Conceptual Clarity on Trafficking*. Kathmandu: WOREC.

Ratts, Alex. 2011. "Os Lugares da Gente Negra: Raca, Genero, e Espaço no Pensamento de Beatriz Nascimento e Lélia Gonzalez." Paper presented at the Congresso Luso Afro-Brasileiro de Ciencias Sociais, Universidade Federal da Bahia, Salvador.

Rebhun, Linda Anne. 2007. "The Strange Marriage of Love and Interest: Economic Change and Emotional Intimacy in Northeast Brazil, Private and Public." In *Love and Globalization: Transformations of Intimacy in the Contemporary World*, ed. Mark Padilla, Jennifer

S. Hirsch, Miguel Muñoz-Laboy, Robert Sember, and Richard G. Parker. Nashville: Vanderbilt University Press.

Reddy, Chandan. 2005. "Asian Diasporas, Neoliberalism, and Family: Reviewing the Case for Homosexual Asylum in the Context of Family Rights." *Social Text* 84–85:101–19.

Reiter, Bernd. 2009. *Negotiating Democracy in Brazil: The Politics of Exclusion*. Boulder, Colo.: First Forum.

Reiter, Bernd, and Gladys Mitchell, eds. 2010. *Brazil's New Racial Politics*. Boulder, Colo.: Rienner.

Robbins, Bruce. 1998. "Comparative Cosmopolitanisms." In *Cosmopolitics: Thinking and Feeling beyond the Nation*, ed. Peng Cheah and Bruce Robbins. Minneapolis: University of Minnesota Press.

Roett, Riordan. 2010. *The New Brazil*. Washington, D.C.: Brookings Institution Press.

Rogers, Chris. 2010. "Brazil's Sex Tourism Boom." BBC News. July 30. http://www.bbc.co.uk/news/world-10764371?.

Romo, Anadelia. 2010. *Brazil's Living Museum: Race, Reform, and Tradition in Bahia*. Chapel Hill: University of North Carolina Press.

Rosaldo, Michelle Z. 1980. "The Use and Abuse of Anthropology: Reflections on Feminism and Cross-Cultural Understanding." *Signs* 5:389–417.

Roseno, R. 2006. "Breves Reflexões sobre as Relações entre Turismo, Infância, e Juventude no Brasil." In *Turismo Social Dialogos do Turismo: Uma Viagem do Inclusão*. Ministério de Turismo, Instituto Brasileiro do Administração Municipal. Rio de Janeiro: IBAM. http://www.livrosgratis.com.br/arquivos_livros/tu000012.pdf.

Ryan, Chris, and Colin Michael Hall. 2001. *Sex Tourism: Marginal People and Liminalities*. London: Routledge.

Salário Mínimo. N.d. http://www.portalbrasil.net/salariominimo.htm#sileiro.

"Salvador Tem Maior Taxa de Desemprego em Junho." 2010. *R7 Noticias*, July 22. http://noticias.r7.com/economia/noticias/salvador-tem-maior-taxa-de-desemprego-em-junho-20100722.html.

Sansone, Livio. 2003. *Blackness without Ethnicity: Constructing Race in Brazil*. New York: Palgrave Macmillan.

Santos, Boaventura de Sousa. 2006. "Globalizations." *Theory, Culture, Society* 23:393–99.

Santos, Cecilia McDowell. 2005. *Women's Police Stations: Gender, Violence, and Justice in São Paulo*. New York: Palgrave Macmillan.

Santos, Sonia Beatriz dos. 2007. "Feminismo Negro Diasporico." *Genero* 8:11–26.

Saraswati, L. Ayu. 2010. "Cosmopolitan Whiteness: The Effects and Affects of Skin-Whitening Advertisements in a Transnational Women's Magazine in Indonesia." *Meridians* 10:15–41.

Sassen, Saskia. 2001. *Globalization and Its Discontents: Essays on the New Mobility of People and Money*. New York: New Press.

Schaeffer-Grabiel, Felicity. 2004. "Cyberbrides and Global Imaginaries: Mexican Women Turn from the National to the Foreign." *Space and Culture* 7:33–48.

———. 2005. "Planet-Love.Com: Cyberbrides in the Americas and the Transnational Routes of U.S. Masculinity." *Signs* 31:331–56.

———. 2006. "Flexible Technologies of Subjectivity and Mobility across the Americas." *American Quarterly* 58:891–914.

Schelp, Diogo. 2003. "Tem de Gostar Muito do Brasil." *Veja*, October 22. http://veja.abril.com.br/221003/p_080.html.

Schifter-Sikora, Jacobo. 2007. *Mongers in Heaven: Sex Tourism and HIV Risk in Costa Rica and the United States*. Lanham, Md.: University Press of America.

Schilt, Kristen, and Laurel Westbrook. 2009. "Doing Gender, Doing Heteronormativity: 'Gender Normals,' Transgender People, and the Social Maintenance of Heterosexuality." *Gender and Society* 23:440–64.

Seabrook, Jeremy. 2001. *Travels in the Skin Trade: Tourism and the Sex Industry*. 2nd ed. London: Pluto.

Sebastiao, Ana Angelia. 2010. "Feminismo Negro e Suas Práticas no Campo da Cultura." *Revista da Associação Brasileira de Pesquisadores Negros* 1:64–77.

Selka, Stephen. 2007. *Religion and the Politics of Ethnic Identity in Bahia, Brazil*. Gainesville: University Press of Florida.

Sepúlveda dos Santos, Myrian. 1999. "Samba Schools: The Logic of Orgy and Blackness in Rio de Janeiro." In *Representations of Blackness and the Performance of Identities*, ed. Jean Muteba Rahier. Westport, Conn.: Bergin and Garvey.

Sexton, Jared. 2008. *Amalgamation Schemes: Antiblackness and the Critique of Multiracialism*. Minneapolis: University of Minnesota Press.

Sharma, Aradhana, and Akhil Gupta. 2006. "Introduction: Rethinking Theories of the State in an Age of Globalization." In *The Anthropology of the State: A Reader*, ed. Aradhana Sharma and Akhil Gupta. Malden, Mass.: Blackwell.

Sharpley-Whiting, T. Denean. 2007. "'I See the Same Ho': Video Vixens, Beauty Culture, and Diasporic Sex Tourism." In *Pimps Up, Ho's Down: Hip Hop's Hold on Young Black Women*. New York: New York University Press.

Sheriff, Robin. 2001. *Dreaming Equality: Color, Race, and Racism in Urban Brazil*. New Brunswick, N.J.: Rutgers University Press.

Silva, Ana da. 2010. "Brazil's Tourism Black and Blues. *Brazzil*, January 24.

Silva, Denise Ferreira da. 2004. "An Introduction: The Predicament of Brazilian Culture." *Social Identities: Journal for the Study of Race, Nation, and Culture* 10:719–34.

Skidmore, Thomas. 1974. *Black into White: Race and Nationality in Brazilian Thought*. New York: Oxford University Press.

Smith, Christen. 2008. "Scenarios of Racial Contact: Police Violence and the Politics of Performance and Racial Formation in Brazil." *E-Misférica* 5.2: *Raza y Sus Otras*. December. http://hemi.nyu.edu/hemi/es/e-misferica-52/smith.

Soares do Bem, Ari. 2005. *A Dialética do Turismo Sexual*. Campinas: Papirus.

Sodré, Muniz. 1999. *Claros e Escuros: Identidade, Povo, e Mídia no Brasil*. Petropolis: Vozes.

Spivak, Gayatri Chakravorty. 2000. "Discussion: An Afterword on the New Subaltern." In *Community, Gender, and Violence*, ed. Partha Chatterjee and Pradeep Jeganathan. New York: Columbia University Press.

Stallybrass, Peter, and Allon White. 1986. *The Politics and Poetics of Transgression*. Ithaca: Cornell University Press.

Stam, Robert. 1997. *Tropical Multiculturalism: A Comparative History of Race in Brazilian Cinema and Culture*. Durham: Duke University Press.

Steiw, Leandro. 2007. "Imagem É Quase Tudo." *Exame, Annuário de Turismo 2007–2008*: 53. São Paulo: Abril. http://exame.abril.com.br/revista-exame/edicoes/0890/noticias/imagem-e-quase-tudo-m0125865.

Stephens, Sharon. 1995. *Children and the Politics of Culture.* Princeton: Princeton University Press.

Sterling, Cheryl. 2010. "Women-Space, Power, and the Sacred in Afro-Brazilian Culture." *Global South* 4:71–93.

Sunder, Rajan. 2003. *The Scandal of the State: Women, Law, and Citizenship in Postcolonial India.* Durham: Duke University Press.

"TAM Apoia Campanha contra Turismo Sexual." 2005. *Diário do Nordeste,* January 14. http://diariodonordeste.globo.com/m/materia.asp?codigo=219018.

A Tarde. 2005. "Turismo Sexual na Mira do Governo." January 11.

Teles dos Santos, Jocélio. 1998. "A Mixed-Race Nation: Afro-Brazilians and Cultural Policy in Bahia, 1970–1990." In *Afro-Brazilian Culture and Politics: Bahia, 1790s to 1990s,* ed. H. Kraay. Armonk, N.Y.: Sharpe.

———. 2005. *O Poder da Cultura e a Cultura no Poder: A Disputa Simbólica da Herança Cultural Negra no Brasil.* Salvador: Edufba.

Telles, Edward. 2004. *Race in Another America.* Princeton: Princeton University Press.

Thayer, Millie. 2010. *Making Transnational Feminism: Rural Women, NGO Activists, and Northern Donors in Brazil.* New York: Routledge.

Thorbek, Susanne, and Bandana Pattanaik, eds. 2002. *Transnational Prostitution: Changing Patterns in a Global Context.* London: Zed.

Trotter, Henry. 2009. *Sugar Girls and Seamen: A Journey into the World of Dockside Prostitution in South Africa.* Johannesburg: Jacana.

Turismo Sustentável e Infância: Colocando na Prática. N.d. Brasilia: Programa Turismo Sustentavel e Infancia, University of Brasilia.

Turner, Victor. 1969. *The Ritual Process: Structure and Anti-Structure.* Chicago: Aldine.

United Nations. 2000. *Protocol to Prevent, Suppress, and Punish Trafficking in Persons, Especially Women and Children, Supplementing the United Nations Convention against Transnational Organized Crime.* www.uncjin.org/Documents/Conventions/dcatoc/final_documents_2/convention_%20traff_eng.pdf.

United Nations Development Programme. 2010. *The Real Wealth of Nations: Pathways to Human Development.* New York: Palgrave Macmillan. http://hdr.undp.org/en/media/HDR_2010_EN_Complete_reprint.pdf.

Urry, John. 1995. *Consuming Places.* London: Routledge.

———. 2002. *The Tourist Gaze.* 2nd ed. London: Sage.

U.S. Department of State. 2009. *Trafficking in Persons Report: Country Narratives—Countries A through C.* www.state.gov/g/tip/rls/tiprpt/2009/123135.htm.

———. 2011. *Trafficking in Persons Report: Country Narratives—Countries A through F.* http://www.state.gov/j/tip/rls/tiprpt/2011/164231.htm.

Valentine, David. 2007. *Imagining Transgender: An Ethnography of a Category.* Durham: Duke University Press.

van der Veen, Marjolein. 2000. "Beyond Slavery and Capitalism: Producing Class Differences in the Sex Industry." In *Class and Its Others,* ed. J. K. Gibson-Graham, Stephen A. Resnick, and Richard D. Wolff. Minneapolis: University of Minnesota Press.

Vargas, João Costa. 2004. "Hyperconsciousness of Race and Its Negation: The Dialectic of White Supremacy in Brazil." *Identities: Global Studies in Power and Culture* 11:443–70.

Vertovec, Steven, and Robin Cohen. 2002. "Introduction: Conceiving Cosmopolitanism." In *Conceiving Cosmopolitanism: Theory, Context, and Practice*, ed. Steven Vertovec and Robin Cohen. New York: Oxford University Press.

Viana, Elizabeth de Espirito Santo. 2010. "Lélia Gonzalez e Outras Mulheres: Pensamento Feminista Negro, Antiracismo, e Antissexismo." *Revista da Associação Brasileira de Pesquisadores Negros* 1:52–63.

Vianna, Hermano. 1999. *The Mystery of Samba: Popular Music and National Identity in Brazil*. Trans. John Charles Chasteen. Chapel Hill: University of North Carolina Press.

Wagley, Charles. 1959. "On the Social Concept of Race in the Americas." *Actas del XXXIII Congreso Internacional de Americanistas* 1:403–17.

Warren, Jonathan. 2000. "Masters in the Field: White Talk, White Privilege, White Biases." In *Racing Research, Researching Race: Methodological Dilemmas in Critical Race Studies*, ed. France Winddance Twine and Jonathan W. Warren. New York: New York University Press.

Wearden, Graeme. 2011. "Brazil Considers Helping Portugal Ease Debt Crisis." *Guardian*, March 30. www.guardian.co.uk/business/2011/mar/30/brazil-considers-helping-portugal/print.

Wekker, Gloria. 2006. *The Politics of Passion: Women's Sexual Culture in the Afro-Surinamese Diaspora*. New York: Columbia University Press.

Werneck, Jurema. 2010. "Nossos Passos Vêm de Longe! Movimentos de Mulheres Negras e Estratégias Políticas Contra o Sexismo e o Racismo." *Revista da Associação Brasileira de Pesquisadores Negros* 1:8–17.

Whitehead, Stephen, and Frank Barrett, eds. 2001. *The Masculinities Reader*. Cambridge: Polity.

Wijers, Marjan, and Marieke van Doorninck. 2002. "Only Rights Can Stop Wrongs: A Critical Assessment of Anti-Trafficking Strategies." Paper Presented at EU/IOM STOP Conference on Preventing and Combating Trafficking in Human Beings—A Global Challenge for the 21st Century, September 18–20, 2002. http://www.walnet.org/csis/papers/wijers-rights.html.

Williams, Erica Lorraine. 2010. "Blonde Beauties and Black Booties: Racial Hierarchies in Brazil." *Ms. Magazine Blog*, June 11. http://msmagazine.com/blog/blog/2010/06/11/blonde-beauties-and-black-booties-racial-hierarchies-in-brazil/.

———. 2011a. "Moral Panic: Sex Tourism, Trafficking, and the Limits of Transnational Mobility in Bahia." In *Policing Pleasure: Sex Work, Policy, and the State in Global Perspective*, ed. Susan Dewey and Patty Kelly. New York: New York University Press.

———. 2011b. "Slut-Walk: Bahia-Style." Ms. Magazine Blog, August 5. http://msmagazine.com/blog/blog/2011/08/05/slutwalk-bahia-style/.

———. forthcoming. "*Mucamas* and *Mulatas*: Black Brazilian Feminisms, Representations, and Ethnography." In "Transatlantic Feminisms: Women and Gender Studies in Africa and the African Diaspora," ed. Akosua Ampofo, Cheryl Rodriguez, and Dzodzi Tsikata. East Lansing: Michigan State University Press.

Wilson, Ara. 2004. *The Intimate Economies of Bangkok: Tomboys, Tycoons, and Avon Ladies in the Global City*. Berkeley: University of California Press.

Wilson, Julee. 2012. "Natural Hair Song by Tiririca Deemed Racist, Sony Music Ordered to Pay $1.2 Million." *Huffington Post*, January 6. http://www.huffingtonpost.com/2012/01/06/natural-hair-racist-_n_1189068.html.

Wilson, Tamar Diana. 2008. "Introduction: Impacts of Tourism in Latin America." *Latin American Perspectives* 35:3–20.

Winant, Howard. 1992. "Rethinking Race in Brazil." *Journal of Latin American Studies* 24:173–92.

Wonders, Nancy A., and Raymond Michalowski. 2001. "Bodies, Borders, and Sex Tourism in a Globalized World: A Tale of Two Cities—Amsterdam and Havana." *Social Problems* 48:545–71.

Woods, Clyde, and Katherine McKittrick. 2007. *Black Geographies and the Politics of Place.* Cambridge, Mass.: South End.

Woods, Jewel, and Karen Hunter. 2008. *Don't Blame It on Rio: The Real Deal behind Why Men Go to Brazil for Sex.* New York: Grand Central .

"World's Gayest Tourism Destinations." 2011. *Out Now*, May 10. http://www.outnow consulting.com/latest-updates/press-centre/worlds-gayest-tourism-destinations.aspx.

Wyler, Liana Sun, and Alison Siskin. 2010. *Trafficking in Persons: U.S. Policy and Issues for Congress.* Washington, D.C.: Congressional Research Service. http://fpc.state.gov/documents/organization/152057.pdf.

Zelizer, Viviana. 2005. *The Purchase of Intimacy.* Princeton: Princeton University Press.

———. 2009. "Dinheiro, Poder, e Sexo." *Cadernos Pagu* 32:135–57.

Index

advertising. *See* sex tourism marketing
Afro-Brazilian culture: attitudes, 171nn14–
15; Bahian tourism, 30–43; Black Mecca
marketing, 29–32; commodification,
21–22; complexity of racial identification,
51–52; cultural elements/sex relationship,
80–81; economic value, 41–42; eroticiza-
tion history, 56–57; hypersexuality-sacred
ritual link representation, 57; "racial de-
mocracy" relationship, 56–57; racialized
eroticization, 5, 16, 56–63; reality of Afro-
Brazilian people vs., 55–56; tourist industry role, 32–34; and women, 50–51, 61–62.
See also Candomblé
Agustín, Laura María, 148, 153
Alexander, M. Jacqui, 5–6, 58, 82, 106, 154
Allen, Jafari Sinclaire, 10, 71, 153, 163
Altman, Dennis, 5, 104
The Anthropology of Sex (Donnan and Mc-
Gowan), 9
Appadurai, Arjun, 6
Aprosba (Association of Prostitutes of
Bahia): accomplishments, 101–3; affilia-
tions, 106–7, 111; citizenship rights, 107;
decriminalization, 104–6; education,
111–13; empowerment, 98, 100, 107–8,
109; enterprises, 107–8; health and safety
information, 111–13; legitimization, 100,
104–6; logo, 113; meetings, 1, 97–98; mem-
ber-to-member support, 97–98; Ministry
of Health and Culture, 175n12; overviews,
97–101, 123–25; research, 12–16; transnational solidarities, 123–24

Araújo, Joel Zito, 76, 105
Assis, Glaucia de Oliveira, 70–71
Association of Prostitutes of Bahia (Aprosba). *See* Aprosba (Association of Prostitutes of Bahia)

Babb, Florence, 10
Bahia: Afro-Brazilian cultural tourism, 22,
30–43; as Black Mecca, 3, 21, 22, 29–32;
Candomblé, 30–31; demographics, 8;
economy, 27–28; ethnicity, 29–30; as gay
tourism mecca, 65; history, 170n12; pov-
erty and inequality, 27–28; racism, 31–32;
Rastafarianism, 30; sex tourism focus in
advertising, 47–48; sex tourism overview,
3–7; as tourism leader, 28–29. *See also*
Salvador
Bahian icons (*baianas*), 32–33
Bahian-ness, 31, 34
Bahians, 37. *See also* Afro-Brazilian culture
Bahia state tourism agency (Bahiatursa),
28, 30–31
Bahiatursa, 28, 30–31
baianas (Bahian icons), 32–33
baianidade (Bahian-ness), 31, 34
Bananas, Beaches, and Bases (Enloe), 69
Barra, 23, 25, 44–45
Barry, Kathleen, 103, 148
Bastide, Roger, 54, 56
Beijo da Rua, 107
Bernstein, Elizabeth, 89
Bevins, Vincent, 166
black gay sex tourism, 65–67, 79–82

black hypersexuality mythology, 2–3, 5, 11–12, 45–46, 59–62
Black Mecca (*also* Black Rome/Roma Negra), 3, 21, 22, 29–32, 170n12
black woman (*escura, negra,* or *preta*), 51–52
Blanchette, Thaddeus, 78, 152, 158
Bocão, Eduardo, 76
Boellstorff, Tom, 161
Boris, Eileen, 139–40
branca (white woman), 40, 52
Brazil, 45, 52–56, 62–63, 172nn11–12
Brazilian Classification of Occupations (*Classificação Brasileira de Ocupações*), 99, 101
Brazilian Network of Prostitutes (*Rede Brasileira de Prostitutas*), 106–7, 108–10
Brazilian women of African descent, 50–52, 85–86, 92–93, 95–96. See also *mulata*
Brennan, Denise, 6, 86, 153
brothel, 36, 88
brown woman (*morena, mulata, negra,* or *parda*), 50, 51–52
Bruner, Edward M., 92
Burdick, John, 51–52
"butt culture," 45

Cabezas, Amalia, 100, 116, 124, 163
caçador (hunter), 12, 20, 43, 44, 134, 161
caça-gringas (hunter of foreign women), 14–15, 19–21, 44–45, 169nn1–2
Caldwell, Kia Lilly, 3, 49
call girls (*garotas de programa*), 25
Camacho, Ernest, 66
Candomblé: commodification for tourism, 30–31, 38–41, 57–58, 171nn17–19; intolerance as racism manifestation, 172n12
capoeira, 21, 33
Carby, Hazel, 154
Cardoso, Fernando Henrique, 54, 55
Carioca School (*Escola Carioca*), 55
Carnaval, 74
Carneiro, Edson, 39
Carneiro, Sueli, 50
casa (house of prostitution), 36, 88
CATW (Coalition Against Trafficking in Women), 48, 103, 177n10
CEDECA, 77
Center for Information for Women from Asia, Africa, and Latin America (FIZ), 144–45
Centro Histórico (Historic Center), 18, 23, 25
CHAME (Humanitarian Center for the Support of Women): anti-trafficking education, 142, 149–53; Aprosba (Association of Prostitutes of Bahia) collaboration, 144; assumptions about low-income Brazilian women of African descent, 149–56, 177–78n8; exploitation vs. *se valorizando*, 136–37; mission, 144; primary functions, 145; research methodology, 12–13; sex tourism research, 70; trafficking definition, 149
chapter overviews, 16–17
Chequer, Pedro, 100
Children and the Politics of Culture (Stephens), 77
child sexual exploitation: complexity and ambiguity, 77, 78; prevention organizations and campaigns, 74–75, 77–78, 173nn8–9, 173n12, 174n3; research and statistics, 74–75, 77, 173nn7–9; sample case, 75–76
Cidade Alta (Upper City), 23
Cidade Baixa (film), 126
Cidade Baixa (Lower City), 23
Cidade des Homens (City of Men), 24
Cinderelas, Lobos, e um Principe Encantado (Cinderellas, Wolves, and a Prince Charming), 76, 105
cis-gender, 60, 172n14
City of God (film), 24
City of Women (Landes), 57
Classificação Brasileira de Ocupações (Brazilian Classification of Occupations), 99, 101
Clifford, James, 166
Coalition against Trafficking in Women (CATW), 103, 148, 177n10
coastline (*orla*), 18–19, 23, 25
Cohen, Cathy, 11
Cohen, Stanley, 153–54
Cohim, Debora, 77
Collins, Patricia Hill, 114
commercial sex transactions (*programas*), 3, 52, 115, 127, 135, 161, 169n3
Committee to Confront Sexual Violence against Children and Adolescents in Bahia, 75
Congress of Brazilian Women, 50
"controlling images," 114–15
Coreia, Sonia, 163, 165
Correio da Bahia, 75–76
Costa, Jô, 77
Crepaldi, Iara, 57

dark woman (*escura*), 51–52
Daspu, 107

Davidson, Julia O'Connell, 117
Davis, Adrienne, 5–6
Davis, Darien, 35
Delegacía da Mulher (Women's Police Station), 102, 174n6
Delegacia de Proteção ao Turista (Delegation for the Protection of Tourists) (Deltur), 14–15, 72, 145
Deltur (Delegation for the Protection of Tourists), 14–15, 72, 145
Desai, Manisha, 123, 124, 161
Dewey, Susan, 118, 167
Doezema, Jô, 86, 103, 148
Donnan, Hastings, 9
Dunn, Christopher, 31, 34
Dzidienyo, Anani, 51, 55, 56

Ebron, Paulla, 139, 154–55, 163
Edmonds, Alexander, 5, 53
Embratur, 29, 47, 73–74, 170n11
Emtursa, 32–33
Enloe, Cynthia, 69
Escola Carioca (Carioca School), 55
Escola Paulista (São Paulo School), 54, 55
escura (dark woman), 51–52
Esteban-Muñoz, José, 121
Esteves, Acúrsio Pereira, 30
ethnoscape, 6
exportation-type mulata (*mulata tipo exportaçao*), 48

feminist scholarship, 24, 63, 98, 103–6, 162, 165, 170n5. *See also specific scholars and specific works*
Fernandes, Florestan, 54
Ferree, Myra Marx, 9–10
Ferreira da Silva, Denise, 53, 55
"fetishized natives," 58–59
Filho, Antonio Jonas Dias, 118–19
FIZ (Center for Information for Women from Asia, Africa, and Latin America, 144–45
Freyre, Gilberto, 39, 49–50, 53, 56, 171n19
Frohlick, Susan, 84, 95, 96

Garcia, Carmen Ines, 74
garotas de programa (call girls), 25
garotos de programa (male prostitutes), 37, 91
Gaudenzi, Paulo, 30
gay and lesbian sex tourism, 65–67, 82, 172nn1–2, 172n4. *See also* black gay sex tourism; GLS (gay, lesbian, and allies) tourism

gendered racism, 3. *See also* sexual stereotyping: by gender
Gille, Zsuzsa, 6
Gilliam, Angela, 22, 47
Global Alliance Against Trafficking in Women, 147–48, 174n8, 176n6
globalization anthropology, 10–11
globalized sex tourism: abolitionists vs. sex workers' rights advocates, 141–48; agency, 162–63; ambiguities, 165–68; Brazilian men vs. foreign tourists, 159–60; Brazilian women vs. European women, 177n2; contemporary economics, 165–66, 177n4; cosmopolitanism, 159–63; as feminism global variant, 162; feminist perspective, 165; and freedom, 160–61; impact on relationships and dating, 159–63; intersectionality, 163–65; laws against, 176n3; national involvements, 165–68; prostitutes as tourists, 141–42; racialized and gendered effects, 163–65; regulationists, 176n3; victimization vs. agency argument, 163–65. *See also* sex tourism; trafficking
Global Sex Worker (Kempadoo), 116
GLS (gay, lesbian, and allies) tourism, 65–67, 172n3. *See also* black gay sex tourism; gay and lesbian sex tourism; *and specific versions of sex tourism*
Goldstein, Donna, 62
Gonzalez, Lélia, 24, 50
gostoso (sexy or tasty), 37, 58, 59, 143
Gregory, Steven, 85, 93, 105, 122
Grewal, Inderpal, 12, 164
gringólogas (women of African descent who go to the Centro to meet *gringos*), 118
gringos (foreign male tourists): advantages, 134–36; cosmopolitanism, 43, 151; economics, 73, 131, 133, 134–35, 137; exploitation, 30, 73; extortion, 126; languages, 13; locations, 3; misinterpretation as trafficking, 49, 139–40; misunderstandings, 37; prestige, 57–58, 61, 134, 137; racial stereotyping, 46, 126; relationships, 3, 14, 26, 118, 127; seasons, 13; social class stereotyping, 85, 137; solicitations, 1; stigma, 133
Guardian (newspaper), 166
Guillermoprieto, Alma, 51
Guimarães, Antonio Sergio Alfredo, 34
Guy-Sheftall, Beverly, 164

Hall, Colin Michael, 82
Hammonds, Evelyn, 63
Hanchard, Michael, 32, 55

Harrison, Julia, 84
Hasenbalg, Carlos, 53
hatred of prostitutes, 2, 169n6
Hautzinger, Sarah J., 117
HIV-AIDS, 111–13
houses of prostitution, 36, 88
Human Development Index, 8, 27–28
Humanitarian Center for the Support of
    Women. *See* CHAME (Humanitarian
    Center for the Support of Women)
Human Rights Caucus, 147–48
hunter (*caçador*), 20, 43, 44, 134, 161. See also
    caça-gringas (hunter of foreign women)
Hunter, Karen, 94–95
hypersexuality. *See* black hypersexuality
    mythology; sexual stereotyping: by race

Ilhéus, a Terra da Gabriela (Ilhéus, the Land
    of Gabriela), 47–48
Inda, Jonathan, 10
International Day to End Violence Against
    Women, 143, 176n2
International Gay and Lesbian Travel As-
    sociation, 67
intimate labor, 139–40
Italian tourists, 64–65, 67–69, 72

Kang, Joo-Hyun, 13
Kaplan, Caren, 12, 164
Kelly, Patty, 118, 167
Kempadoo, Kamala, 86, 98, 116, 117–18, 139,
    163, 165
Kincaid, Jamaica, 58–59
Kondo, Dorinne, 139

Landes, Ruth, 57
Lei Maria da Penha (Brazil's Federal Law
    11340), 117
Leite, Gabriela, 103, 104, 138, 167
Leite, Jacqueline, 70, 78, 136–37, 143–44, 155
Lipsitz, George, 25
Lofgren, Orvar, 85
Lower City, 1, 23
"low Other," 115–16
Lucinda, Elisa, 90
Lula da Silva, Luíz Ignácio, 55
Lusotropicalism, 53–56
Lyrio, Alexandre, 76

MacCannell, Dean, 88
Maciel, Guilherme, 57
Magalhães, Antonio Carlos, 41
Magowan, Fiona, 9

Making Transnational Feminism (Thayer), 123
male prostitutes (*garotos de programa*), 37, 91
Manalansan, Martin, 136
Manifesto of Black Women, 50
Marcus, George, 166
marinheiros (foreign seamen/ship workers),
    127, 130, 136
Massey, Doreen, 22
McCallum, Cecilia, 8
McClintock, Anne, 132, 139
McKittrick, Katherine, 22, 25, 61–62
mestiçagem (racial and cultural mixing),
    53–56. *See also* "racial democracy" my-
    thology
michê (man who has commercial sex with
    men but does not identify as gay), 99, 118,
    169n1, 173–74n14, 175n11. *See also* black
    gay sex tourism
Miller-Young, Mireille, 11, 164–65
Ministry of Health and Culture, 175n12
Ministry of Tourism, 29
Miranda, Carmen, 33–34
miscegenation mythology, 51
Mitchell, Gladys, 12
Mitchell, Gregory, 80, 99–100
Mohanty, Chandra Talpade, 85, 148,
    176–77n8
Montgomery, Heather, 77
moral panics, 153–56, 158, 177n3
morena (brown woman), 51
morenidade (brownness), 52
mulata (woman of black and white racial
    ancestry), 46–53, 171n1. *See also* sexual
    stereotyping: by race
"*Mulata Exportação*/Mulata Exportation"
    (Lucinda), 90
mulata-ness (*mulatice*), 50
mulata shows, 48–49
mulata tipo exportaçao (exportation-type
    mulata), 48
mulatice (*mulata*-ness), 50

Nagel, Joane, 95
namoros (open-ended relationships), 3, 52,
    115, 127, 135, 161
Nash, Dennison, 29
National Plan for Confronting Commercial
    Sexual Exploitation of Children and Ado-
    lescents in Tourism, 74
*National Tourism Plan: A Journey towards
    Inclusion*, (2007–2010), 29, 166, 170n19
Negotiating Democracy in Brazil (Reiter), 99
negra (black/brown woman), 50, 51–52

Negras in Brazil (Caldwell), 3
Negreiros, Adriana, 70

Olivar, José Miguel Nieto, 70–71
Oliveira, Waldemar, 75
Ó Riain, Seán, 6
open-ended relationships (*namoros*), 3, 52, 115, 127, 135, 161
Opperman, Martin, 64, 71, 138
orla (coastline), 18–19, 23, 25
outlaw heterosexuals, 11
The Out Traveler, 66

Padilla, Mark, 5, 12, 122
parda (brown woman), 51–52
Parreñas, Rhacel Salazar, 139–40
Patil, Vrushati, 165
Pattanaik, Bandana, 147
Pedroso, Marcelo, 29
pega-turistas (tourist grabber), 20. See also *caça-gringas* (hunter of foreign women)
Pelourinho, 23, 24–25, 26
Pereira, 170n9
Pierson, Donald, 54
Piscitelli, Adriana, 68, 70–71
Policing Pleasure (Dewey and Kelly), 118
pontos (points where sex workers solicit clients), 15. See also sexual stereotyping: by location
Praça da Sé, 23, 25
Pratt, Marie Louise, 87
Pravaz, Natasha, 50, 53, 163–64
preta (black woman), 51–52
Pretty Modern (Edmonds), 5
privilege manifestation, 83–91, 93–94, 115–16
Prodetur (Program for the Development of Tourism), 28–29, 170nn8–9
professional do sexo (sex worker): abolitionist perspectives, 103–4, 174n7; categorization schemes, 119–20; class politics, 119–20; "controlling images," 114–15; economics, 21, 26, 105–6, 107, 170n3; government classification, 99, 103, 174n4; high-end vs. low-end, 119–20; human rights issue, 103–4; as "low Other," 115–16; marginalization, 107, 174n10; racial disparities, 114–15; stigmatization, 117–18; terminology, 118–19, 120–22; violence against women, 100–101, 102, 116–18, 175n13. See also *prostituta* (prostitute)
programas (commercial sex transactions), 3, 52, 115, 127, 161, 169n3
Programa Sentinela, 173n12

Program for the Development of Tourism (Prodetur), 28–29, 170nn8–9
Projeto sem Vergonha (Without Shame Project), 108–10
promotion. *See* sex tourism marketing
prostituta (prostitute): agency, 131, 133; ambiguity of meaning, 88, 89, 120, 121; Aprosba (Association of Prostitutes of Bahia) terminology, 98, 108, 111; Candomblé priestess vs., 57; dancer association, 58; as exploited, 46, 103; feminist rejection of term, 116; interracial relationship association, 1, 60, 88; legal definition in Brazil, 78; as legitimate, 136–37; marginalization, 105; *mulata* synonymity, 49; politics of naming, 17; racial implications, 3, 59, 60; self-worth, 132; stigma, 2; stigma elimination, 12, 108, 109; STIs (sexually transmitted illnesses), 167; trafficking vs., 147; as victim, 147. See also *professional do sexo* (sex worker)
Prostitution, Power, and Freedom (Davidson), 117
Puar, Jasbir K., 10, 81
putaphobia (hatred of prostitutes), 2, 169n6

"racial democracy" mythology, 51, 53–56, 62–63, 172n11
racial identification, 49–53, 171n7, 172n8
racialized eroticization. *See* black hypersexuality mythology; sexual stereotyping: by race
Radio Zona, 107–8
Rastafarianism, 30
Rede Brasileira de Prostitutas (Brazilian Network of Prostitutes), 106–7, 108–10
Reiter, Brend, 12, 51, 99
Richetti, Wilson, 119
Rio de Janeiro, 27, 48
Romo, Anadelia A., 28, 31, 33, 55
Rosaldo, Renato, 10
Rosário, Mario do, 74
Ryan, Chris, 82

sailors (*marinheiros*), 127, 130, 136
Sales, João de, 66
Salvador: Afro-Brazilian cultural tourism, 30–43; economic history, 27–29; as gay tourism mecca, 65; guidebook representation, 57; sex tourism–black women association, 59–62; sex tourism zones, 18–26; as "site of desire," 5; zones of class and race, 23–26. *See also* Bahia
samba, 35

Sansone, Livio, 31, 59

Santos, Boaventura de Sousa, 161

Santos, Cecilia McDowell, 117

São Paolo, 27

São Paulo School (Escola Paulista), 54, 55

Sargentelli, Oswaldo, 48–49

Schaeffer-Grabiel, Felicity, 91

scopophilia, 49, 171n2

Scowscill, David, 166

seamen/shipworkers (*marinheiros*), 127, 130, 136

Secretariat for the Promotion of Racial Equality, 55

Secretariat of Culture and Tourism, 30

self-respect. See *se valorizando* (valuing oneself)

Selka, Stephen, 40

Sena, Edna, 75

Serviço Nacional de Aprendizagem Comercial (National Service of Commercial Learning), 69, 172n5

se valorizando (valuing oneself): charging money vs. not charging money for sex, 132–34, 137–38; complexity of relationships involved, 139–40; cosmopolitanism, 134; feeling needed and valued, 132–34; "girlfriends" vs. prostitutes, 136–37; *gringos* (foreign male tourists) vs. locals, 134–36; *intimate labor*, 139–40; limitations, 130–31, 139, 175n5; *namoros vs. programas* (relationships vs. sex transactions), 127–28; prostitutes as tourists, 132, 135; researcher considerations, 130; terminology, 175n4

sexscapes, 6

Sexton, Jared, 62

sex tourism: ambiguities, 69–73, 82, 84–85, 146; anxiety, 7; arguments, 9–12; black women association, 59–62; complexities, 69–73, 82; defined and explained, 5–6, 70–72, 95–96; economics, 21, 26, 73, 170n3; as exploitation, 136–37; facilitators, 78; globalization, 69–73; history, 70; interviewees, 14–15; locations worldwide, 7; male ego and bonding, 91–95; negative interactions result, 60–62; privilege manifestation, 83–84; reciprocity concept, 87–90; research methodologies, 12–16; social class aspects, 67–69; stereotype reinforcement, 7; structure, 78–82; theoretical framework, 9–12; Third World "other," 87; trafficking vs., 142–43, 156–58; varieties, 65–66, 69–73. See also globalized sex tourism; *specific sex tourism types*

sex tourism marketing: "Afro-ethnic tourism" initiative, 41; Bahian-ness, 34–35; Bahian state tourism agencies, 47; black body, 21, 25; Black Mecca, 21, 25, 29–32, 163, 170n8, 170n12; Candomblé, 33, 38–39; celebrity involvement, 85; culture, 35, 42, 47–49; effects, 58, 78–79; history, 62–63; *mulatas*, 47–49, 62, 63; research, 12. *See also* "racial democracy" mythology; *specific organizations and agencies*

sex trafficking. *See* trafficking

sexually transmitted illnesses (STIs), 111–13

sexual stereotyping: by gender, 47–51, 59–62, 84–87, 114–16; by location, 59–60, 84–87, 114–16; by nationality, 58–59; by physical appearance, 15, 169n8; by profession, 58; by race, 47–51, 59–62, 84–87, 89–91, 114–16, 171n1; by social class, 67–69. *See also* black hypersexuality mythology; *and specific locations* {Is the latter necessary?}

sex worker. See *professional do sexo* (sex worker)

Sharpley-Whiting, T. Denean, 85

Sheriff, Robin, 54

Silva, Anna Paulo da, 78, 152, 158

Silva, Claudio da, 41

Slut Walks, 117, 175n15

A Small Place (Kincaid), 58–59

Smith, Christen, 62–63

social class, 65, 83–84. *See also* sexual stereotyping: by social class

spa, 88

Spivak, Gayatri Chakravorty, 157

Stallybrass, Peter, 115

Stam, Robert, 54

Statement of Principles (of *Rede Brasileira de Prostitutas*), 106–7

Stephens, Sharon, 77

Sterling, Cheryl, 39

Steve Biko Cultural Institute, 23, 170n4

Stewart, Charles Samuel, 56–57

STIs (sexually transmitted illnesses), 111–13

Suplicy, Marta, 65

Sustainable Tourism and Childhood program, 74

Teles dos Santos, Jocélio, 30

Telles, Edward, 34–35

termas (spa/brothel), 88

terreiros. See Candomblé

Third World "other," 85–87

Thorbek, Suzanne, 147

tour guides, 78, 91–92

tourism: marketing and promotion, 170nn7–9; propaganda, 59–62; statistics, 170n11; studies and research, 8–9; workers, 170–71n3, 172n5

tourist grabber (*pega-turistas*), 20

"touristic intimacy," 84, 96

touristscape, 6, 45–46

trabalhadora do sexo (sex worker). See *professional do sexo* (sex worker); *prostituta* (prostitute)

trafficking: abolitionists vs. sex workers' rights advocates, 141–48; CHAME assumptions about low-income Brazilian women of African descent, 149–56, 176–77n8; complexities, 147; conflicting approaches, 147–48; consent vs. nonconsent, 157–58; definitions, 147, 176n4, 177n11; history, 146; identification complexity, 147, 157–58, 176n4; moralizing discourses, 156–58; moral panics aspect, 153–56, 177n3; overviews, 141–43, 158; present-day, 146–47; research perspectives, 147–48, 177n11; sex tourism vs., 142–43, 156–58; transnational mobility vs., 142

Trafficking in Persons (TIP) Report, 74

transgender, 120–21

transnational male sociality, 91–95

transnational tourism propaganda, 59–62

travesti (gay man who lives primarily as a woman), 60–61, 172n13

Tripp, Aili Mari, 9–10

Turismo Étnico-Afrio, 69

UNESCO World Heritage Site, 24–25

UN Trafficking Protocol, 147–48, 157, 176n5

Upper City, 23

Valenssa, Valéria, 49, 50, 171n5

Valentine, David, 120

valuing oneself. See *se valorizando* (valuing oneself)

van der Veen, Margolein, 103

Vargas, Getúlio, 34, 35, 53, 171n16

Veja, 70

violence against women, 100–101, 102, 116, 175n13

Wagner, Jacques, 41

Warren, Jonathan, 90–91

Wekker, Gloria, 11, 122

What's Love Got to Do With It? (Brennan), 6

White, Allen, 115

white woman (*branca*), 40, 52

whore, 121. See also *professional do sexo* (sex worker); *prostituta* (prostitute)

Without Shame Project (Projeto sem Vergonha), 108–10

Women Are Equal in Whatever Profession, 109

Women's Police Station, 102, 174n6

Woods, Clyde, 22

Woods, Jewel, 94–95

World Code of Ethics in Tourism, 74

World Heritage Site, 24–25

World Tourism Organization, 71–72

ERICA LORRAINE WILLIAMS is an assistant professor of anthropology at Spelman College.

The University of Illinois Press
is a founding member of the
Association of American University Presses.

Composed in 10.5/13 Adobe Minion Pro
by Lisa Connery
at the University of Illinois Press
Manufactured by Thomson-Shore, Inc.

University of Illinois Press
1325 South Oak Street
Champaign, IL 61820-6903
www.press.uillinois.edu